DEDICATION

Setting: Pompano Beach, Florida. Event: February, 2011 speech by freshman Congressman Allen West.

Confrontation: Qur'an-wielding CAIR-person demanding to know: "Where in the Qur'an does it say to carry out attacks against Americans and innocent people?"

First response from the Congressman: "It cannot possibly say that because America was not around when it was written." The CAIR heckler kept at it until Congressman West finally said (ending confrontation):

"Don't come up here and try to blow sunshine up my butt!"

ACKNOWLEDGMENTS

Specific people have been a big help in pulling this compilation together. My grateful thanks to: Amil Imani, Diala Rihani (especially for being willing to "get creative" with Arabic when there were no terms in existence in Islam for a concept like "critical thinking,"), Jane Hogan (for feeling free to say "Egad, no!"), and Johny Elbitar.

And of course to all the friends who helped with the editing and had suggestions and were willing to take calls and just listen. I would hope you know who you are: Fighters in the cause. Thanks.

And special thanks to Sonja L., without whom I could never have gotten the whole thing laid out better than a kindergartner.

HANDFUL OF BIBLE/QUR'AN COMPARISONS

The Bible

(Matt. 5:7) Blessed are the merciful for they shall obtain mercy.

(Matt. 5:9) Blessed are the peacemakers.

(Matt.5:44) Love your enemies, bless them that curse you, do good to them that hate you, pray for them that spitefully use you.

(Matt. 6:14) Forgive and you shall be forgiven.

(Matt.7:1-2) Judge not that ye be not judged.

(Matt. 25:40) Feed the hungry, clothe the naked, visit the sick, whatever you do to the very least you have done unto me.

(Luke 6:27-36) "The Golden Rule." Treat others the same way you would have them treat you.

The Qur'an

(2:191) Kill the disbelievers wherever you find them.

(4:101) Infidels are your sworn enemies.

(5:51) Take neither the Jews nor the Christians for your friends.

(5:33) Those who make war upon Allah . . . have their hands and feet of alternate sides cut off.

(9:29) Fight those who believe not in Allah and the Last Day.

(9:123) Make war on the infidels who dwell around you.

(28:86) Never be a helper to the disbelievers. Be ruthless to the infidels.

(66:9) Fight the unbelievers and the hypocrites and be severe with them.

Hadith

(Al-Bukhari 1:3:111) No Muslim should be killed for killing an infidel.

(Al-Bukhari 9:84-57) If someone stops believing in Allah, kill him.

"What a powerful resource! A combination dictionary/encyclopedia English-to-Arabic/Arabic-to-English for Islamic history, words, phrases, and world-wide organizations that all people can keep at their fingertips. I am especially pleased that the author is one of ACT! for America's long-time leaders! Good job, Dorrie."
—Brigitte Gabriel, President/CEO, ACT! for America

"This is a most useful handbook and primer for some of the fundamentals about Islam and Islamic terrorism. As a desktop reference, it will be THE one to reach for whenever a quick check for a definition or term is needed."
—Clare M. Lopez, Sr. Fellow, Center for Security Policy

"500+ Islamic Words is a reference book that is as handy as a pocket in a shirt. It is interesting to poke around in it and let serendipity rule. If you have a basic knowledge about Islam, reading it is like playing Trivial Pursuit with yourself, saying: 'I didn't know that.' 500+ Islamic Words is a fun read because it has a sense of irony and a touch of ridicule that makes the book not a pure dictionary, or at least, it is a dictionary with a little attitude—a good addition to your library."
—Bill Warner, PoliticalIslam.com, and author of *Sharia Law for the Non-Muslim*, and many others.

"This is a superb reference work that will be of great use for anyone who wants to understand the threats we face in America and the West."
—Christopher Holton, Vice President with the Center for Security Policy and the Director of its Divest Terror Initiative.

"Dorrie O'Brien has been a champion of gloves-off truth-telling, and gives us all a great example of what one American with guts, intellect, integrity, and tenacity can do. She is a Patriot, and we should be grateful she stands on the wall and consistently puts the spotlight on the enemies of our great Republic."

—John Guandolo, national security expert and co-author of *Sharia: The Threat to America* and *Raising A Jihadi Nation*

"In her work, Dorrie O'Brien has created a long-overdue and valuable tool—a reference for professionals and laymen alike that further defines the enemy camp by providing insight as to the true meaning of the diction that they employ against us."

—Jeff Epstein, America's Truth Forum

"There has been no reference guide to Islam which would aid the researcher in finding and deciphering key Islamic terminology up to now. With Ms. O'Brien's book, we are now able to reference Islamic terms in English, not just by the words, but by category. This book is a boon to all Americans who have the courage to confront the threat of Islam."

—Eric Martin, playwright; "Stragglers"; narrator, the King James, the New King James, and the New America bibles

"Dorrie O'Brien's work in this handy new resource enables you to quickly get a glimpse into the mindset that began 1400 years ago through common words and concepts that are used throughout the world today. Understanding that mindset is a necessary step if we are to survive the all-encompassing threat of radical Islam."

—Kelly Cook, Executive Director, ACT! for America

500+
ISLAMIC WORDS
YOU SHOULD KNOW

AN ENCYCLOPEDIA OF ISLAM

Dorrie O'Brien

DGE

Dobrien Global Enterprises, Inc.

ISBN 978-0-9888612-0-6
First edition, April, 2013
Updated, January, 2014
Copyright © 2013 by Dorrie O'Brien

Dobrien Global Enterprises, Inc.
Grand Prairie, Texas 75052
dorrieobrien2011@gmail.com

Cover Art: Gail Cross, Desert Isle Design, Mesa, Arizona
Printed in the U.S.A. by Lightning Source, Inc.

INTRODUCTION

As the Bard said, the eyes are the windows to a man's soul.

It is equally true that words are the windows to a man's thinking. Nothing could be a better example of that than Islam's collection of its three doctrinal books: the Qur'an, the *ahadith*, and the *sirat*, from which Islamic law, the Sharia, flows. If you know how to listen, you can clearly hear the call to war against all *kuffar* until the world is conquered under Allah. America is its biggest battlefield.

Most Westerners can't hear that call to conquest because of the difference in the sound of the mother language, Arabic. It goes in one ear and out the other; it's like Greek or Chinese to us. We probably understand those better, in fact. How many of you remember the bar scene in *Star Wars* (IV, if you're a *SW* purist)? You probably laugh, but it's indicative of how far apart we are from understanding Islam.

It is a world apart (this is a creed that sanctions fathers and mothers selling, maiming, and killing their daughters, and husbands beating and killing their wives)—and they know that, and they use it to their advantage against their enemy by twisting up words we commonly use, e.g.: truth, justice, peace, oppression, treaty, blasphemy, slander, and others to make them sound like we're talking the same language. These words, in their understanding are, in fact, inimical to Western life, and Westerners can easily be (and consistently are) fooled by that. All *kuffar* need to be wary of this.

Muhammad was wont to say: "They [non-Muslims] are a people without understanding." He's correct; we have no clue about the guile Islam employs to devastate non-Islamic peoples. They tell us, but we just don't hear it.

So to quote from *Mad Max Beyond Thunderdome*: "Here be the right of it."

There's no good way to put a ton of Qur'anic verses in this reference primer (though there certainly are many in here), but one of the worst of the propaganda fool-ya verses is surah 5:32 (chapter 5, verse 32). I was disgusted on Christmas Eve, 2012, when attending a children's movie with my eight-year-old granddaughter and was assaulted with an interfaith ad that included this ubiquitous and out-of-context verse, Q5:32, commonly quoted as ". . . [W]hosoever kills a human being . . . it shall be like killing all humanity; and whosoever saves a life, saves the entire human race." It makes Islam sound so mainstream reasonable and world-class humanitarian, huh? It's not. It's a classic example of the duplicity active in Islam.

The actual verse comes from Babylonian Talmud, Mishnah Sanhedrin 37a: "For this reason was man created alone, to teach thee that whosoever destroys a single soul of Israel, scripture imputes (guilt) to him as though he had destroyed a complete world; and whosoever preserves a single soul of Israel, scripture ascribes (merit) to him as though he had preserved a complete world since all mankind originated from one man."

Q5:32 reads in whole: *"Because of that We ordained for the Children of Israel that if anyone killed a person not in retaliation of murder, or (and) to spread mischief in the land—it would be as if he killed all mankind, and if anyone saved a life, it would be as if he saved the life of all mankind. And indeed, there came to them Our Messengers with clear proofs, evidences, and signs, even then after that many of them continued to exceed the limits (e.g. by doing oppression unjustly and exceeding beyond the limits set by Allah by committing the major sins) in the land!"* [www.thenoblequran.com]

So Q5:32 was originally from God to the Jews, Muhammad lifted it and added some thoughts of his own, attributes it to Allah, and then adds verse Q5:33 (which is *never* mentioned in *kuffar* hearing), which is the basis of the Sharia reasoning for what happens to *anyone* if they "spread mischief in the land": Q5:33: "The recompense of those who wage war against Allah and His Messenger [an overriding meme in the Qur'an is that Muhammad is 1B in importance forever] and do mischief in the land [fitna] is only that they shall be killed or crucified or their hands and their feet be cut off on the opposite sides, or be exiled from the land. That is their disgrace in this world, and a great torment is theirs in the Hereafter."

It's a great example of *muruna*, lying in a big, monster way. The very fact that it's used is in-your-face stealth jihad, because of the constant complaints that non-Muslims are always taking words from the Qur'an out of context and here they are, doing it themselves.

It is why we must understand what they are saying.

The Harvard School of Law put up a stone tablet in January, 2013, of a Qur'anic verse that is so egregiously wrong, especially considering that Harvard started as a Christian college, it's hard to find words of outrage significant enough: Q4:135: "O you who believe [Muslims only], be custodians of justice [Sharia law] and witnesses for Allah even though against yourselves [Muslims who don't want to commit jihad] or your parents or your relatives [Muslims who don't want to fight against their families]. Whether a man be rich or poor Allah is his [the Muslim's] greater well-wisher than you. So follow not the behests of lusts lest you swerve from justice [the Muslim could be seduced away from believing that only Allah has the right of it in all matters and manners] and if you prevaricate or avoid (giving evidence) [taking part in jihad] Allah is cognizant of all that you do. [The constant threat that Allah will punish a Muslim with Hell if he dare think for himself.]"

It's not that Harvard hadn't already gone Left. One indication might be William A. Graham's, Dean, Harvard Divinity School, name on one of the more egregious appeasement vehicles ever (see Da'wah/Interfaith Dialogues], "Loving God and Neighbor Together" put out by the Yale Divinity School in 2007, in response to A Common Word Between Us and You, put out by Royal al-Bayt Institute of Islamic Thought of Jordan. But now here's what looks like the result of the Saudi royal family's generous gifts to Harvard's coffers.

When I put out an email blast with the above interpretation, a friend of a friend made these corrections, and asked why his take wouldn't be equally valid: Q4:135: "O you who believe (Christians), be custodians of justice (U.S. laws) and witnesses for Allah (God) even though against yourselves or your parents or your relatives. Whether a man be rich or poor Allah (God) is his (the Christian's) greater well-wisher than you. So follow not the behests of lusts lest you swerve from justice and if you prevaricate or avoid (giving evidence) Allah (God) is cognizant of all that you do."

His take wouldn't be valid because: 1) God and Allah are not interchangeable; 2) justice does not have the same meaning in Arabic and English; and, 3) Islam rejects U.S. laws.

He doesn't know that. Neither do millions of other Americans. There is certainly nothing unintentional about keeping Americans ignorant. If you can get your hands on *The Methodology of Dawah Elallah in American Perspective*, published in 1989, you will see how well-thought-out the intention was to dull our minds and bring us down as a nation within 20-25 years of going to press. Now, let's see, that would make the outside date for America's destruction in 2014, right? A midterm election year.

Do you think they have to conquer the country through overt jihad to take over? No. They just need nine people/friends in the right positions to destroy us. So, who could those be? The President. The Vice President. The Secretary of State. The Secretary of Defense. The Director of the CIA. The Director of Homeland Security. The U.S. Attorney General. The Senate Majority Leader. The Speaker of the House. Then maybe your next level might be the Chairman of the Joint Chiefs of Staff. It would be perfect to have Democrat majorities in both houses of Congress, too.

"Just sayin'," to quote the Beck.

Well, more than that. Going into 2014, the only true, demonstrable miss the Islamists have had is that the Democrats do not control both house of Congress. Don't believe me that they've been that successful? I'm sorry, you're in for a Great Awakening any time now.

This compilation is designed for the layman to get a quick handle on most things Islamic through Islam's own words. It's an easy "look-up" reference book for the casual and even not-so-casual study of Islam. It's also a story. If you read the Alpha Islamic section from beginning to end you'll eventually have the whole story of Islam, its beliefs, and its unchanging goals beginning in 610, right up to today.

You can do the fast track. There are eleven words to read first, in this order, to understand Islam; if you master these and the concepts behind them, the rest of the words are just more proof of the Islamic *raison d'etra*: *Qur'an*, *Al-Fatiha* (opening *surah* of the Qur'an), *Hadith*, *Fitna* (oppression), *Al-Nasikh wal-Mansukh* (abrogation), *Adl* (justice), *Hourria* (freedom), *Jihad, Sharia, Mosques*, and *Auliya* (friends). And for one more to show that Islam isn't "just a religion," you might check out *Jenseyyah* (nationality), too.

Totalitarian cultures, creeds, and ideologies cannot survive the scrutiny of their tenets by those who understand and reject them and actively enlighten others to the true meaning behind what, in this totalitarian creed's case, these Islamists say.

There may indeed be Muslims in the world who don't want to kill or enslave non-Muslims, and there are serious, conscientious Muslims who are trying to bring modernity to Islam and stop the jihad, but they are far outnumbered by the fundamentalists who use their language to strip you of yours.

You have to learn it, own it, use it; you have to understand it to effectively use your voice against it. This is my attempt to do so.

—Dorrie (spelled Yrwd, in Romanized Arabic) O'Brien
January, 2014

HOW TO USE THIS BOOK

There are three sections to the book:
1. Alpha English to Islamic Terms, Words, Phrases
2. Alpha English Topics to Islamic Terms, Words, Phrases
3. Alpha Romanized Islamic Terms, Words, Phrases to English

Either of the first two sections will lead to the third, where all the definitions or explanations or lists are.

If you know the English word but don't know the Islamic word, look it up in Alpha English. If you can't remember the English word, but have a general idea that it might be a piece of clothing, for instance, use the Alpha Topics list to find it. If you know the Islamic word, but don't know what it means in English, go to the third section.

Even if you know the English word, don't overlook Topics, as I'm sure you'll be surprised by how many other words there are for the same thing, practice, or place, which will lead you to many more Islamic terms, words, and phrases.

For instance:
Alpha English: **Apostate**. Law. *Murtad.*
Alpha Topic: **Law.** Apostate. *Murtad.*
Alpha Islamic to English: **Murtad**: Apostate.
(Followed by the explanation.)

Or:

Alpha English: **Averroes**, aka ibn Rushd. Notables.

Alpha Topic: **Notables**. Averroes, aka ibn Rushd.

Alpha Islamic to English: **Averroes**, aka ibn Rushd.

(Followed by full description.)

Or:

Alpha English: **7 Major Battles Muhammad fought**. Battle.
Muhammad's Aljihad al-Akbar

Alpha Topic: **Battle**. 7 Major Battles Muhammad fought:
Muhammad's Aljihad al-Akbar

Alpha Islamic to English: **Muhammad's Aljihad al-Akbar**:
Muhammad's 7 Major Battles: (followed by list)

There are 20 major topics:

Battle	House	Notables
Book	Ideology	People
Charity	Law	Phrase
Clothing	Islamic org.	Prayer
Evil	Islamic sect	Rites
Fighting	Leadership/title	Scholar
Holy Site	Month	

Choosing the topics for the Topics section and what belonged in which was admittedly arbitrary. You might think something belongs better in one list than another, and you could be correct, too. There is a very thin line between ideology and Sharia law, or no line at all, sometimes.

There is no topic for "history." It is woven within the explanations.

Note that I use numbers for words which begin with first (1st), or second (2nd) or third (3rd) and the like. If appropriate, a section begins with those.

Quickie Contents Guide:

ALPHA ENGLISH TO ISLAMIC

1-sentence Testimony of Faith. Prayer. *Shahada*

1st and 2nd Jihads. Battle. *Auwal and Tani Jihads*

1st Holiest Night of Prayer. Night of Power. Prayer. *Lailatul Qadr*

1st Month of the Islamic calendar. Month. *Muharram*

1st Most Sacred Mosque. (AKA the Grand Mosque.) Holy site. *Masjid al-Haram*

1st Surah of the Qur'an. Prayer. *Al Fatihah*

2nd Holiest Night of Prayer in Islam. Prayer. *Lailat al-Baraat*

2nd Most Sacred Mosque. Holy site. *Masjid al-Nabawi*

3rd Jihad. Battle. *Thaaleth Jihad*

3rd Most Sacred Mosque. Holy site. *Al-Aqsa Mosque*

4 Sacred Months. Month. *Alashor Alharam*

4 Schools of Islamic Jurisprudence. Law. See: Sharia law

5 Daily Prayers. Prayer. *Salaat al-yawmi al-Khamsat.*

5 Fundamental Islamic Needs. Notables. *Daruriyat al Khams*

5 Pillars of Islam. Rites. *Arkan al-Islam al-Khamsat*

6 Articles of Faith. Notables. *Aqidah*

6 Fundamentals of Islamic Belief. Ideology. *Setta Kalimat*

7 Major Battles Muhammad fought. Battle. *Muhammad's Aljihad al-Akbar*

8th Month in the Islamic Calendar. *Lailat al-Baraat* happens in this month. Month. *Sha'aban*

9th Month of the Islamic Calendar. Month. *Ramadan* (falls annually during this month)

10 Failures of U.S. Government on the Domestic Islamist Threat. Notables. *Fashal Altasallul*

10 People Muhammad Assured Would Enter Paradise. Notables. *Al-asharatu mubashshirun*

10th Day of Muharram. Month. *Ashura*

11 Women Victims of Honor Killings in the U.S. Notables. *AHada-'Ashar Imra'a Maiyit Qatl al-Sharf*

12 Months in Islamic Calendar. Month. *Hijra*

18 Major Jihad Attempts/Attacks

on U.S. soil since 9/11. Notables. *Aljihad al-Akbar*

610. Notables. *Bi'thah*

622. Notables. After Hijra. *Ba'd Alhijra*

622. Notables. Before Hijra. *Qabl Hijra*

Abdullah Azzam. Notables.

Abdullah Azzam Brigades. Islamic org. AAZ

Ablution pre-prayers. Prayer. *Wudhu*

Abraham. Notables. Ibrahim and *Sa'ee*

Abrogation. Law. *al-Nasikh wal-Mansukh*

Abu Dawud. Notables.

Accusation of fornication or adultery. Law. *Qathf*

ACLU. See: CAIR

Adultery, fornication. Law. *Zinaa*

Age of responsibility to Islam. Law. *Sin al bulugh*

Ahmadiyya. Islamic sect.

Aisha. Notables.

Al Arabiyya News. Islamic org.

Al-Ghazali, aka Algazel. Notables.

Al-Islamiyin. Islamic org.

Al-Jazeera. Islamic org.

All of Islam (The). Ideology. *Deen*

Allah, Glorified and exalted be He, or, ***Allah, May he be glorified and exalted***. Phrase. *Allah Subhanahu wa Ta'ala*

Allah has willed it. Phrase. *Masha Allah*

Allah is the greatest. Phrase. *Allahu Akbar*

Allah/Lord. Notables. *Rabb*

Allowed, approved. Law. *Halal*

Al Nusra. Islamic org. *Jabhat al-Nusra*. Listed under *Al Nusra*

Al-Qaeda. Islamic org. The Base.

Al-Qaeda in the Arabian Peninsula. Islamic org. AQAP

American-Arab Anti-Discrimination Committee. Islamic Org. ADC

American-Arab Institute. Islamic org. AAH

American Islamic Forum for Democracy. Islamic pro-democracy org. AIFD

American Islamic Leadership Coalition. Islamic pro-democracy org. AILC

American Muslim Advisory Council. Islamic org. AMAC

American Muslim Council. Islamic org. AMC

American Muslim Taskforce. Islamic org. AMT

American Muslims for Palestine. Islamic org. AMP

American Society for Muslim Advancement (The). Islamic org. ASMA

Analogy. Ideology. *Qiyas*

Angel Gabriel. Notables. Ji'bril

Apostate. Law. *Murtad*

Apostate. Law. *Murtad milli*

Apostate. Law. *Ridda*

Apostate. Law. *Takfir*

Army of the Righteous. Islamic org. *Lashkar-e-Taiba*

Assembly of Muslim Jurists in America. AKA: The Group of Lawyers for Sharia in America. *Majama Fuqaha Shariah B'America.* Islamic org. AMJA.

Atheist. Ideology. *Zindiq*

Atheist. Ideology. *Molhid*

Authentic/Authority. Scholar. *Sahih*

Authors of tafsir. Notables. *Mufassir*

Averroes, aka ibn Rushd. Notables.

Avicenna, aka ibn Sina. Notables.

Badr. See: Battle of Badr

Baha'i. Islamic sect.

Barracks, stronghold, mosque. Battle. *Ribat*

Base/Foundation. Islamic org. *Al-Qaeda*

Battle of Badr. Battle.

Battle of Constantinople. Battle.

Battle of Karbala. Battle.

Battle of Lepanto. Battle.

Battle of Poitiers. Battle.

Battle of Vienna. Battle. See: Gates of Vienna

Be. Ideology. *Kun*

Behead/Decapitation. Fighting.

Biographies of Muhammad. Book. *Sira.*

Black Flag of Islam. Notables. *Ar-Raya* or *al-Uqab.* See Black Flag of Islam.

Black slaves. People. *Abeed*

Black Stone, The. Holy site. *Al Hajar al Aswad.* Listed as Black Stone.

Blasphemy. Law. *Tajdif*

Body robe for men. Clothing. *Jalabiya*

Bond for revenue. Finance. *Sukuk*

Book. Book. *Kitaab*

Book. Book. *Mushaf*

Bow low. Ideology. See: *As salaam*

Bridges. Notables. *Jusur*, but, see Qutb, Seyyid.

By the grace of Allah, or, *If it be the will of Allah*. Phrase. *Insh'allah*

By the mercy of Allah. Phrase. *Rahimullah*

Caliphate. Ideology. *Khilafah*

Call for the crowd to shout "Allahu Akbar!" Rites. *Takbir*

Caller for daily prayers. Prayer. (Arabic) *Mu'adhin*; (Turkish) *Muezzin*

Carnal self or desires. Ideology. *Nafs*

Catastrophe; misery. *Naqba*

Cave of Hira. Holy site. *Kahef Hira*

Center for Muslim Christian Understanding. Islamic Org. CMCU

Center for the Study of Islam and Democracy. Islamic org. CSID

Chapter in Qur'an. Book. *Surah*

Charity. Charity. *Sadaqqa*

Chief or leader. Leadership/title. *Shaikh*

Citizenship. Notables. *Jenseyyah*

Civilizational Islam. Islamic org. *Islam Hadhari*

Civilizational jihad. See: *Mosques*

Cleric or teacher. Scholar. *Imam*

Close proximity. Law. *Khalwat*

Commander of all the faithful. Leadership/title. *Amir al-mu'mineen*

Commendable or recommended. Ideology. *Mandub* and *Mustahab*

Companions of pleasure in Paradise. Ideology. *Hourris*

Complete way of life. Ideology. Islam

Conceal, cover, keep secret (thoughts/knowledge). Law. *Kitman*

Conceal, cover up (body). Law. *Awrah*

Conquer by force. Battle. *Anwatan*

Conquest. Battle. *Fath*

Conquest. Battle. *Futuh*

Consensus on Islamic law among the *ulema*. Scholar. *Ijma*

Constantinople. See: Battle of Constantinople

Consultation/Counsel. Law. *Shura*

Contempt for free inquiry. Scholar. *Al-elmo noktatan Katharoho al-jaheloon*

Controversy, dispute, discord. Ideology. *Khilaf*. Also, *Fitna*

Corruption, forgery, fake. Ideology. *Tahrif*

Council of American Islamic Relations. Islamic org. CAIR

Council on Pakistani American Affairs. Islamic org. COPAA

Covenant. Ideology. *Misaq*

Critical thought. Ideology. *Fikir ejramy*

Cycles of prayer. Prayer. *Raka'at*

Daily Call to Prayers. Prayer. *Adhan*

Daughter of. People. *Bint*

Day of Mourning. Notables. *Ashura*

Death. Ideology. *Maut*

Death Sentence. Law. *Fatwa*

Deficient as Qur'anic scholar. Scholar. *Naqis*

Deny, reject, resistance to Islam. Ideology. *Juhud*

Deobandi. Islamic org.

Desk Reference of Islamic law. Book. *Reliance of the Traveller: Umdat-al-Salik*

Devil. Notables. *Iblis.*

Devil. Notables. *Shaitan*

Devil/Idol mentioned in Qur'an. Notables. *Jibt*

Devoted to Allah. People. *Muslims*

Direction to Mecca. Rites. *Qibla*

Disciplines of the mind and manner. Ideology. *Adab al-Islam*

Disobedience. Law. *Fasiq*

Divine blessings. Prayer. *Barakah*

Divorce. Law. *Talaq*

Doctrine. Islamic law. *Mazhab*

Dogs. See: *Ahl al-Kitaab*

Dome of the Rock. Holy site. The *Sakhirah Mosque*, but, see *Al-Aqsa Mosque*

EEOC. See CAIR

Egyptian Freedom Party. Islamic org. *Hizb al-Hori'at fe Meser*

Enchanting. See: **Adhan**

Embrace Islam and be safe! Phrase. *Aslim taslam!*

Emigration, flight from danger. Ideology. *Hijra*

Establishment of Islamic System of Life. Ideology. *Iqamat-ud-Deen*

Etiquette; niceties of war. Fighting. *Adab al Qitaal*

Eve (as in Adam and Eve). Notables. Hawwa

Evil. Vermin. *Fuwaysiqah*

Evil-doer, wicked. *Fajir*

Evil doings. *Munkar*

Evil, prohibited, dreadful. *Nukra*

Excommunication and Exodus. Islamic org. *Takfir wal-Hijra*

Explanatory Memorandum. Notables. See: HLF/Holy Land Foundation Trial and *Mosques*

Faith. Ideology. *Imaan*

Faithful. People. *Mu'minim*

Faith, values, and soul of Islam. Ideology. *Deen*

False, void. Ideology. *Batil*

Falsehood, dishonesty, hypocrisy. Law. *Nifaq*

Fanatic. *Mut'asibun*

Fasting. Rites. *Sawm*

FATAH/Palestinian National Liberation Movement. Islamic org. FATAH

Fate, predestination. Ideology. *Taqdir*

Fate, predestination: Ideology. *Qadar*

Father, father of. People. *Abu*

Federation of Islamic Organizations in Europe. Islamic org. FIOE

Female circumcision, aka female genital mutilation (FGM). Law. *Khafd*

Female full body-covering robe. Clothing. *Burqa.* And see *Awrah*

Female full body-covering robe. Clothing. *Chador.* And see *Awrah*

Female full-dress outer garment. Clothing. *Abayah.* And see *Awrah*

Female head-covering. Clothing. *Niqab.* And see *Awrah*

Festival of the Sacrifice. Rites. *Eid al Adha*

Festival to Break the Fast at End of Ramadan. Rites. *Eid al Fitr*

Fighting in mortal combat for the sake of Allah. Law. *Jihad*

Filth. Ideology. *Najisun*

Finance: Mutual, cooperative insurance plans: *Takaful*

Forbidden. Law. *Haram*

Forum of European Muslim Youth & Student Organization. Islamic org. FEMYSO

Freedom. Ideology. *Hourria*

Freedom. Ideology. *Tahrir*

Freedom and Justice Party (Egyptian). Islamic org. *Al-hori'at wa' ladalat*

Freedom Party. Islamic org. *Hizb ut-Tahrir*

Free Speech. Ideology. *Hurr Khalam*

Free Will. Ideology. *Al-Mashi'a*

Friday Prayers: Prayer. *Jummah salat*

Friend(s). Ideology. *Auliya*

Gates of Vienna. See Battle at Gates of Vienna.

God, deity. Ideology. *Ilah*

"Group," "society," "organization" Islamic org. The words often used in titles of Islamic orgs: *Jamaat; Gama'a*

Guidance. Ideology. *Huda*

Guide (Shi'a). Notables. *Mahdi*

Hadith and Sira. Book. *Sunnah*

Hajj ritual. Rites. *Sa'ee*

Hamas/Palestinian Islamic Resistance Movement. Islamic org.

Harakat al-Muqawama al-Islamiyya. HAMAS

Hassan al-Banna. Notables.

Head-covering for men. Clothing. *Keffiyeh*

Heavenly abode. Ideology. *Baytul M'amuh*

Hell. Ideology. *Jahannam*

Hell. Ideology. *Sidjin*

Hello; welcome. Phrase. *As-Salaam Alaikum*

Helpers; specifically Muslims in Medina. Notables. *Ansar*

Hereafter, or eternal life. Ideology. *Akhirah*

Heresy, apostasy. Law. *Zandaqa*

Heretic, apostate. Law. *Muhartiq*

Hizballah (or Hezbollah). Islamic org. Party of Allah ("god"). *Hizballah*

HLF/Holy Land Foundation Trial. Notables. *Moasesset al'arazi al-Moghadaseh.* HLF

Holidays/Festivals. See: Rites in Alpha Topics.

Holy War. Fighting. *Jihad.*

Holy War. Ideology. *Jihad.*

Holy War. Law. *Jihad*

Holy warriors, strivers. Battle. *Mujahedeen*

Homegrown Jihad Camps. See *MOA/Jamaat al-Fuqra*

Honor killing. Law. Urdu/Pakistani: *Karo-kari.* Arabic: *Qatl al sharf.* See Honor killings.

House for Muslim concubines. *Harem*

House/mosque/masjid of a lower level. Holy site. *Musallah*

House of Allah. *Mosque*

House of Disbelief. *Dar al Kuffar*

House of Islam. *Dar al Islam*

House of Peace. *Dar al Sohl*

House of Preaching. *Dar al Da'wah*

House of Refuge. *Dar ul Aman*

House of War. *Dar al Harb*

Human rights. Ideology. *Huquq al Insan*

Hypocrites. Law. *Munafiqun*

Ibn Ishaq. Notables.

Ibn Kathir. Notables.

Ibn Khaldun. Notables.

Ibn Rushd, aka Averroes. Notables.

Ibn Sina, aka Avicenna. Notables.

Ibn Tamiyya. Notables.

Icon on Muslim Brotherhood sign: Ideology. *Waidu.* See *Ikhwan al Muslimin*

Ideology. Ideology. *Fiqra*

Idolatry, idolatrous, impurity. Ideology. *Taghut*

Idolatry, impurity. Ideology. *Tawagheet*

Ignorance of Islam. Ideology. *Jahiliyah*

Illiterate people. People. *Ummi, ummiyyun*

Imitation. Scholar. *Taqlid*

Immigrants. Notables. *Muhajiroon*

Impure/impurities. Ideology. *Najasa*

Infidel. People. *Kafir; pl., kuffar*

Infidel leader. Notables. *Rayyis al-Kuffar*

Inner struggle. Ideology. *Jihad*

Inner struggle. Law. *Jihad*

Innocent. Ideology. *Barii*

Institute for Muslim Minority Affairs. Islamic org. IMMA

Institute on Religion and Civic Values. Islamic org. IRCV

Insurgency, rebellion. Fighting. *Baghawat*

Intelligence, intellect. Ideology. *Aql*

Interest payments, usury. Finance. *Riba*

Interfaith dialogues. See: *Da'wah.*

International Institute of Islamic Thought. Islamic org. IIIT

Interpretation: Mystical interpretation of the Qur'an. Scholar. *Ta'wil*

Interpretation of Qur'an. Scholar. *Tafsir*

Inter-Securities Intelligence. Islamic org. ISI

In the name of Allah. Phrase. *Bishmillah*

In the name of Allah, most gracious, most merciful. Phrase. *Basmala*

In the Way of Allah. Phrase. *Fi sabil Allah*

Invasion. Battle. *Fatteh*

Invitation to join Islam. Ideology. *Da'wah*

Islam: Ideology. To submit. Also: A complete way of life

Islamic Association of North America. Islamic org. IANA

Islamic Association for Palestine. Islamic org. IAP

Islamic banking. Finance. *Muamalat*

Islamic Circle of North America. Islamic org. ICNA

Islamic determination. Ideology. *Azimah*

Islamic Jihad in Motion. (Pakistani). Islamic org. HuJI: *Harkat-ul-Jihad-al Islami*

Islamic jurisprudence. Law. *Fiqh*

Islamic law. Law. *Sharia*

Islamic law by Ibn Abbas. Law. *Fiqh as-Sunna*

Islamic New Year. See *Hijra*

Islamic Pious Forefathers. Notables. *As-Salaf as-Saalih*

Islamic Relief USA. Islamic org. IRUSA

Islamic Religious Police (Indonesian). Islamic org. *Jakim*

Islamic Republic of Iran Broadcasting. Islamic org. IRIB

Islamic scholars trained in Islamic law. Scholar. *Ulema*

Islamic Society of North America. Islamic org. ISNA

Islamic U.S. advisory group. Law. *Majlis ash-Shura*

Islamic world. Ideology. *Ummah*

Islamophobia. Ideology. See IIIT

Ismaili. Islamic sect.

Israel's annihilation. (Shi'a) Ideology. *Al-Quds (Day)*

I will not submit to Islam. Phrase. *Lan astaslem*

Jesus. Notables. Isa

Judge in Islamic Law. Scholar. *Qadi*

Judgment Day. Holy site. Arafat (plains of).

Judgment Day. Ideology. *Qiyamah*

Just and noble. Ideology. *Wasat*

Justice. Ideology. *Qist*

Justice. Law. *Adl*

Karbala. See: Battle of Karbala. Also see *Ashura*.

Khadija. Notables.

Kill. Fighting. *Qitaal*

Killing. Ideology. *Qatlu*

Kill them all, or, *Then kill them*. Phrase. *Faq'tuluhum*

King or prince (Ismaili). Leadership/title. *Aga*

Kneeling down. Rites. *Rakat Salah*

Law. Law. (In Urdu) *Tashri. Fiqh*, but commonly *Sharia*

Lay sermon and prayer leader at mosques. Prayer. *Khatib*

Leader of Jummah (Friday) prayers. Prayer. *Khutbah*

Leader of the Believers. Leadership/title. *Amuril Mu'minin*

Leader of the Muslim Brother hood. Leadership/title. Supreme Guide. *Morshed-al-ala*. See Supreme Guide.

Leader of the Shi'a. Leadership/title. *Ayatollah.*

Leader of the Ummah/ Muhammad's rightful follower. Leadership/title. *Khalif*

Leader, ruler, commander, nobleman. Leadership/title. *Emir*

Learned interpreter of the law (Shi'a). Scholar. *Mujtahid*

Learned person. Scholar. *Maw'lawi*

Learned person. Scholar. (Shi'a) *Mullah*

Lepanto. See: Battle of Lepanto.

Loyalty *and* **enmity.** Ideology. *Wala wa bara*

Lying/cheating (between Muslims only). Ideology. **Dajjal**

Lying/deceit. Ideology. *Dharura*

Lying/deceit. Ideology. *Muruna*

Lying/deceit. Ideology. *Taqiyya*

Lying/deceit. Ideology. *Tawriya*

Mahdi. Guide, the Lord of the Age. *Sahib-ul-Zaman.* Listed under *Mahdi.* More information under *La ilaha illah Allah,* and the *Twelvers*

Making prayer. Prayer. *Namaz*

Marriage ceremony. Rites. *Nikah*

Martyr. Law. *Shahid*

Martyrdom. Law. *Istishhad*

Mary. Notables. Maryam

Maududi, Abul A'la. Notables.

May Allah be glorified and exalted, or, *May he be glorified and exalted.* Phrase. *Allah Subhanahu wa Ta'ala*

May Allah protect you. Phrase. *Fi Amanillah*

May the blessing and the peace of

Allah be upon him. Phrase. (For Muhammad only): *Sallallahu alaihi wa salaam*

May the blessings of Allah be upon you. Phrase. *Barakallah*

May you enjoy a blessed festival. Phrase. *Eid Mubarak*

Meal after sunset during Ramadan. Rites. *Iftar*

Meal before sunrise to make the Ramadan fast (*sawm*) **easier.** Rites. *Suhur*

Mecca. Holy site.

Medina. Holy site.

MeK (sometimes **PMOI**). Islamic pro-democracy org. The People's Mujahedeen (Holy Warriors) for Iran. *Mujahedeen-e-Khalq*

Memorize the Qur'an. Prayer. *Hifz al-Qur'an*

Methodology/Principles of Islamic Jurisprudence. Ideology. *Usul al-Fiqh.* See: *Hisbah* and *Minhaj*

Migration, flight from danger. Ideology. *Hijra*

Minhaj-ul-Quran Int'l. Islamic org. Reforming rules of Qur'an. MQI

Minorities. People. *Aqaliyyat*

Miracle. Book. *Ayah*

Miracle of the Qur'an. Book. *Ijaz*

Misunderstand. See *Da'wah (#6)* and *IIIT* (for Islamophobia)

Mobilization of the Oppressed (morality police). Iranian/Shi'a. Islamic org. *Basiji*

Monotheist: Ideology: *Hanif*

Mortal combat. Fighting. *Qitaal* and *Jihad*

Mortgage. Finance. *Murabaha*

Moses. Notables. Musa

Mother. People. *Om*

Muhammad. Notables.

Muhammad: Messenger of Allah. Notables. *Rasulallah*

Muhammad, perfect man. Notables. *al-Insan al-Kamil*

Muhammad: Seal of the Prophet. Notables. *Khatam al-nabiyyin*

Muhammad's companions. Notables. *Sahabah*

Muhammad's descendants. Notables. *Seyyid*

Muhammad's first choice for God. Ar Rahman. See: *La ilaha illah Allah*

Muhammad's ggg-grandfather Qusayy. See *Mecca*, and *La ilaha illah Allah*

Muhammad's rightly guided successors. Notables. *al-Khulafaa al-Raashidoon*

Murder. Law. *Qatl*

Muslim. People. *Muslim*

Muslim Alliance in North America. Islamic org. MANA

Muslim American Society. Islamic org. MAS

Muslim Brotherhood. Islamic org. *Ikhwan al Muslimin*

Muslim Brotherhood top man: *Supreme Guide.*

Muslim Canadian Congress. Islamic pro-democracy org. MCC

Muslim Community Association. Islamic org. MCA

Muslim Proselytizer Involved in Da'wah. One who calls others to Islam. Ideology. *Da'ee*

Muslim Public Affairs Council. Islamic org. MPAC

Muslim Students Association. Islamic org. MSA

Muslim Students Society (UK). Islamic org. MSS

Muslim World League. Islamic org. MWL, but see *Al-Haramain*

Muslims of America. Islamic org. MOA

Nakedness. Law. *Awrah*

Name of the Islamic god. Notables. Allah

National Iranian American Council. Islamic org. NIAC

National Progressive Unionist Party. Islamic org. *Hizb al Tagammu al Watani al Taqadomi al Wahdawi*

National Ummah Movement. Islamic org. NUM

Natural Religion. Ideology. *Fitra*

Night Journey. Ideology. *Isra'a*

Noah. Notables. Nuh

No Interest (as in payment). Islamic org. *LARIBA*.

Non-consensus of opinion. Scholar. *Ikhtilaf*

Non-equality of gods with Allah. Ideology. *Shirk*

North American Imam Federation. Islamic org. NAIF

North American Islamic Trust. Islamic org. NAIT

O Allah! Phrase. *Alluhumma*

Oath of Allegiance. Notables. *Bai'a*

Obedience (total) to Allah. Ideology. *Ebaadah*

Obedience (simple)ds. Ideology. *Ta'aa*

Obligatory or mandatory. Law. *Wajib*. Most common, *Fard*

OIC/Organization of Islamic Cooperation. Islamic org. *Moassesseh Ta'awon al-Islamiyya.* OIC

One. None like Allah. Notables. *Ahad*

One God, the unity of the God-head. Ideology. *Tawhid*

One who has memorized the Qur'an. Notables. *Hafiz*

On Him (Muhammad) are the blessings and the peace of Allah. Phrase. *Alaihissalatu Wassalam*

Oppression, tumult. Ideology. *Fitna*

Order within the laws of Allah. Ideology. *Hisbah*

Osama bin Laden. Notables.

Pakistani Islamic Group. Islamic org. *Jamaat-e-Islami*. JEI

PA/Palestinian Authority. Islamic org. *As-Sultah Al-Wataniyyah Al-Filastiniyyah*. PA

Pact of Umar. Law. *Al-Uhda Al-Uhmariyya*. See: Pact of Umar

PIJ/Palestinian Islamic Jihad. Islamic org. *Harakat al-Jihad al-Islami fi Filastiniyya* PIJ

PLO/Palestinian Liberation Organization. Islamic org. *Munazzamat at-Tahrir al-Filastiniyyah*. PLO

PNA/Palestinian National Authority. Islamic org. PNA

Paradise. Ideology. *Illiyoun*

Paradise. Ideology. *Jannah*

Party of Allah (Shi'a). Islamic org. *Hizballah*

PBUH. *Peace be upon him.* Phrase. *Salla Allahu alaihi wa salaam*

Peace. Ideology. *As salaam*

Peace. Ideology. *Sohl*

Peace be upon him (PBUH). Phrase. *Salla Allahu alaihi wa salaam*

Peace be upon them. Phrase. *Alayhis Salaam*

Pedophilia. Notables. See: Aisha

People. Notables. *Ahl*

People of ignorance. People. *Ahl al-Fetrah*

People of opinion. People. *Ahl ar'ar'y*

People of the book. Book (Qur'an). *Ahl al-Kitaab*

People of the House. Notables. Literally, Muhammad's descendants. *Ahl al-Bayt*

People's Mujahedeen (Holy Warriors) for Iran. Islamic Pro-democracy Org. *Mujahedeen-e-Khalq:* MeK

Permitted, lawful. Law. *Mandub.*

Permitted, lawful. Law. *Halal*

Permitted, lawful. Law. *Mustahab*

Person who wages war against Allah. Notables. *Muharebeh*

Pilgrimage reward. Rites. *Hajj Mabrur*

Pilgrimage. Rites. *Hajj*

Political party: *Hizb*

Polytheists. Law. *Mushrikoon*

Praise be to Allah. Phrase. *Hamdellah*

Prayer of Sincerity. Prayer. *Surat al-Ikhlas*

Prayer meeting. Prayer. *Usra*

Preparation for Battle. Battle. *I'dad Al-'oda*

Prepare (You). Ideology. *Waidu.* See: Muslim Brotherhood: *Ikhwan al Muslimin*

Prince, commander, leader. Leadership/title. *Amir*

Prison Converts. See *Da'wah/* Prison Da'wah/Prislam

Promise. Ideology. *Wa'ed*

Prophets. Notables. *Nabi*

Proselytization (Da'wah) **Training.** Ideology. *Tarbiya*

Protected, second-class non-Muslim in an Islamic nation-state. Law. *Dhimmi*

Punishment (corporal). Law. *Tazir*

Punishment. Law. *Hadd*

Purification of the soul. Charity. *Tazkiyah*

Purify, to make new. Ideology. *Tajdid*

Questionable/abhorrent. Ideology. *Makrooh*

Qur'an. Book. *Qur'an* or *Koran*

Qur'an, original. Book. *Umm al-kitaab*

Qutb, Seyyid. Notables.

Raids/raiding. Fighting. *Ghazwat*

Ramadan. Month. Islamic holy month.

Ramadan prayers. Prayer. *Tarawih Salah*

Ransom/blood money. Law. *Diyya*

Read or recite. Book. *Iqraa*

Reason (human ability to). Ideology. *Istidlaal*

Reasons for Qur'anic revelations. Book. *Asbab al-Nuzul*

Rebel/Rebellion. Fighting. *Tamarod*

Recitation. Book. *Talawa*

Recitation (complete) of the Qur'an during Ramadan. Rites. *Khatm*

R4BIA. Notables. See: *Ikhwan*

Reform in Islamic law. Scholar. *Ijtihad*

Relax Sharia compliance. Law. *Taysir*

Religious duty. Law. *Fard.*

Religious endowment. Law. *Waqf*

Religious innovation, bad. Scholar. *Bi'dah sayyi'ah*

Religious innovation, good. Scholar. *Bi'dah hananah*

Religious police. *Mutawe'e*

Remembrance of Allah. Ideology. *Dhikr*

Resurrection (The). Ideology. *Mi'ad*

Retribution, retaliation. Law. *Qisas*

Return of the Shi'a Mahdi. Ideology. *al-Faraj*

Return/Revert. Ideology. *Awdah*

Ridda Wars/War of the Apostates. Battle. *Hurub al-Ridda*

Rites. Prayers: *Salah*

Ritual animal slaughter. Rites. *Zabiha*

Rope around male head-coverings. Clothing. *Iqal*

Rule. Ideology. *Hukumat*

Rule/ruling by Sharia jurist only. Scholar. *Fatwa*

Rule/ruling from Sharia. Law. *Bayah*

Rule/ruling from Sharia. Law. *Siyasa*

Rules. Scholar. *Minhaj*

Sacred, holy. Ideology. *Haram*

Sacrifice. Ideology. *Udhiyah*

Salafi. Islamic sect.

Saudi Arabia's highest religious council. Scholar. *Majlis al-Ifta al-A'ala*

Saudi religious police. Islamic org. *Mutawe'e*

SAWS. Phrase. *Sallallahu 'alaihi wa salaam*

Scarf. Female head-covering. Clothing. *Hijab.* And see *Awrah*

Scarf. Female head-covering. Clothing. *Jilbab.* And see *Awrah*

Scarf. Female head-covering. Clothing. *Khimar.* And see *Awrah*

Scholar. Scholar. (Shi'a) *Mufti*

Scholars specializing in Sharia. Scholar. *Fukaha'a*

School or university. Scholar. *Madrassa*

Servant. People. *Abdu*

Sex slave. Law. *Melk al-yamin*

Sexual exploitation of boys. Ideology. *Bacha Bazi*

Sharia for minorities. Law. *Fiqh al-aqaliyyat*

Shi'a. Islamic sect.

Shi'a school of law. Law. *Ja'afari*

Sign of God (Shi'a). Notables. *Ayatollah*

Slander. Law. *Ghiba*

Slave. People. *Abd*

Slaves, black. People. *Abeeb*

Social cohesion, group-consciousness. Ideology. *Asabiyyah*

Society for Spreading the Faith (or: Congregation for religious propaganda). Islamic org. *Tablighi Jamaat*

Son of. People. *Bin*

Son of. People. *Ibn*

Special worship during Ramadan. Rites. *Lbadat*

Spirit/breath. Ideology. *Ruh*

Spoils of war. Battle. *Ghanimah*

State of Islam. *Dawlat al Islam*

State. State, as in nation. *Dawla*

State treasury in an Islamic nation. Finance. *Bayt al-mal*

Stoning. Law. *Rajm*

Struggle. Law. *Jihad*

Students. Scholar. *Taliban*

Submission to Allah. Notables. *Islam*

Submit to Islam and you will be spared. Phrase. *Aslim Taslam!*

Submit to the will of Allah. Notables. *Taslim*

Success. Ideology. *Falah*

Successorship of Muhammad. (Shi'a) Leadership/title. *Imamate*

Sufi teacher. Scholar. *Murshid*

Sufi. Islamic sect.

Suicide. Law. *Qatlu nafsi-hi*

Sunni. Islamic sect.

Supernatural creatures in the Qur'an. *Djinn* or *Jinn*

Supererogatory prayers. Prayer. *At-tatawwu.*

Supererogatory prayers. Prayer. *Nawafil*

Supplication to Allah. Prayer. *Du'a*

Supreme Court definition of religion. Notables. See: *Mosques*

Supreme Guide. Notables. *Moshed-al-ala*

Sword of Islam. Notables. *Saif al-Islam*

SWT. Glorified and exalted be He, or, May he be glorified and exalted. Phrase. *Subhanahu wa Ta'ala*

Tax. Law. *Zakat*

Tax. Law. *Jizya*

Tax on dhimmis' land. Law. *Kharaj*

Tax "one/fifth." Law. *Khums*

Teacher of Islam. Scholar. *Pir*

Temple/Shrine. Holy site. *Ka'aba*

Temporary marriage. Law. Arabic: *Misyar*; Shi'a: *Mut'ah*

Temporary wife. Islamic Law. *Seeghe*

Terrorist. Ideology. *Irhabi*

The Emigrants. Islamic org. *Al-Muhajiroun*

The Islamic Group. Islamic org. *Al-Gama'a Al-Islamiya*

The Light. Islamic org. *Al-Nour*

The name of god is Allah. Phrase. *La ilaha illah Allah*

There is no god but Allah and Muhammad is his messenger. Phrase. *La ilaha illallah muhammad ur rasulullah*

There is no god but Allah. Phrase. *La ilaha il Allah*

The Truth. Islamic Org. *Al Haqiqa*

The Truth. Phrase. *Al-Haqiqa*

The Twelfth Imam. Notables. *Mahdi*

The Vanguard. Islamic org. *As-Sabiqun*

The Youth. Islamic org. *Al-Shabaab*

This life, worldly affairs. Ideology. *Dunya*

Tolerance. Ideology. *Tasamouh*

Tower. Holy site. *Minaret*

Traditions. Book. *Hadith*, pl., *ahadith*

Treaties. Law. *Mu'ahadat*

Truce, ceasefire. Law. *Hudna*

Truce of Hudaibiya. Battle. *Hudna min Hudaibiya*

Truth, justice. Ideology. *Haq*

Tumult, Oppression. Ideology. *Fitna*

Twelvers. Shi'a. Islamic sect. *Ithna Ashariyya*

Uprising/Shake off. Fighting. *Intifada*

Verse in Qur'an. Book. *Ayah*

Verse of the Sword. Notables. *Ayah al-Saif,* Q9:5

Vienna. See Battle at Gates of Vienna.

Void. Law. *Hadr*

Wahhabi. Islamic sect.

World Association of Muslim Youth. Islamic org. WAMY

Water well in Mecca, under the Ka'aba. Holy site. Well of ZamZam

Western Education Is Sin. Islamic org. *Boko Haram*

Wisdom. Ideology. *Hikmah*

Words on Muslim Brotherhood icon: Ideology. *Waidu*

Words on Black Flag of Islam: *Shahada*

Worlds. All that exists. Ideology. *Alamin*

Yusuf al-Qaradawi. Notables.

Zakat Foundation of America. Islamic org. ZFA.

ALPHA ENGLISH TOPIC

Battle. 1st and 2nd Jihads: *Auwal* and *Tani Jihads*

Battle. 3rd Jihad: *Thaaleth Jihad*

Battle. 7 Major Battles Muhammad fought: Muhammad's *Aljihad al-Akbar*

Battle. Barracks, stronghold, mosque: *Ribat*

Battle. Battle at Gates of Vienna

Battle. Battle of Badr

Battle. Battle of Constantinople

Battle: Battle of Karbala

Battle. Battle of Lepanto: *Qitaal Lepanto*

Battle. Battle of Poitiers

Battle. Conquer by force: *Anwatan*

Battle. Conquest: *Fath*

Battle. Conquest: *Futuh*

Battle. Holy warriors, strivers: *Mujahedeen*

Battle. Invasion: *Fatteh*

Battle. Preparation for: *I'dad Al-'oda*

Battle. The Ridda Wars, aka, The Wars of the Apostates: *Hurub al-Ridda. See Auwal & Tani* Jihads

Battle. Truce of Hudaibiya: *Hudna min Hudaibiya*

Battle. Spoils of war: *Ghanimah*

Book. Book: *Kitaab*

Book. Book: *Mushaf*

Book. Biographies of Muhammad: *Sirat*

Book. Chapter in Qur'an: *Surah*

Book. Desk Reference of Islamic law: *Reliance of the Traveller: Umdat-al-Salik*

Book. *Hadith* and *Sira: Sunnah*

Book. Miracle: *Ayah*

Book. Miracle of the Qur'an: *Ijaz*

Book. Original version of the Qur'an: *Umm al-kitaab*

Book. People of the Book (Qur'an): *Ahl al-Kitaab*

Book. *Qur'an* or *Koran*

Book. Read or recite: *Iqraa*

Book. Reasons for Qur'anic Revelations: *Asbab al-Nuzul*

Book. Recitation: *Talawa*

Book. Traditions: *Hadith*. Plural: *Ahadith*

Book. Verse in Qur'an: *Ayah*

Catastrophe, misery: *Naqba*

Charity. Charity: *Sadaqqa*

Charity. Purification of the soul: *Tazkiyah*

Clothing. Body robe for men: *Jalabiya*

Clothing. Female full body-covering robe: *Burqa*

Clothing. Female full body-covering robe: *Chador*. And see *Awrah*

Clothing. Female full-dress outer garment: *Abayah*. And see *Awrah*

Clothing. Female head-covering: *Niqab*. And see *Awrah*

Clothing. Head-covering for men: *Keffiyeh*

Clothing. Rope around male head-coverings: *Iqal*

Clothing. Scarf. Female head-covering: *Hijab*. And see *Awrah*

Clothing. Scarf: Female head-covering: *Jilbab*. And see *Awrah*

Clothing. Scarf: Female head-covering: *Khimar*. And see *Awrah*

Evil-doer, wicked: *Fajir*

Evil doings: *Munkar*

Evil, dirty talk: *Laghw*

Evil, prohibited, dreadful: *Nukra*

Evil, vermin: *Fuwaysiqah*

Fighting: *Behead/Decapitation*

Fighting. Etiquette; niceties of war: *Adab al Qitaal*

Fighting. Insurgency, rebellion: *Baghawat*

Fighting. Holy War: *Jihad*

Fighting. Kill: *Qitaal*

Fighting. Mortal combat: *Qitaal*

Fighting. Raids: *Ghazwat*

Fighting. Rebel/Rebellion: *Tamarod*

Fighting. Uprising/"shake off": *Intifada*

Finance. Bond for revenue: *Sukuk*

Finance. Interest payments, usury: *Riba*

Finance. Islamic banking: *Muamalat*

Finance. Mortgage: *Murabaha*

Finance. Mutual, cooperative, insurance plans: *Takaful*

Finance. State treasury in an Islamic nation: *Bayt al-mal*

Holy site. 1st most Sacred Mosque, in Mecca (aka the Grand Mosque): *Masjid al-Haram*

Holy site. 2nd Most Sacred Mosque in Medina: *Masjid al-Nabawi*

Holy site. 3rd most sacred mosque in Jerusalem: *Al-Aqsa Mosque*

Holy site. Black Stone, The. *Al Hajar al Aswad*. Listed as Black Stone

Holy site. Cave of Hira: *Kahef Hira*

Holy site. Dome of the Rock. See: *Al-Aqsa Mosque*

Holy site. Houses of Allah. Places of worship/forts: *Mosques/masjids*

Holy site. Arafat (Plains of)

Holy site. Mecca

Holy site. Medina

Holy site. Mosque/masjid of a lower level: *Musallah*

Holy site. Temple/Shrine: *Ka'aba*

Holy site. Tower: *Minaret*

Holy site. Well in Mecca under the Ka'aba: Well of ZamZam

House for Muslim concubines: *Harem*

House of Allah: *Mosque*

House of Disbelief: *Dar al Kuffar*

House of Islam: *Dar al Islam*

House of Peace: *Dar al Sohl*

House of Preaching: *Dar al Da'wah*

House of Refuge: *Dar ul Aman*

House of War: *Dar al Harb*

Ideology. 6 Fundamentals of Islamic Belief: *Setta Kalimat*

Ideology. "All of Islam." Faith, values, and perspective of Islam: *Deen*

Ideology. Analogy: *Qiyas*

Ideology. Atheist: *Molhid*

Ideology. Atheist: *Zindiq*

Ideology. "Be": *Kun*

Ideology. Bow low. *As Salaam*

Ideology. Caliphate: *Khilafaf*

Ideology. Carnal self or desires: *Nafs*

Ideology. Commendable or recommended. *Mandub* and/or *Mustahab*

Ideology. Companions of pleasure in Paradise: *Hourris*

Ideology. Complete way of life: *Islam*

Ideology. Controversy, dispute, discord: *Fitna*

Ideology. Controversy, dispute, discord: *Khilaf*

Ideology. Corruption, forgery, fake: *Tahrif*

Ideology. Covenant: *Misaq*

Ideology. Critical thought/thinking. *Fikir ejramy*

Ideology. Death: *Maut*

Ideology. Deny, reject, resistance to Islam: *Juhud*

Ideology. Disciplines of the mind and manner: *Adab al-Islam*

Ideology. Emigration. Flight from danger: *Hijra*

Ideology. Establishment of Islamic System of Life: *Iqamat-ud-Deen*

Ideology. Faith: *Imaan*

Ideology. False, void: *Batil*

Ideology. Fate, predestination: *Qadar*

Ideology. Fate, predestination: *Taqdir*

Ideology. Female Circumcision: *Khafd*

Ideology. Filth: *Najisun*

Ideology. Freedom: *Hourria*

Ideology. Freedom: *Tahrir*

Ideology. Free Speech: *Hurr Khalam*

Ideology. Free Will: *Al Mashi'a*

Ideology. Friend(s): *Auliya*

Ideology. God, deity: *Ilah*

Ideology. Guidance: *Huda*

Ideology. Heavenly abode: *Baytul M'amuh*

Ideology. Hell: *Jahannam*

Ideology. Hell: *Sidjin*

Ideology. Hereafter, or eternal life: *Akhirah*

Ideology. Holy; sacred: *Haram*

Ideology. Holy War: *Jihad*

Ideology. Human rights. *Huquq al Insan*

Ideology. Ideology: *Fiqra*

Ideology. Idolatry, idolatrous: *Taghut*

Ideology. Idolatry, impurity: *Tawagheet*

Ideology. Ignorance of Islam: *Jahiliyah*

Ideology. Impure/impurities: *Najasa*

Ideology. Inner struggle: *Jihad*

Ideology. Innocent: *Barii*

Ideology. Intelligence, intellect: *Aql*

Ideology. Interfaith dialogues. See: *Da'wah*

Ideology. Invitation to join Islam: *Da'wah*

Ideology. Islamic determination: *Azimah*

Ideology. Islamic world: *Ummah*

Ideology. Islamophobia: See IIIT

Ideology. Israel's annihilation: Shi'a: *Al-Quds* (Day)

Ideology. Judgment Day: *Qiyamah*

Ideology. Just and noble: *Wasat*

Ideology. Justice: *Qist*

Ideology. Killing for the sake of Allah: *Qatlu*

Ideology. Loyalty *and* enmity: *Wala wa bara*

Ideology. Lying/cheating (between Muslims only): *Dajjal*

Ideology. Lying/deceit: *Dharura*

Ideology. Lying/deceit: *Muruna*

Ideology. Lying/deceit: *Taqiyya*

Ideology. Lying/deceit: *Tawriya*

Ideology: Migration. Flight from danger: *Hijra*

Ideology: Monotheist: *Hanif*

Ideology: Mortal combat: *Jihad*

Ideology. Muslim proselytizer involved in Da'wah: One who calls others to Islam: *Da'ee*

Ideology: Natural Religion: *Fitra*

Ideology. Night Journey: *Isra'a*

Ideology. Non-equality of gods with Allah: *Shirk*

Ideology. Obedience: *Ta'aa*

Ideology. Obedience (total): *Ebaadah*

Ideology. One God; the unity of the Godhead: *Tawhid*

Ideology. Oppression, tumult: *Fitna*

Ideology. Order, within the laws of Allah: *Hisbah*

Ideology. Paradise: *Illiyoun*

Ideology. Paradise: *Jannah*

Ideology. Peace: *As Salaam*

Ideology. Peace: *Solh*

Ideology. Promise: *Wa'ed*

Ideology. Proselytization (Da'wah) training: *Tarbiya*

Ideology. Purify, to make new: *Tajdid*

Ideology. Questionable/abhorrent: *Makrooh*

Ideology. Reason (human ability to): *Istidlaal*

Ideology. Remembrance of Allah: *Dhikr*

Ideology. Resurrection (The): *Mi'ad*

Ideology. Return of the Shi'a Mahdi: *Al-Faraj*

Ideology. Return/Revert: *Awdah*

Ideology. Rule: *Hukumat*

Ideology. Sacrifice: *Udhiyah*

Ideology. Sexual exploitation of boys: *Bacha Bazi*

Ideology. Social cohesion, group consciousness: *Asabiyyah*

Ideology. Spirit/breath: *Ruh*

Ideology. Submission: *Islam*

Ideology. Success: *Falah*

Ideology. Terrorist: *Irhabi*

Ideology. This life, worldly affairs: *Dunya*

Ideology. Tolerance: *Tasamuh*

Ideology. Truth, justice, inevitable, the word of Allah: *Haq*

Ideology. Methodology/Principles of Islamic Jurisprudence. *Usul al-Fiqh*. See: *Hisbah*, and *Minhaj*

Ideology. Tumult, oppression: *Fitna*

Ideology. Wisdom: *Hikmah*

Ideology. Worlds; all that exists: *Alamin*

Islamic org. *Abdullah Azzam Brigades: AAZ*

Islamic org. *Al Arabiyya News*

Islamic org. *Al-Islamiyin*

Islamic org. *Al-Jazeera*

Islamic Org. *Al-Nusra*

Islamic org. Al-Qaeda

Islamic org. Al-Qaeda in the Arabian Peninsula: AQAP

Islamic Org. American-Arab Anti-Discrimination Committee: ADC

Islamic org. American-Arab Institute: AAH

Islamic org. American Muslim Advisory Council: AMAC

Islamic org. American Muslim Council: AMC

Islamic org. American Muslim Taskforce: AMT

Islamic org. American Muslims for Palestine: AMP

Islamic org. American Society for Muslim Advancement: ASMA

Islamic org. Army of the Righteous: *Lashkar-e-Taiba*

Islamic org. Assembly of Muslim Jurists in America; AKA, The Group of Lawyers for Sharia in America: *Majama Fuqaha Shariah B'America*: AMJA.

Islamic org. Base/Foundation: *Al-Qaeda*

Islamic org. Center for Muslim Christian Understanding: CMCU

Islamic org. Center for the Study of Islam and Democracy: CSID

Islamic org. Civilizational Islam: *Islam Hadhari*

Islamic org. Council of American Islamic Relations: CAIR

Islamic org. Council on Pakistani American Affairs: COPAA

Islamic org. *Deobandi*

Islamic org. Egyptian Freedom Party: *Hizb al-Hori'at fe Meser*

Islamic org. Excommunication and Exodus: *Takfir wal-Hijra*

Islamic Org. FATAH/Palestinian National Liberation Movement. FATAH

Islamic org. Federation of Islamic Organizations in Europe: FIOE

Islamic org. Forum of European Muslim Youth & Student Organization: FEMYSO

Islamic org. Freedom and Justice Party (Egyptian): *Al-hori'at wa'ladalat*

Islamic org. Freedom Party: *Hizb ut-Tahrir*

Islamic org. "Group," "society," "organization." Words often used in titles of Islamic orgs: *Jamaat; gama'a*

Islamic org. HAMAS/Palestinian Islamic Resistance Movement. *Harakat al-Muqawama al-Islamiya.* HAMAS

Islamic Org. Party of Allah ("god"). *Hizballah*

Islamic org. HuJI/Islamic Jihad in Motion (Pakistani). *Harkat-ul-Ji-had-al-Islami:* HuJI

Islamic org. Institute for Muslim Minority Affairs: IMMA

Islamic org. Institute on Religion and Civic Values: IRCV

Islamic org. International Institute of Islamic Thought: IIIT

Islamic org. Inter-Securities Intelligence: ISI

Islamic org. Islamic Association for Palestine: IAP

Islamic org. Islamic Association of North America: IANA

Islamic org. Islamic Circle of North America: ICNA

Islamic org. Islamic Relief USA: IRUSA

Islamic org. Islamic Religious Police (Indonesian): *Jakim*

Islamic org. Islamic Republic of Iran Broadcasting: IRIB

Islamic org. Islamic Society of North America: ISNA

Islamic org. Mobilization of the Oppressed (morality police) (Iranian/Shi'a): *Basiji*

Islamic org. Muslim Alliance in North America: MANA

Islamic org. Muslim American Society: MAS

Islamic org. Muslim Brotherhood: *Ikhwan al Muslimin*

Islamic org. Muslim Community Association: MCA

Islamic org. Muslim Public Affairs Council: MPAC

Islamic org. Muslim Students Association: MSA

Islamic org. Muslim Students Society (UK): MSS

Islamic org. Muslim World League: MWL, but, see *Al Al-haramain*

Islamic org. Muslims of America: MOA

Islamic org. National Iranian American Council (Shi'a): NIAC

Islamic org. National Progressive Unionist Party: *Hizb al Tagammu al Watani al Taqadomi al Wahdawi*

Islamic org. National Ummah Movement: NUM

Islamic org. "No Interest": LARIBA

Islamic org. North American Imam Federation: NAIF

Islamic org. North American Islamic Trust: NAIT

Islamic org. OIC/Organization of Islamic Cooperation (UN): *Moassesseh Ta'awon al-Islamiyya OIC*

Islamic org. Pakistani Islamic Group. *Jamaat-e-Islami*: JEI

Islamic org. PA/Palestinian Authority. *As-Sultah Al-Wataniyyah Al-filastiniyyah*: PA

Islamic org. PIJ/Palestinian Islamic Jihad. *Harakat al-Jihad al-Islami fi Filastiniyyah*: PIJ

Islamic org. PLO/Palestinian Liberation Organization. *Munazzamat at-Tahrir al-Filastiniyyah*: PLO

Islamic org. PNA/Palestinian National Authority: PNA

Islamic org. Rules reform in Qur'an: *Minhaj-ul-Quran Int'l*: MQI

Islamic org. Saudi religious police: *Mutawe'e*

Islamic org. Party of Allah (Shi'a): *Hizballah*

Islamic org. Society for Spreading the Faith (or: Congregation for Religious Propaganda): *Tablighi Jamaat*

Islamic org. The Emigrants: *Al-Muhajiroun*

Islamic org. The Islamic Group: *Al-Gama'a Al-Islamiya*

Islamic org. The Light: *Al-Nour*

Islamic org. The Truth: *Al Haqiqa*

Islamic org. The Vanguard: *As-Sabiqun*

Islamic org. The Youth: *Al-Shabaab*

Islamic org. Western Education Is Sin: *Boko Haram*

Islamic org. World Association of Muslim Youth: WAMY

Islamic org. Zakat Foundation of America: ZFA

Islamic pro-democracy org. American Islamic Forum for Democracy: AIFD

Islamic pro-democracy org. American Islamic Leadership Coalition: AILC

Islamic pro-democracy org. Muslim Canadian Congress: MCC

Islamic pro-democracy org. People's Mujahedeen for Iran (PMOI) (Shi'a): *Mujahedeen -e-Khalq*: MeK

Islamic sect: *Ahmadiyya*

Islamic sect: *Baha'i*

Islamic sect: *Ismaili*

Islamic sect: *Salafi*

Islamic sect: *Shi'a*

Islamic sect: *Sufi*

Islamic sect: *Sunni*

Islamic sect: The Twelvers (Shi'a): *Ithna Ashariyya*

Islamic sect: *Wahhabi*

Law. 4 Schools of Islamic Jurisprudence: See: Sharia law

Law. Abrogation: *Al-Nasikh wal-Mansukh*

Law. Accusation of fornication or adultery: *Qathf*

Law. Adultery, fornication: *Zinaa*

Law. Age of responsibility to Islam: *Sin al bulugh*

Law. Allowed, approved: *Halal*

Law. Apostate: *Murtad*

Law. Apostate: *Murtad milli*

Law. Apostate: *Ridda*

Law. Apostate: *Takfir*

Law. Blasphemy: *Tajdif*

Law. Close proximity (Indonesian): *Khalwat*

Law. Commendable or recommended: *Mandub* and/or *Mustahab*

Law. Conceal, cover, keep secret (thoughts/knowledge)(Farsi): *Kitman*

Law. Conceal, cover up body, as in clothing: *Awrah*

Law. Consultation/Counsel: *Shura*

Law. Death sentence: *Fatwa*

Law. Disobedience: *Fasiq*

Law. Divorce: *Talaq*

Law. Doctrine: *Mazhab*

Law. Falsehood, dishonesty, hypocrisy: *Nifaq*

Law. Female circumcision aka female genital mutilation (FGM): *Khafd*

Law. Fighting in mortal combat for the sake of Allah: *Jihad*

Law. Forbidden: *Haram*

Law. Heresy. Apostasy: *Zandaqa*

Law. Heretic. Apostate: *Muhartiq*

Law. Holy War: *Jihad*

Law. Honor killing: Urdu/Pakistani: *Karo-kari* Arabic: *Qatl al sharf*. See Honor Killing

Law. Hypocrites: *Munafiqun*

Law. Inner struggle: *Jihad*

Law. Islamic advisory group: *Majlis ash-Shura*

Law. Islamic jurisprudence: *Fiqh*

Law. Islamic law: *Sharia*

Law. Islamic law by Ibn Abbas: *Fiqh as-Sunna*

Law. Justice: *Adl*

Law. Law (Urdu: *Tashri*): *Fiqh*. Most common: *Sharia*

Law. Lawful, permitted: *Halal*

Law. Martyr: *Shahid*

Law. Martyrdom: *Istishhad*

Law. Mortal combat: *Jihad*

Law. Murder: *Qatl*

Law. Nakedness: *Awrah*

Law. Obligatory or mandatory: *Wajib.* Most common: *Fard*

Law. Pact of Umar. *Al-Uhda Al-Uhmariyya.* See: Pact of Umar

Law. Polytheists: *Mushrikoon*

Law. Protected, second-class non-Muslim person in an Islamic nation-state: *Dhimmi*

Law. Punishment (corporal): *Tazir*

Law. Punishment: *Hadd*

Law. Ransom/blood money: *Diyya*

Law. Relax Sharia compliance: *Taysir*

Law. Religious duty, or an obligatory action: *Fard*

Law. Religious Endowment: *Waqf*

Law. Retribution, retaliation: *Qisas*

Law. Rule/ruling from Sharia: *Bayah*

Law. Rule/ruling from Sharia: *Siyasa*

Law. Sex slave: *Melk al-yamin*

Law. Sharia for minorities: *Fiqh al-aqaliyyat*

Law. Slander: *Ghiba*

Law. Stoning: *Rajm*

Law. Suicide: *Qatlu nafsi-hi*

Law. Tax: Income tax: *Zakat*

Law. Tax on dhimmis' land: *Kharaj*

Law. Tax "one/fifth": *Khums*

Law. Tax. Poll tax on dhimmis: *Jizya*

Law. Temporary marriage: Arabic: *Misyar*; Shi'a: *Mut'ah*

Law. Temporary wife: *Seeghe*

Law: Shi'a school: *Ja'afari*

Law. Treaties: *Mu'ahadat*

Law. Truce; ceasefire: Hudna

Law. Void. *Hadr*

Leadership/title. Chief or leader: *Shaikh*

Leadership/title. Commander of all the faithful: *Amir al-mu'mineen*

Leadership/title. Highest position in Shi'a leadership: *Ayatollah*

Leadership/title. King or prince (Ismaili): *Aga*

Leadership/title. Leader of the Believers (Sunni): *Amuril Mu'minin*

Leadership/title. Leader of the Muslim Brotherhood. Supreme Guide: *Moshed-al-ala*

Leadership/title. Leader of the ummah/Muhammad's rightful follower: *Khalif*

Leadership/title. Leader, ruler, commander, nobleman: *Emir*

Leadership/title. Prince, commander, leader: *Amir*

Leadership/title. Successorship of Muhammad: (Shi'a) *Imamate*

Month. 1st month of the Islamic calendar: *Muharram*

Month. 4 sacred months: *Alashor Alharam*

Month. The 8th month in the Islamic calendar: *Sha'aban*

Month. The 9th month of the Islamic calendar hosts *Ramadan*

Month. 10th Day of Muharram: *Ashura;* also: Battle of *Karbala*

Month. 12 months in Islamic Calendar: *Hijra*

Notables. 3rd Jihad. *Thaaleth Jihad*

Notables. 5 fundamental Islamic needs: *Daruriyat al Khams*

Notables. 6 Articles of faith: *Aqidah*

Notables. 10 Failures of U.S. government on the domestic Islamist Threat: *Fashal Altasallul*

Notables. 10 people Muhammad assured would enter Paradise: *Al-asharatu mubashshirun*

Notables. 11 Women Victims of Honor killings in the U.S.: *AHada-'Ashar Imra'a Maiyit Qatl al-Sharf*

Notables. 18 Jihad attempts/ attacks on U.S. soil since 9/11: *Aljihad al-Akbar*

Notables. 610: *Bi'thah*

Notables. 622: After Hijra (AH): *Ba'd Alhijra*

Notables. 622: Before Hijra: (CE) *Qabl Hijra*

Notables. Abdullah Azzam

Notables. Abraham: Ibrahim (and see *Sa'ee*)

Notables. Abu Dawud

Notables. Aisha

Notables. Al-Ghazali, aka Algazel

Notables. Allah/Lord: *Rabb*

Notables. Angel Gabriel: Ji'bril

Notables. Ar Rahman. See *La ilaha illah Allah*

Notables. Authors of tafsir: *Mufassir*

Notables. Averroes, aka ibn Rushd

Notables. Avicenna, aka ibn Sina

Notables. *ar-Raya or al-Uqab:* Black Flag of Islam.

Notables. Bridges. *Jusur*, but, see Qutb, Seyyid

Notables. Citizenship. *Jenseyyah*

Notables. Day of Mourning: Ashura; also: Battle of Karbala

Notables. Devil: *Iblis*

Notables. Devil: *Shaitan*

Notables. Devil/Idol mentioned in Qur'an: *Jibt*

Notables. Dogs. See: *Ahl al-Kitaab*

Notables. Eve (as in Adam and Eve): *Hawwa*

Notables. Explanatory Memorandum. *See: HLF/Holy Land Foundation Trial*

Notables. Guide (Shi'a): *Mahdi*

Notables. Hassan al-Banna

Notables. Helpers; specifically Muslims in Medina: *Ansar*

Notables. Holy Land Foundation Trial: *Moasesset al'arazi al-Moghadaseh* HLF

Notables. Ibn Ishaq

Notables. Ibn Kathir

Notables. Ibn Khaldun

Notables. Ibn Rushd, aka Averroes

Notables. Ibn Sina, aka Avicenna

Notables. Ibn Tamiyya

Notables. Immigrants: *Muhajiroon*

Notables. Infidel leader: *Rayyis al-Kuffar*

Notables. Islamic creed: *Aqidah*

Notables. Islamic Pious Forefathers: *As-Salaf as-Saalih*

Notables. Jesus: Isa

Notables. Khadija

Notables. Mahdi, the Lord of the Age: *Sahib-ul-Zaman*. See, *Mahdi*. And *La ilaha illah Allah*, and *Twelvers*

Notables. Mary: Maryam

Notables. Maududi, Abul A'la

Notables. Moses: Musa

Notables. Muhammad

Notables. Muhammad, Messenger of Allah: *Rasulallah*

Notables. Muhammad, perfect man: *Al-Insan al-Kamil*

Notables. Muhammad, Seal of the Prophet: *Khatam al-nabiyyin*

Notables. Muhammad's companions: *Sahabah*

Notables. Muhammad's descendants: *Seyyid*

Notables. Muhammad's favorite god: Ar Rahman. See *La ilaha illah Allah*

Notables. Muhammad's ggg-grandfather Qusayy: See *La ilaha illah Allah*, and Mecca

Notables. Muhammad's rightly guided successors: *Al-Khulafaa al-Raashidoon*

Notables. Name of the Islamic god: Allah

Notables. Noah: Nuh

Notables. Noble person. Literally, prophets. *Nabi*

Notables. Oath of Allegiance: *Bai'a*

Notables. One who has memorized the Qur'an. *Hafiz*

Notables. One. None like Allah: *Ahad*

Notables. Osama bin Laden

Notables. Pedophilia. See: Aisha

Notables. People of the House. Literally, Muhammad's descendants: *Ahl al-Bayt*

Notables. People: *Ahl*

Notables. Person who wages war against Allah: *Muharebeh*

Notables. Qusayy (King). Muhammad's ggg-grandfather. See: *La ilaha illah Allah* and *Mecca*

Notables. Qutb, Seyyid

Notables: R4BIA: See: *Ikhwan*

Notables. Submission to Allah: *Islam*

Notables. Submit to the will of Allah: *Taslim*

Notables. Supreme Court definition of religion. See: *Mosques*

Notables. Supreme Guide: *Morshed-al-ala*

Notables. Sword of Islam: *Saif al-Islam*

Notables. Twelfth Imam. *Mahdi*

Notables. Verse of the Sword: *Ayah al-saif,* Q9:5

Notables. Yusuf al-Qaradawi

People: Black slaves: *Abeeb*

People. Daughter of: *Bint*

People. Devoted to Allah: *Muslim*

People. Faithful: *Mu'minim*

People. Father, father of: *Abu*

People. Illiterate people: *Ummi, ummiyyun*

People. Infidel: *Kafir*

People. Minorities: *Aqaliyyat*

People. *Moslem*: See *Muslim*

People. Mother: *Om*

People. *Muslim*

People. Of Ignorance: *Ahl al-Fetrah*

People. People of Opinion: *Ahl ar-ra'y*

People. Servant: *Abdu*

People. Slave: *Abd*

People. Son of: *Bin*

People. Son of: *Ibn*

Phrase. "Allah has willed it": *Masha Allah*

Phrase. "Allah is the greatest": *Allahu Akbar*

Phrase. "By the grace of Allah"; "If it be the will of Allah": *Insh'allah*

Phrase. "By the mercy of Allah": *Rahimullah*

Phrase. "Embrace Islam and be safe!": *Aslim taslam!*

Phrase. "Hello, welcome": *As-Salaam Alaikum*

Phrase. "In the name of Allah": *Bishmillah*

Phrase. "In the name of Allah, most gracious, most merciful": *Basmala*

Phrase. "In the way of Allah": *Fi sabil Allah*

Phrase. "I will not submit to Islam": *Lan astaslem*

Phrase. "Kill them all," or, "Then kill them": *Faq'tuluhum*

Phrase. "May Allah be glorified and exalted": *Allah Subhanahu wa Ta'ala*

Phrase. "May Allah protect you": *Fi Amanillah*

Phrase. "May the blessing and the peace of Allah be upon him (Muhammad)": *Sallallahu alaihi wa salaam*

Phrase. "May the blessings of Allah be upon you": *Barakallah*

Phrase. "May you enjoy a blessed festival": *Eid Mubarak*

Phrase. "O Allah!": *Alluhumma*

Phrase. "On Him (Muhammad) are the blessings and the peace of Allah": *Alaihissalatu Wassalam*

Phrase. "Peace be Upon Him (PBUH): *Salla Allahu alaihi wa salaam*

Phrase. "Peace be Upon Them": *Alayhis Salaam*

Phrase. "Praise be to Allah": *Hamdellah*

Phrase. *SAWS: Sallallahu alaihi was salaam*

Phrase. "Submit to Islam and you will be spared": *Aslim Taslam*

Phrase. *SWT*: Glorified and exalted be He": *Allah Subhanahu wa Ta'ala*

Phrase. "The name of god is Allah": *La ilaha illah Allah*

Phrase. "There is no god but Allah and Muhammad is his messenger": *La ilaha illallah muhammad ur rasulullah*

Phrase. "There is no god but Allah": *La ilaha il Allah*

Political party: *Hizb*

Prayer. 1-sentence statement of faith: *Shahada*

Prayer. 1st holiest night of prayer in Islam: Night of Power: *Lailatul Qadr*

Prayer. 1st surah of the Qur'an: *Al Fatihah.*

Prayer. 2nd holiest night of prayer in Islam: *Lailat al-Baraat*

Prayer. 5 Daily Prayers: *Salaat al-Yawmi al-Khamsat.*

Prayer. Ablution pre-prayers: *Wudhu*

Prayer. Blessing, divine grace: *Barakah*

Prayer. Caller for daily prayers: (Arabic) *Mu'adhin*; (Turkish) *Muezzin*

Prayer. Cycles of prayer: *Raka'at*

Prayer. Daily call to prayers: *Adhan*

Prayer: Friday prayers: *Jummah salat*

Prayer. Lay sermon and prayer leader at mosques: *Khatib*

Prayer. Leader of Jummah (Friday) prayers. *Khutbah*

Prayer. Making prayer: *Namaz*

Prayer. Prayer meeting: *Ursa*

Prayer. Memorize the Qur'an: *Hifz al-Qur'an*

Prayer. Prayer of Sincerity: *Surat al-Ikhlas*

Prayer. Ramadan prayers: *Tarawih Salah*

Prayer. Supererogatory prayers: *At-tatawwu*

Prayer. Supererogatory prayers: *Nawafil*

Prayer. Supplication to Allah: *Du'a*

Rites. 5 Pillars of Islam: *Arkan al-Islam al-Khamsat*

Rites. Call for the crowd to shout "Allahu Akbar!" *Takbir*

Rites. Direction to Mecca: *Qibla*

Rites. Fasting: *Sawm*

Rites. Festival of the night Allah sent down the Qur'an through the Angel Gabriel: *Ramadan*

Rites. Festival of the Sacrifice: *Eid al Adha*

Rites. Festival to Break the Fast at end of Ramadan: *Eid al Fitr*

Rites. Hajj ritual: *Sa'ee*

Rites. Kneeling down: *Rakat Salah*

Rites. Marriage ceremony: *Nikah*

Rites. Meal after sunset during Ramadan: *Iftar*

Rites. Meal before sunrise to ease the fast (*sawm*) during Ramadan: *Suhur*

Rites. Pilgrimage: *Hajj*

Rites. Prayers: *Salah*

Rites. Recitation (complete) of the Qur'an during Ramadan: *Khatm*

Rites. Reward of pilgrimage: *Hajj Mabrur*

Rites. Ritual sacrifice: *Udhiyah*

Rites. Ritual animal slaughter: *Zabiha*

Rites. Shi'a Day of Mourning. *Ashura*

Rites. Special worship during Ramadan: *Lbadat*

Scholar. Authentic/Authority: *Sahih*

Scholar: Cleric or teacher: *Imam*

Scholar: Consensus on Islamic law among the ulema: *Ijma*

Scholar. Contempt for free inquiry: *Al-elmo noktatan katharoho al-jaheloon*

Scholar. Deficient as Qur'anic scholar: *Naqis*

Scholar: Imitation: *Taqlid*

Scholar. Interpretation: Mystical interpretation of the Qur'an: *Ta'wil*

Scholar. Interpretation of Qur'an: *Tafsir*

Scholar. Islamic scholars trained in Islamic law: *Ulema*

Scholar: Judge in Islamic Law: *Qadi*

Scholar. Learned interpreter of the law (Shi'a): *Mujtahid*

Scholar: Learned person: *Maw'lawi*

Scholar. Learned person (Shi'a): *Mullah*

Scholar: Non-consensus of opinion: *Ikhtilaf*

Scholar: Reform in Islamic law: *Ijtihad*

Scholar. Religious innovation, bad: *Bi'dah sayyi'ah*

Scholar. Religious innovation, good: *Bi'dah hananah*

Scholar. Rule/ruling by Sharia jurist only: *Fatwa*

Scholar. Rules: *Minhaj*

Scholar. Saudi Arabia's highest religious council: *Majlis al-Ifta al-A'ala*

Scholar. Scholars specializing in Sharia: *Fukaha'a*

Scholar. School or university: *Madrassa*

Scholar. Students: *Taliban*

Scholar. Sufi teacher: *Murshi*

Scholar: Teacher of Islam: *Pir*

State. State, as in nation: *Dawla*

State of Islam: *Dawlat al Islam*

Supernatural creatures in the Qur'an: *Djinn* and *Jinn*

Worlds. All that exists: *Alamin*

ALPHA ISLAMIC TO ENGLISH

AAH: American Arab Institute. Civil rights organization. Also works to find electable Muslims, as does the **AMT** (American Muslim Taskforce). Muslim Brotherhood [**Ikhwan**] front.

AAZ: Abdullah Azzam Brigades: Global **jihad**ist organization, designated U.S. federal terrorist organization, and affiliated with **al-Qaeda**. See Abdullah Azzam.

Abayah: Full covering garment for females. See **Awrah/nakedness.**

Abd: Slave (in a name., i.e., "Abdullah," the name translates to Slave of Allah). Ibn Arabi, a **Sufi** scholar, is cited for having defined freedom as "being perfect slavery to Allah." He took that from the many **ahadith** that say that the perfect Muslim becomes a slave to Allah. Also means black. Slave and black are synonymous in Arabic. Slaves and slavery are a common fact of life in Islam, and would be more common if it weren't for the **kuffar** and their unreasonable humanitarian rules against it. Muhammad had slaves, so all Muslims can have slaves, especially slave girls/women: Q4:3: "those whom your right hand possesses."

Given the rate at which American blacks revert [**awdah**] to Islam, this following insight into Islam is fascinating: "Muslims usually come from tribal cultures with extended family groups. Despite its claims of transnationalism and multiculturalism, Islam is an ethnic ideology with the descendants of Mohammed elevated over everyone else, the families in the region of his first conquests elevated over other Arabs, Arabs elevated over non-Arabs, Asian Muslims over African Muslims and African Muslims over Western converts to Islam." http://www.frontpagemag.com/2014/dgreenfield/the-muslim-suicide-convert/?utm_source=FrontPage+Magazine&utm_medium=email&utm_campaign=d208ef51a0-Mailchimp_FrontPageMag&utm_term=0_57e32c1dad-d208ef51a0-156518973. See **Abeed.**

Abdu [pro: *abdoh*]: Servant.

Abdullah Azzam. (Palestinian; 1941-1989). One of the least known but most influential of all the fundamentalist Islamists who started the present-day Third Jihad [**thaaleth jihad**]. According to Steve Emerson, Investigative Project on Terrorism: "The Muslim leader most responsible for expanding the jihad into a full-blown international holy war without borders was not **Usama Bin Laden**, or Shaikh Omar Abdul Rahman (the radical Islamic cleric most known to the American public for his conviction in the 1993 World Trade Center bombing trials), but a leader whose name remains today virtually unknown to the West—Shaikh Abdullah Azzam, the "father of **al Qaeda**," who galvanized the Muslim masses to wage an international holy war against all infidels and non-believers until the enemies of Islam were defeated." He hated the United States, yet found his most fertile ground there. He hated Jews without ever having met one. He declared war on every non-Muslim for no reason other than that they were not Muslim. He was killed in a bomb blast. No one knows who set up the bomb, but U.S. operatives have always been blamed. http://www.investigativeproject.org/profile/103

Abeed [var. sp.: *abid*]: a derogatory term in Arabic meaning "slave" and is usually applied as an insult to blacks to invoke stereotypes, particularly to blacks in Somalia and the Sudan. The name has been explained as an allusion to the submission that Muslims owe to Allah.

Abu: Father/Father of. If using "father of," it's generally put before the first born son's name, i.e.: Laden abu Usama.

Abu Dawud (d.889): Abu Dawud Sulayman ibn al-Ash'ath al-Azdi as-Sijistani. Noted Persian collector of prophetic **hadith**, compiled the third of the six canonical hadith collections recognized by **Sunni** Muslims, the Sunan Abi Dawud. He was primarily interested in jurisprudence, and as a result his collection focuses largely on legal hadith (and note that he would have been squarely involved with the first formal compilations of Islamic jurisprudence during his working years, with his death being in 889). He is considered the most traveled of the hadith scholars, visiting Iraq, Egypt, Syria, Hijaz, Tihamah, Khurasan, Nishapur, and Marv among other places in order to collect hadith.

Adab al Qitaal (var. sp.: Aadaab al Qitaal): Etiquette; niceties of war; proper way of fighting/killing in war.

Adab al-Islam: Proper disciplines of the mind and manner; good education and good breeding, politeness, deportment, a mode of conduct or behavior as behooves Islamic practices.

ADC: American-Arab Anti-Discrimination Committee. Claims to be civil rights organization. Is pro-**Hamas**, anti-Israel. Is a Muslim Brotherhood [**Ikhwan**] front with close ties to **CAIR** and other Muslim Brotherhood front groups.

Adhan [pro: *aathan*] (var. sp.: aadhan, adhaan, azan, athan): Five daily calls (the "enchanting") to prayers.

Adl [pro: *adel*]: Justice in Islamic law is from Allah alone; nothing man made about it—social, economic, political, and environmental justice. This means that Muslims will never recognize the U.S. Constitution, the Bill of Rights, or English Common Law as having any relevance in their lives, and in fact, having the opposite. It is man-made law, so all are considered *in*justice. **Sharia** law is the only acceptable law for the entire world. Period. Think about that.

Reliance of the Traveller (the handbook of Islamic law) opens Section O, "Justice," with the legal rulings of "injurious crimes" (AKA murders) for which no one may seek retaliation against the killer (there are 5; I'll list 4, as appropriate for this book), in other words, there's no punishment for: a Muslim for killing a non-Muslim; a **dhimmi** or a Muslim for killing an apostate [**ridda** or **murtad**]; a parent for killing a child or children for bringing embarrassment on him/her or Islam; and, a husband killing his wife for bringing embarrassment on him or Islam.

Section O of *Reliance of the Traveller* is one every non-Muslim should be very familiar with. The stark difference in how Western law and Islamic law operates is proof of the mind chasm between us.

Aga (var. sp.: Agha): King or prince or **imam** in Ismaili sect.

AH: After Hijra. See: **Ba'd Alhijra** and **Hijra**.

Ahad: One. One alone. None like Allah.

AHada-'Ashar Imra'a Maiyit Qatl al-Sharf: 11 Women Victims of Honor Killings in the U.S. (through December, 2013):
11/1989, MO: Palestina Issa (16), Palestinian father stabbed her to death while her mother (Brazilian) held her down; Palestina got a part-time job, and she dated a black non-Muslim. FBI were taping the father's terrorist activities when this happened; no one was on duty at the time of the murder.
1/1/2008, TX: Amina (16) and Sarah (17) Said. Father shot them to death in the back of his taxi for liking and dating American boys.
7/2008, GA: Sandela Kanwal (25), father strangled her for not marrying the man he wanted her to.
2/2009, NY: Aayisa Hassan (37), (Palestinian) husband cut her head off for asking for a divorce.

10/2009, AZ: Noor Amaleki (20), Iraqi father ran over her with his car for because she refused to marry a man he'd picked out for her.

4/2011, MI: Jessica Alfetlawi (20), stepfather shot her for not being Islamic enough.

5/2011, FL: Fatimah Abdullah (48): severe head trauma. According to police report: "She hit her head on the coffee table until she was dead." Maybe it was gas fumes from cleaning. Her death followed a "community-shocking" divorce.

7/2011, NJ: Shazmina Khan (31): estranged husband stabbed her and sliced her throat, probably for trying to divorce him.

3/2012, CA: Shaima Alawadi (32), Iraqi husband beat her to death for wanting to divorce him.

It is Islamic law (*Reliance of the Traveller*, Section O. Justice,1.2(4): "There can be no retribution for a father or mother (or their fathers or mothers) for killing their offspring, or offspring's offspring;" . . . if those children are "shaming" Allah. O1.2(5) is no better: "nor is retaliation permissible to a descendant for (A: his ancestor's) killing someone whose death would otherwise entitle the descendant to retaliate, such as when his father kills his mother."

This report from Atlas Shrugs is not unusual: http://atlasshrugs2000.typepad. com/atlas_shrugs/honor_killings_islam_misogyny/ ". . . It was posted in five local mosques during Friday prayer [see **Jummah Salat** and **Mosques**] and signed by more than 50 relatives, including Abed Al-Rahman Zeidan, a Palestinian lawmaker. 'My husband was under tremendous pressure,' said Ms. Zeidan's mother, Laila. 'The family wanted to banish us from the West Bank and people started rumors that my husband wasn't mentally stable.' Reacting to demands to restore the family's honor, Munther killed his daughter."

An ideology that ranks men's honor higher than their children's lives, or demands proof of loyalty to its god from its believers by killing one's *own* child or wife is one whose believers will kill non-believers in an eye-blink. Until Islam strips Islamic law of all segments of (*at least*) the whole of Section O in *Reliance of the Traveller* (or any other of its law books) Islams adherents have no right to sit at any table with civilized human beings, and certainly not to be involved in determining human rights violations.

Ahl [pro: *ahel*] (var. sp.: ahla, ahle): People. The vowel is added when referring to a group, as opposed to specific people, i.e., *ahla* Sunni, or *ahle* Shi'a, or *ahle* American. (Sometimes. Not always.)

Ahl al-Fetrah [pro: *ahel alfatrah*]: People of ignorance. People who live in ignorance of the teachings of the revealed religion, Islam.

Ahl al-Kitaab [pro: *ahel elketab* (or) *al-nasarah*] (var. sp.: Ahl al-Kitab): People of the Book. (Sometimes also Children of the Book.) Qur'anic term for Christians, Jews, Zoroastrians, and Hindus. The Qur'an further defines Jews as apes and pigs, and Christians as dogs. Working dogs are acceptable in Islam; otherwise, dogs are considered unclean, so no pets. Working dogs would include those who guide the blind, which puts the lie (for instance) to the Muslim cabbies in Minneapolis in 2007 who refused to take passengers who had dogs with them as wholesale "being against their religion."

The connection between dogs and Christians comes from Qur'an **surah** (chapter) 18, verses 9-26, but there are more references to Muhammad's dislike of dogs in the **hadith**: "Once Gabriel promised the Prophet (that he would visit him, but Gabriel did not come) and later on he said, 'We, angels, do not enter a house which contains a picture or a dog.'" -- **Sahih** Bukhari 4.54.50

"Abdullah (b. Umar) (Allah be pleased with them) reported: Allah's Messenger (may peace be upon him) ordered the killing of dogs and we would send (men) in Medina and its corners and we did not spare any dog that we did not kill, so much so that we killed the dog that accompanied the wet she-camel belonging to the people of the desert." -- Sahih Muslim 10.3811

"Ibn Mughaffal reported: The Messenger of Allah (may peace be upon him) ordered killing of the dogs, and then said: What about them, i.e., about other dogs? And then granted concession (to keep) the dog for hunting and the dog for (the security) of the herd, and said: When the dog licks the utensil, wash it seven times, and rub it with earth the eighth time." -- Sahih Muslim 551

Ahl ar-ra'y [pro: *ahel alra'y*]: People of Opinion. Scholars [**Ulema**].

Ahl al-Bayt [pro: *ahel albayt*]: People of Muhammad's Household. Infallible, spiritually pure.

Ahmadiyya [pro: *almadeyyeya*]: "Renewing." This sect believes in the death and return of Jesus, that **jihad** can be a peaceful format, and that there can be more prophets after Muhammad, especially the founder,

Mirza Ghulam Ahmad, who claimed he was both the **Mahdi**, and the second coming of Jesus [**Isa**]. Orthodox Muslims consider all Ahmadis to be apostates [**ridda, murtad**].

AIFD: American Islamic Forum for Democracy. Founded by Dr. Zuhdi Jasser of Phoenix, AZ in 2003. It is anti-political Islam, pro-democracy.

AILC: American Islamic Leadership Coalition. Founded in September, 2010 in Washington, D.C. Mission is to defend the U.S. Constitution, uphold religious pluralism, protect American security, and cherish genuine diversity in the practice of [the Islamic] faith. It is anti-political Islam, pro-democracy.

Aisha bint Abu Bakr: (612-678) Muhammad's third and youngest wife. A baby bride, in fact: "The Prophet wrote the (marriage contract) with Aisha "while she was six years old and consummated his marriage with her while she was nine years old and she remained with him for nine years (i.e. until his death)." (Bukhari 7.62.88) It is from this marriage that pedophilia became a sanctioned activity in Islam. There is no set age when a girl is considered too young to be married, and no set age when she is considered too young for the "husband" to have sex with her; the time is often determined by weight—can the child bear the weight of the man on top of her? This brings some intensely revolting and cruel images to mind. The Messenger did it, though, so it's okay.

Akhirah: The afterlife.

Al Arabiyya News: "The Arabic One." A pro-caliphate [**khilafah**] and Sharia Pan-Arabist Saudi-owned Arabic-language television news channel based in Dubai Media City, United Arab Emirates, and is majority-owned by the Saudi broadcaster Middle East Broadcasting Center (MBC).

Alaihissalatu Wassalam [pro: *alayehi assalato walsalam*]: "On Him (Muhammad) are the blessings and the peace of Allah."

Alamin [pro: *alameen*]: Worlds. All that exists, anywhere, everywhere. And Allah is in charge of all of it, even where nobody wants him. Just read the Qur'an. He'll tell you.

Al-Aqsa Mosque [pro: *masjed alaska*]: The Farthest Mosque in Jerusalem. First there was Solomon's Temple on the Mount (the mount is just what it sounds like: a big hill that overlooks all of Jerusalem, even now) built in 957 BC and destroyed by the Babylonians in 586 BC. A second temple was constructed by Zerubbabel (returned with Joshua after the exile) in

516 BC and destroyed by the Roman Empire in 70 AD. The Jews have not rebuilt anything there, but the land is called the Temple Mount (in Arabic, *Haram Ash-Sharif*), on which the Sakhirah Mosque, the Dome of the Rock, was built. The rock is sacred for the hoofmark that Muhammad's horse-mule-angel, Buraq, left when he took Muhammad up to Paradise in the Night Journey, **Isra'a**. [There are many in the non-Muslim world who don't believe this *was* only a dream.] After the Muslim conquest of Jerusalem in 637, the Umayyad caliphs [**khalif**[commissioned the construction of the Al-Aqsa Mosque and Dome of the Rock on the site. The Dome was completed in 692, making it one of the oldest extant Islamic structures in the world, after the **Ka'aba**. The Al-Aqsa Mosque sits at the southern side of the Mount, facing Mecca. The Dome of the Rock currently sits in the middle, where the Bible mandates the Holy Temple is to be rebuilt.

Al-asharatu mubashshirun [pro: *al asharato almobashereen*]: The ten (and only) people Muhammad assured would enter Paradise. Abu Bakr, Umar, Uthman, Ali, Abdur Rahman ibn Awf, Abu Ubaydah ibn al-Jarrah, Talhah ibn Ubaydullah, az-Zubayr ibn al-Awwam, Sa'd ibn Abi Waqqas, Sa'id ibn Zayd. Four became the Rightful Caliphs (*Al-Khulafaa-e-Rashideen*) after Muhammad was assassinated (Abu Bakr, Umar, Uthman, and Ali). All but Abu Bakr of the four Rightful Caliphs were assassinated, too.

Alashor Alharam: 4 Sacred Months (during which the Arabic tribes could not fight one another, as set up by tradition long before Muhammad's arrival): 1st month: *Muharram;* 7th month: *Rajab;* 11th month: *Dhu al-Qi'dah;* 12th month: *Zhu-l-Hijjah.* See **Hijra**.

Alayhis Salaam (AS) [pro: *alayhee assalam*]: "Peace be Upon Them." Used when referring to the lesser prophets of Islam: Jesus [**Isa**], for instance.

Al-elmo noktatan katharoho al-jaheloon [pro: *alelmo noktatan katheroho aljheloon*]: Contempt for free inquiry. "Knowledge is only one dot, expanded by the ignorant." Could be interpreted as New Ideas Unwelcome Here. Or, Muhammad Said It, That's All You Need to Know.

Al-Faraj: The return of the Shi'a **Mahdi**. He is to show up with Jesus [**Isa**] and Muhammad (as the **Mahdi**) after the world has been destroyed and issue in a new Islamic era of all things going completely according to Allah.

Al-Fatihah: "The Opening." The central prayer of faith. Opening **surah** (chapter) in Qur'an and said at the beginning of every prayer session.

Praise of Allah and Muhammad, plus this disclaimer as to who Allah is talking about in the Qur'an: "Show us to the straight path [Islam], The Way of those on whom You [Allah] have bestowed Your Grace [the Believers], not (the way) of those who earned Your Anger [the Jews], nor of those who went astray [the Christians or apostates (**ridda or murtad**)]." Straightforward statement of/call for hate forever. Brainwashing. Mind control. What, after all, would you believe if you repeated something five times a day, every day, your entire life? Chances are it's not going to be something opposite of that.

Al Gama'a Al-Islamiya—The Islamic Group. Islamic organization led by Omar Abdel Rahman, the notorious "Blind Shaikh" currently serving a life sentence in U.S. federal prison for his leading role in forming the jihadist cell that carried out the 1993 World Trade Center bombing and was later thwarted while attempting simultaneously to bomb several other New York City landmarks. Also responsible for slaughtering about 60 European tourists in the 1997 Luxor Massacre. Its goal was to replace the Egyptian government with an Islamic state.

Al-Ghazali, aka **Algazel** (1058-1111). Abu Hamid Muhammad ibn Muhammad al-Ghazali. **Sufi** Islamic philosopher who argued that the faith or mysticism of Islam should take precedent over the science (orthodoxy) of Islam.

Al-Haqiqa: [pro: *alhakika*]: "The Truth." Egyptian TV station.

Al-Haqiqa: [pro: *alhakika*]: "The truth." There is no truth to any other belief system in the world except Islam and there is no truth to be had from any book or saying or law unless it comes from the Sharia or the Qur'an or a **Hadith**.

Al Haramain: Muslim World League. MWL. The MWL was started by the Saudi government in 1962 with Muslim Brotherhood [**Ikhwan**] members in key leadership positions. It has served as the principal vehicle for the propagation of Islamic supremacism by the Saudis and the Brotherhood. The MWL spawned the **MSA** in America, as just one example. It funds terrorism through "humanitarian relief" fronts:
1- Bosnia Canadian Relief Association
2- Canadian Relief Foundation (CRF)
3- Human Concern Int'l (HCI)
4- Kashmiri-Canadian Council(KCC)
5- Life for Relief & Development(LIFE)
6- North American Muslim Foundation (NAMF)

7- ICNA Relief (ICNA) [and there it is, the U.S. **Ikhwan** connection]
8- Int'l Dev. & Relief Foundation (IDRF)
9- Int'l Relief Fund for Afflicted and Needy (IRFAN-CANADA)

Al-Insan al-Kamil [pro: *elensan alkamel*]: The perfect man (Muhammad).

Al-Islamiyin: "Islamists." Adamant Muslims, as opposed to less rigid Muslims who favor less rigorous application of Sharia law.

Al-Jazeera News. "The Island." A broadcasting company owned by the state of Qatar through the Qatar Media Corporation and headquartered in Doha, Qatar. As of January, 2013, Al-Jazeera bought Al Gore's Current TV (which was failing in the States) for something like $60M-$100M, putting Al-Jazeera directly into American homes.

Aljihad al-Akbar: 18 major jihad attempts/deadly attacks in the U.S. since 9/11:

12/2001, FL: Richard Reid, British revert [**awdah**]. Attempted to detonate explosives packed into the shoes he was wearing, while on American Airlines Flight 63 from Paris to Miami.

8/2005, CA: Kevin James, *prisoner*; accused of founding a radical Islamic group called J.I.S. (Jam'iyyat Ul-Islam Is-Saheeh, Arabic for "Assembly of Authentic Islam") from his cell in Folsom Prison in California, and of recruiting fellow inmates to join his mission to kill infidels. See: **Da'wah/ Prison Da'wah/Prislam.**

3/2006, NC: Mohammed Reza Taheri-Azar, Iranian. Attempted murder as he used his taxi to run down and injure 9 people a the University of NC at Chapel Hill.

7/2006, WA: Naveed Haq, Pakistani. Shot six people, killing one, at the Jewish Federation of Greater Seattle building in the Belltown, near Seattle.

5/2007, NJ, The Fort Dix Six; six jihadis from Yugoslavia, Jordan, and Turkey, conspired to stage an attack with AK-47s , and M-16s, against U.S. military personnel stationed at Fort Dix, close to Trenton.

6/2009, AR: Abdulhakim Mujahid Muhammad (Carlos Bledsoe), American revert [**awdah**]. Shot and killed one soldier and wounded another at military recruiting station in Little Rock.

9/2009, TX: Hosam Smadi, Jordanian. Attempted to blow up a skyscraper in downtown Dallas.

9/2009, NY, Najibullah Zazi, Afghanstani. Attempted to blow up NY subway system.

11/2009, TX: Nidal Hasan, American Muslim; also, major in U.S.

Army. Shot and killed 13, and wounded 32 people on the Ft Hood military base, Killeen.

12/2009, MI: Umar Farouk Abdulmutallab, Nigerian. Attempted to detonate plastic explosives hidden in his underwear while on board Northwest Airlines Flight 253, en route from Amsterdam to Detroit, Michigan, on Christmas Day.

5/2010, NY: Faisal Shahzad, Pakistani. Attempted to blow up Times Square with a car bomb.

11/2010 OR: Mohamed Mohamud, Somali. Attempted car bombing at a Christmas tree lighting ceremony at a shopping mall in Portland.

12/2010, MD: Muhammad Hussain (Antonio Martinez), American revert [**awdah**]. Attempted bombing of military recruitment center in Catonsville.

2/2011, TX: Khalid Aldawsari, Saudi Arabian. Plotted to blow up nuclear plants, and one of President George W. Bush's homes.

5/2011, NY: Ahmed Ferhani (Nigerian) and Mohamed Mamdouh (Moroccan). Attempted to blow up a NYC synagogue.

7/2011, TX: Jason Abdo, American Muslim revert [**awdah**]. Attempted to kill soldiers off base near Ft. Hood, Killeen.

4/2013, MA: Tamerlan and Dzhokhar Tsarnaev, Chechnian. Used two pressure-cooker bombs along the Boston Marathon route, killing 3 people and injuring hundreds of others. Tamerlan was killed by police when trying to get out of Boston. Dzhokhar awaits trial.

12/2013, KS: Terry Lee Loewen, American revert [**awdah**]; attempted bombing of Kansas Midcontinent Airport in Wichita.

Note: 104 people attempted jihad attacks of some kind in the U.S. between 2009 & 4/2011. Of those, 62 (60%) were Americans. See www.religionofpeace.com for an updated list of all Islamic terrorist activities since 9/11.

See http://www.heritage.org/research/reports/2013/07/60-terrorist-plots-since-911-continued-lessons-in-domestic-counterterrorism for a complete list of 60 U.S. jihad attacks since 2001 (as of December, 2013).

I also recommend the Christian Action Network's DVD, *Homegrown Jihad*, to see just how many smaller jihads have been carried out or attempted in the U.S. for about a decade. The original, long version has a list of the names of Muslim-on-Muslim deaths the MOA is responsible for. You can watch the shorter, 32-minute version on-screen at:
http://www.youtube.com/watch?v=IjML6FN8yjo

Aljihad al-Akbar certainly includes 9/11/2001 in NYC, NY; 3/11/2004, Madrid, Spain; 7/7/2005, London, England, the Mumbai Massacre, November 26-29, 2008, and the recent September, 2013, Nairobi, Kenya, Westgate Shopping Mall attack that left 67 dead and 200 injured. There are many earlier than 2001 and many between 2008-2013. Israel suffers almost daily attacks from Hamas, the PA, the PIJ, or the PLO (and then blames them on Israel). The world, it seems, has become inured to jihad and turns a blind eye to all but the most egregious attacks. America's present leadership has stepped down from leadership. The world, consequently, flounders.

Al-Khulafaa al-Raashidoon [pro: *alkholafaa' alrashedoon*]: Muhammad's successors, called the Four Rightly Guided Caliphs: Abu Bakr, father-in-law; Umar, one of Muhammad's first companions; Uthman, friend of Abu Bakr's and 4th person to revert [**awdah**] to Islam; and Ali ibn Abni Talib, Muhammad's son-in-law and cousin. Ali is considered by the Shi'a to be the First Imam and should have been First Rightful Caliph. See **Battle of Karbala**, and **Ashura**.

Allah Subhanahu wa Ta'ala [pro: *allah sobhanaho wata'ala*]: "May Allah be glorified and exalted"; or, "May he be glorified and exalted."

Allah: Name of the Islamic god. Was also the name of the Arabic pagan moon god.

Allahu Akbar [pro: *Allahoo akbar*]: "Allah is the greatest."

Alluhumma: "O Allah."

Al Mashi'a: Free will, as in: You have the free will to join Islam. Free will is not available for use to leave Islam. Any Muslim who thinks he has free will can be considered a heretic [**Muhartiq**], because only Allah has "will." Only he can determine fate.

Al-Muhajiroun [pro: *al mohajeroon*]: The Emigrants. Salafist organization, started in and then banned in UK. Headed up by Anjem Choudary along with Omar Bakri Mohammed.

Al-Nasikh wal-Mansukh [pro: *nasekh wal mansookh*] (var. sp.: nashk): "The rejected law and the process to reject it." "The abrogator and that which is abrogated (nullified, voided, changed)." Simply put: The verse in the Qur'an that's been thrown out or tweaked, and the verse that threw it out or tweaked it. Abrogation is one of the toughest subjects for the non-Muslim to tackle and explain why it's so bad for the **kafir**.

The words and phrases and verses that have been nullified or rejected are still in the Qur'an, because nothing Allah said is ever deemed wrong, he simply added these nullified words and phrases and verses and told Muhammad to say something better, but the old are still true. Many of the words and verses that have been nullified are all the patient things that Allah said while Muhammad was in **Mecca** (613-621), trying to garner reverts [**awdah**] to his new religion, Islam. That clearly wasn't working; Muhammad only gathered 150 followers in the 10 years he was preaching. So Allah told Muhammad to move up to **Medina** and simultaneously unveiled **fitna** and **jihad**. Clearly, this new tack was bent on revenge, so the tolerant, inclusive verses had to go.

The Qur'an's 114 verses are not laid out in chronological order. If it were, the book would be split into the **Mecca**n (the early, patient period) and the **Medina**n (second, jihad time) periods and it would be obvious that the correctly arranged chapters 1-86 (Meccan period) are largely unrepresentative of the true Islam as practiced today. The present chapter 2 would be #87 (the first year in Medina) and chapter 113 would hold the data from chapter 9, which are the last words from Allah before Muhammad was assassinated.

Chapter 9, verse 5 is the Verse of the Sword (**Ayah al saif**); it alone abrogates 124 words, phrases, or verses in the book, of the total 225 that have been rejected but are still in the book. Only 43 chapters have not been messed with, but the non-Muslim does not know which (or even that that's the case); this is gold for the Islamic **da'ee**. He can show the unwary **kafir** (heads of state, politicians, clergy, women thinking to marry good-looking Arab men who promise to take care of them, prisoners, useful idiots/enablers) all the tolerant, nice verses (Islam is a religion of peace!) and not actually be lying, though surely concealing [**kitman**] the fact that those verses are no longer in use in Islam.

Islam is about conquering and controlling the world. The Qur'an, in its incomprehensible order, and the Doctrine of Abrogation, are two of its best tools for accomplishing that.

Al-Nour: The Light. Egyptian **Salafi**st (Islamic purists) political party, established in January, 2011.

Al-Nusra Front: "The Support Front for the People of Levant." *Jabhat al-Nusra / Jabhat an-Nus'rah li-Ahl ash-Sham* is a branch of Al Qaeda operating in Syria. It was created in January, 2012 to be a "rebel" force against the Syrians. It has been designated a terrorist organization by the UN, the U.S., the UK, and Australia. Al Nusra's leader, Abu Mohammad al-Jawlani, affirmed its allegiance to Al-Qaeda leader Ayman al-Zawahiri. By May, 2013, a faction of Jabhat loyal to the Islamic State of Iraq leadership began acting under the name of the "Islamic State of Iraq and the Levant." Starting around November 2013, members of the group in Syria, and supporters on line, began circulating banners, flags, and flyers using the name *Tanzim Qa'edat Al-Jihad fi Bilad Al-Sham* or *Al-Qaeda in Syria* instead of, or in addition to, the name Jabhat al-Nusra.

Al-Qaeda: The Base. Started in November, 1988. Al-Qaeda was the brainchild of three men, Ayman al-Zawahiri, **Usama bin Laden**, and Seyyid Imam al-Sharif (AKA "Dr. Fadl"), all adherents to **Seyyid Qutb**'s books and lectures on the need for a rebirth of Islam. It is beyond the scope of this primer to get into the depth of al-Qaeda. But, a note: "Many do not realize that the ideology of al Qaeda started in the United States in 1987, nearly ten years before Usama bin Laden declared war on America. The creation of al Qaeda in America by Muslim brother Mohamed Akram may be traced back to the May 19, 1991 document *An Explanatory Memorandum on the General Strategic Goal for the Brotherhood in North America*. **The Explanatory Memorandum** [see **HLF**] has been characterized as the Muslim Brotherhood's [**Ikhwan**] Declaration of Independence from the U.S. and the U.S. Constitution. Mohamed Akram, its author, is referred to as the Muslim Brotherhood's Thomas Jefferson."—Dr. Richard Swier: http://watchdogwire.com/florida/2013/03/18/did-you-know-al-qaeda-started-in-the-united-states/

Al-Quds (usually left unsaid: **Yaum = Day**). "Jerusalem Day," August 17th, an annual Iranian anti-Zionist event established in 1979 by Ayatollah Khomeini. The Iranian leader, Mahmoud Ahmadinejad, said on 8/3/12: "Quds Day is not merely a strategic solution for the Palestinian problem, it is to be viewed as a key for solving the world's problems. Anyone who loves freedom [**hourria**] and justice [**adl**] must strive for the annihilation of the Zionist regime in order to pave the way for world justice and freedom." Also see: **Intifada**.

Al-Shabaab [pro: *ashabab*] (var. sp.: al-Shabab): The Youth. Somalian/al-Qaeda Islamic group.

Al Uhda al-Umariyya. See: **Pact of Umar**.

AMAC: American Muslim Advisory Council. Its motto: "Engage and educate law enforcement and other government agencies [to everything that is unreal about Islam]." The intent is to "help these agencies better [mis]understand the Muslim communities through an [in]accurate understanding of religious and cultural traditions." Muslim Brotherhood [**Ikhwan**] front.

AMC: American Muslim Council. Muslim Brotherhood [**Ikhwan**] front.

Amir [pro: *ameer*] (var. sp.: ameer, emir): Prince, commander, leader.

Amir al-mu'mineen [pro: *ameer almo'meneen*]: Commander of all the faithful.

AMJA: Assembly of Muslim Jurists in America; aka: American Muslim Jurists Assembly. AMJA is also known as The Group of Lawyers for Sharia in America: *Majama Fuqaha Shariah B'America*. AMJA's stated purpose is to "clarify the rulings of the **Sharia** which are relevant for those who live in America." For instance: Can Muslims be American citizens? Response: Only as long as there's no intention to follow American laws. Muslim Brotherhood [**Ikhwan**] front. Note that Sohail Mohammed, a justice on the New Jersey Superior Court, is a member of AMJA, and put forth for ratification by the NJ senate by Governor Chris Christie.

AMP: American Muslims for Palestine. Muslim Brotherhood [**Ikhwan**] front.

AMT: American Muslim Taskforce. Muslim Brotherhood front. Tasked with finding electable Muslims in any position, but primarily on city councils, America's most vulnerable and easily assailed political bodies. Consider what city councils control: The money. The police. The zoning and the planning boards. Public utilities.

Also think of this: *Once elected, they get to make American laws which will be based on Sharia laws.* And repeal those they don't like, as a long-term goal. Get enough of them in the right legislatures, like the U.S. House and Senate, along with major state legislatures like California, Florida, Texas, Virginia (one might look at Dearborn, Michigan just to see how a Sharia-compliant U.S. city works) and who knows how fast the Constitution unravels, along with all other civilized practices, like parliamentary procedures, *Roberts Rules of Order* . . . common decency . . . .

And if that doesn't impress you, perhaps copying this link into your 'Net connection will show you how BIG they're thinking (it's a picture): http://www.radicalislam.org/news/muslim-inauguration-gala-promo-shows-minaret-over-white-house/#fm

Amuril Mu'minin: Leader of the Believers. In fact, the title for the leader of the **Sunni** Muslims only, until 1924 and the fall of the Ottoman / Turkish Empire.

Ansar: Helpers. Specifically Muslims in **Medina**. These Medinan Muslims helped Muhammad and his followers when Muhammad emigrated (see **Hijra**) from **Mecca** to Medina. If one looked closely, one could see a band of cutthroat brigands at work, there. Muhammad did not say them nay.

Anwatan: To conquer by force. As opposed to stealth.

Aqaliyyat [pro: *akalleyyat*]: Minorities. There are no divisions of Muslims (like youth or females or blacks], so minorities are the "protected" **dhimmis**.

AQAP: Al-Qaeda in the Arabian Peninsula. Likely behind the failed attempt by the Christmas "Underwear Bomber" in 2009 to blow up an American airliner, another attempt in May, 2012, and again in June, 2012. It is also suspected of having a hand in a 2010 attempt to blow up cargo planes heading to the United States with explosives concealed in printer cartridges.

Aqidah [pro: *akeedah*](var. sp.: akidah): The Islamic creed: The 6 articles of faith: the belief in: 1) Allah, 2) Angels, 3) Messengers and Prophets; 4) Scriptures, 5) the Day of Judgment, and 6) Destiny.

Aql [pro: *akel*]: Intelligence, intellect, mind, understanding. The **Shi'a** define this as divine wisdom.

Arafat: A plain north of **Mecca** where humanity will be raised on the Day of Judgment. Muslim pilgrims gather here on the ninth day of Zhu-l-Hijjah [the last month of the Islamic calendar, see **Hijra**], as part of the **Hajj** ritual, which makes it a holy site.

Arkan al-Islam al-Khamsat (also *Rukn*, and *Mabade' aleslalm*): 5 Pillars of Islam. Testifying that there is no god except Allah (**Shahada**), the obligatory 5 daily prayers (**Salat al-Yawmi al-Khamsat**), paying the alms tax (charitable giving, **Zakat**), the fast (**Sawm**) of **Ramadan**, and making pilgrimage (**Hajj**) to **Mecca**.

Asabiyyah [pro: *asabeyyah*]: Tribal loyalty or nationalism, social solidarity with an emphasis on unity, group consciousness, and social cohesion, originally in a context of "tribalism" and "clan-ism," but sometimes used for modern nationalism. Thinking on that, really, un-fancied up, it means they are all (supposed) to do the same things at the same time and in the same way . . . considering the dedication to the five prayer times a day, and consistent adherence to other Islamic rules, it seems they *do* more than they *don't*.

Asbab al-Nuzul [pro: *asbab alnozool*]: "The reasons for revelations." Considered a science to determine why Allah sent down a verse to Muhammad. It is the basis of figuring out why some verses are abrogated, and others not. *Ma'rifat asbab al-nuzul:* "The knowledge of the reasons of revelations." [Sometimes it's difficult to keep a straight face on these words and phrases. "A science"? They can say on one hand that Allah knows all and is all, which no one can question, and on the other, they want to figure out the "why" of Allah?]

Ashura: Shi'a Day of Mourning: (though this event lasts for 2 months and 8 days) the Shi'ite mourning festival—which includes men and boys, some quite young, with long, sharp instruments on chains that they sling around themselves about the head, neck and body, punishing themselves for not being there to save Ali—marking the death of the Shi'a leader Hussain bin Ali in the battle of **Karbala** against the Umayyad opposing force in the year 680. Ashura begins on the 10th day of Muharram, the first month in the Islamic calendar [see: **Hijra**].

The Shi'a re-enact this in many Iranian cities, but it also happens in the U.S.: http://creepingsharia.wordpress.com/2013/12/26/atlanta-shia-muslims-beat-themselves-bloody-in-another-ritual/. That particular ritual was for Arbaeen, which follows Ashura by 40 days, but it is still a mourning for Ali.

Aslim taslam! [pro: *aslem taslam*] "Embrace Islam and be safe!" Don't, and die? Yes. Another translation: "Submit to Islam and you will be spared." So much for "Islam is a religion of peace."

ASMA: The American Society for Muslim Advancement. Formed specifically to "sell" the Cordoba **Mosque** in NYC to the public in 2010. Re-named the Park51 Mosque (popularly called the Monster Mosque) when public outcry over a mosque at the site of the 9/11 attacks seriously halted Muslim Brotherhood-connected [**Ikhwan**] Faisal Abdul Rauf and his wife, Daisy Khan's, efforts to establish it. Rauf claims he is not part of the MB and the push to get the mosque in the old Burlington Coat Factory building established was simply his benign way of helping all humanity to get along. But the ties cannot be dismissed: Faisal is the son of Muhammad Abdul Rauf, a contemporary of Hassan al-Banna, who founded the **Ikhwan al-Muslimin;** Muhammad taught at Al Azhar University in Cairo at the same time as did al-Banna. Faisal's book: *What's Right with Islam*, has been translated into many languages (in Indonesia's Bahasa, its title translates as *The Call from the WTC Rubble*) was backed by the Islamic Society of North America [**ISNA**] and the Islamic Circle of North America [**ICNA**], both co-conspirators in the Holy Land Foundation trial [**HLF**]. Rauf was one of the signers of "A Common Word," one of the most successful ISNA **da'wah** efforts in the U.S., developed in 2007. See **Da'wah/Interfaith Dialogues.**

Asr: Late afternoon (4th) obligatory prayer of the day.

As-Sabiqun [pro: *assabekoon*]: The Vanguard. "Re-Africanization of the Islamic Movement in the USA." Founded in 1990s in Philadelphia by Imam Musa, an ex-convict who reverted [**awdah**] to Islam in prison. It is now firmly established in several major U.S. cities, including Los Angeles and Washington, DC. Muslim Brotherhood [**Ikhwan**] front.

As salaam [pro: *assalaam*]: Commonly: "Hello," or "Peace to you." But more seriously, it also means to "bow low." Fitting, considering that Islam fancies itself supreme in all things, so everyone must bow to it. The lower the better.

As Salaam: Peace. Also means to bow low in humility and subservience. (Islam means "to submit," after all.) Most importantly, Islamic ideology insists that there will be no peace in the world until every single living human being has accepted Allah as the one god and Muhammad as his prophet. Until that day comes, **fitna** will reign in **Dar al Harb** and there must always be **jihad**. Any means to attain this peace (trickery, lies, war, subterfuge, mass killings/genocide) is acceptable. Westerners believe that peace means we all get along in our different ways (we play "nice" together). Believers know that peace means we can only get along in one way— their way.

As-Salaam Alaikum [pro: *assalahm alaykom*]: "Hello"; "Welcome"; "May peace be with you," an expression Muslims say when they meet one another, a greeting with peace. This is not said to a Christian or Jew.

As-Salaf as-Saalih [pro: *assalaf assaleh*]: Islamic pious forefathers: prophets who held the way for Allah, i.e., Noah, Abraham, Moses, Joseph, Jesus

. . . Any prophet mentioned in the Bible, in fact, is considered a place-holder for Muhammad until Allah reappeared to announce himself as the first and only god of the world and Muhammad his "voice."

At-tatawwu [pro: *attatawwo*], or **nawafil**; supererogatory prayers. If a Muslim has not made enough of the obligatory (**fard**) prayers in his life, Allah will check into his supererogatory prayers, and if the Muslim has made enough of those (generally in the house, but certainly outside of the mosque), those prayers can be used to balance the books and the Muslim *may* be allowed to enter Paradise.

Auliya: Friend(s). Q5:51: "O you who believe! Take not the Jews and the Christians as *Auliya* (friends, protectors, helpers, etc.), they are but *Auliya* to one another. And if any amongst you takes them as *Auliya,* then surely he is one of them. Verily, Allah guides not those people who are the *Zalimun* (polytheists and wrong-doers and unjust)."

Q5:57: "O you who believe! Take not for *Auliya* (protectors and helpers) those who take your religion for a mockery and fun from among those who received the Scripture (Jews and Christians) before you, nor from among the disbelievers; and fear Allah if you indeed are true believers."

Q60:1: "O you who believe! Take not my enemies and your enemies (i.e. disbelievers and polytheists, etc.) as friends, showing affection towards them, while they have disbelieved in what has come to you of the truth (i.e. Islamic Monotheism, the Qur'an, and Muhammad), and have driven out the Messenger (Muhammad) and yourselves (from your homeland) because you believe in Allah your Lord! If you have come forth to strive in My Cause and to seek My Good Pleasure, (then take not these disbelievers and polytheists, etc., as your friends). You show friendship to them in secret, while I am All-Aware of what you conceal and what you reveal. And whosoever of you (Muslims) does that, then indeed he has gone (far) astray (away) from the Straight Path."

It should be clear. There is more, in case it's not: Muslims are not to hang out with the **kuffar**. Unless, of course, it's to further the cause of Islam and then shoot, party hearty, anything goes, as long as the Muslim is holding hatred in his heart for the fool of a **kafir** who's buying his bag of goods.

But wait. What if a Muslim in Western lands befriends or aids local authorities (such as ICE) and is discovered, and the local Muslims simply are in no position to kill him? There are worse punishments: The man can be ostracized from **mosque** attendance. He is an outcast. He can't attend **Jummah** [Friday] prayers (risking all hope of going to Paradise [**Jannah**]). If he has a business, the community will not buy his product. If he is an employee, he will be fired and cannot be rehired. His family members are punished with beatings. His wife can be refused entrance to the mosque, too, or if she is allowed in, she carries home the opprobrium of the community. If he has not yet received naturalization status, local Muslim Brotherhood [**Ikhwan**] members can make sure that never happens. The clan's condemnation can become so intense that to overcome it, the man can be forced into some form of **jihad** for restitution and reinstatement into the community.

Auwal and Tani Jihads: 1st (632-732) and 2nd (923-1683) Jihads: The **Ridda** [Apostate] Wars, aka: The Wars of the Apostates. When the word of Muhammad's death spread in June, 632, millions of "Muslims" in the Arabic Peninsula who had been reverted [**awdah**] by Muhammad's sword took it as an opportunity to turn back to their old beliefs. Muhammad's first successor, Abu Bakr, needed to bring these people back into Islam in order to retain power. It took a year, from 632-633 to put down the "rebellion" against Islamic rule, by killing those who would not re-revert, which gave rise to the Sharia law that apostates must be put to death.

Abu Bakr (d. 634) then turned his attention to further Islamic conquest by attacking the Persian Empire in the northeast and the Byzantine Empire in the northwest. He died before the news came that the Muslims had captured Damascus in September, 634. His successors and various dynasties for the next 100 years followed his pattern. They beat the Romans in 638 and lay claim to Jerusalem. Constantinople is besieged in 639 and finally goes down for good in 716. North Africa goes under between 639-707, with Egypt falling in 659. Muslims spread into and conquer the Lower Indus Valley between 710-713. They invade and conquer Spain by 713 and set up Cordoba in 719 as the Islamic seat of government. Spain will remain in Islamic hands until 1492 and the final battle of the Reconquista. The 1st Islamic **jihad** is stopped from going any farther north by Charles Martel at the **Battle of Poitiers** in 732.

"By . . . 923, jihad wars had expanded the Muslim empire from Portugal to the Indian subcontinent. Subsequent Muslim conquests continued in Asia, as well as Eastern Europe. Under the banner of jihad, the Christian kingdoms of Armenia, Byzantium, Bulgaria, Serbia, Bosnia, Herzegovina, Croatia, and Albania, in addition to parts of Poland and Hungary, were also conquered and Islamized by waves of Seljuk, or later Ottoman Turks, as well as Tatars. Arab Muslim invaders engaged, additionally, in continuous jihad raids that ravaged and enslaved Sub-Saharan African animist populations, extending to the southern Sudan. When the Ottoman Muslim armies were stopped at the gates of Vienna in 1683, over a millennium of jihad had transpired. These tremendous military successes spawned a triumphalist jihad literature. Muslim historians recorded in detail the number of infidels slaughtered, or enslaved and deported, the cities, villages, and infidel religious sites which were sacked and pillaged, and the lands, treasure, and movable goods seized."—Andrew Bostom, blog, 6/12/12: "Mohammed Zuhdi Jasser's Koran."

Averroes, aka **ibn Rushd** (1126-1198). Full name: Abu al-Walid Muhammad ibn Ahmad ibn Rushd. Spanish Islamic philosopher (during the Islamic "Golden Age"), postulated that Muslims have the right and duty to interpret the Qur'an in order to understand it. Primarily known for his interpretations of Aristotle's philosophy.

Avicenna, aka **ibn Sina** (930-1037). Full name: Abu Ali Al-Husayn ibn Ad Allah ibn Sina. Considered the premier Islamic Persian philosopher during the Islamic "Golden Age."

Awdah [pro: *al aoudah*] (var. sp.: Aloodeh): Return or revert. People revert to Islam, not convert. All people are born into the **deen** of Islam; only ignorance of the true deen keeps them out. When they realize the truth, they revert from whatever beliefs they held to come to the true and only way of life. This idea comes thinly from Q30:30, but also from the many (and varying) explanations of how *Allah* gave life to Adam, certainly not God/Yahweh, as the Jews and Christians who corrupted the story and hid Allah's existence, will tell you.

Awrah (var. sp.: Aurah): Nakedness. Parts of the body that are not supposed to be exposed to others. For men this is from the navel to the knee. For the women it is all of her body, except the hands, feet, and face (depending on where on the Earth she is), and thus the development of the **chador/burqa**, what Westerners call the "canvas prison." Refer to ***Reliance of the Traveller***, Book M, Marriage, (2.7-8) to get the whole flavor of the restrictions on women.

Q33:59: "O Prophet! Tell your wives and your daughters and the women of the believers to draw their cloaks (veils) all over their bodies (i.e. screen themselves completely except the eyes or one eye to see the way). That will be better, that they should be known (as free respectable women)[as opposed to slave women] so as not to be annoyed [raped]. And Allah is Ever Oft-Forgiving, Most Merciful."

Ayah: (var. sp.: aya, ayyah): Miracle. And (most common): All verses in the Qur'an. Plural: Ayat. The Qur'an is considered to be a miracle. Each verse or sentence is called an ayah or a miracle. Ayah can also mean "message."

Ayah al-saif: Verse of the Sword: Q9:5. "When the sacred months are over, slay the idolaters wherever you find them. Arrest them, besiege them, and lie in ambush everywhere for them. If they repent and take to prayer and render the alms [**jizya**] levy, allow them to go their way." Note that the last line does not mean the idolaters are free; it means they've accepted **dhimmi status**. Ayah 9:5 **abrogates** 124 of the tolerant or patient verses in the Qur'an, denuding the Qur'an of any possibility of getting along with any other peoples in the world. **Ibn Kathir** has a **tafsir** that IDs and explains 149 verses of the sword in the Qur'an.

Ayatollah (Farsi/**Shi'a**): Sign of God. A senior clerical rank in the Shi'a hierarchy achieved only after many decades of pious devotion to Islam and intensive theological scholarship, including teaching. Only a Grand Ayatollah ranks above an Ayatollah. The Ayatollah Ruhollah Khomeini was a Grand Ayatollah, but the current Supreme Leader of Iran, the Ayatollah Ali Khamenei, was only a Hojjatolislam, a middle rank, when Khomeini died in 1989 and had to be elevated artificially and without the requisite scholarship to the rank of ayatollah in order to be named Supreme Leader. This is the beauty of the **fatwa,** of course; the scholars can make one up on the spot as needed. No messy precedent to follow as in Western jurisprudence.

Azimah: Eloquent determination. If a Muslim has this, he can overcome all attacks against Islam. True of Christians and Jews and Republican Conservatives and the United Kingdom Independent Party, and the Congress Party in India, too, but it's not like you'll catch any of them saying "Eloquent determination for me!" out loud, more's the pity.

Bacha Bazi: [pro: *botchuh bahtzi*] Sexual exploitation of boys (Arabic); playing with children (Iranian), playing with boys (Afghani), but meaning "dancing boys," the sexually-exploited prepubescent and pubescent boys trained to dance like females, wearing female clothing and makeup, for the entertainment of Afghan, especially Pashtun, men whose cultural and Islamic ideology teach them that women are unclean.

Ba'd Alhijra (AH): After Hijra. Used in Arabic calendar, which began in 622. See **Hijra**.

Baghawat: Insurgency; rebellion. Specifically, against a legitimate government. No government is legitimate in Muslim eyes except one that is Islamic. However, see **Tamarod**.

Baha'i. The Baha'i Faith was founded in 1863 by Baha'u'llah: "The Glory of God," a member of the Persian nobility who claimed *he* was the last prophet. Baha'u'llah was exiled to the prison city of Akka in Palestine. There are no clergy in the Baha'i Faith; all decision-making power devolves upon the elected assemblies. The Baha'i community has survived intense persecution in its Iranian homeland, but has spread worldwide, and is second only in spread to Christianity. It claims 2,100 ethnic, racial, and tribal groups and is the most diverse organized body of people on the planet. Orthodox Muslims kill them as quickly as they kill Jews and Christians.

Bai'a [pro: *bayah* or *bayat*]: Pledge, Oath of Allegiance. Made by Muhammad's companions to Muhammad's successors. Will be made by all Muslims to the next caliph [**khalif**] if there is another one.

Baitullah [pro: *baytoallah*]: **Mosque**/House of Allah. Specifically, the **Ka'aba**. AKA *Baitul Gaffar*: House of the Creator. Allah ordered Adam to build this house of worship. Muhammad also said that Abraham and Ishmael built it. *Baitul M'amuh*: Heavenly abode. Allah's home in Paradise.

Barakah: Blessing, divine grace. The holy spirit, breath of life.

Barakallah: "May the blessings of Allah be upon you."

Barii. Innocent. The oft-heard statement that **jihad**ists do not kill innocent people is true, if the speaker is referring to Muslims. Non-Muslims are never considered innocent because the True Religion exists and is available for all to partake of. If a non-Muslim does not revert [**awdah**], he or she should be killed or enslaved, or agree to accept **dhimmi** status.

Basiji (Basij-e Mostaz'afin): Mobilization of the Oppressed. A paramilitary volunteer militia established in 1979 by order ["volunteers ordered"] of the Islamic Revolution's leader Ayatollah Khomeini. A subset of the Iranian Revolutionary Guards. Commonly called the "Islamic morality police."

Basmala: "In the name of Allah, most gracious, most merciful." Each **surah** (chapter) in the Qur'an starts with the Basmala, except the 9th [chronologically the last chapter in the Qur'an, in which Muhammad, ahem, Allah, declares hatred and death against every **kafir** everywhere for all time, or at least until Muhammad (as the **Mahdi [Shi'a]**) gets his shot at coming back with **Isa** [Jesus] and picking and choosing what souls go to hell [**Jahannam**] or Paradise [**Jannah**].

Batil: false, void; false religion: All religions are false except the **deen** of Allah.

Battle at the Gates of Vienna, *Ikinci Viyana Kusatması* (Turkish). September 11-12, 1683. Vienna had been besieged by the Ottoman / Turkish Empire [see **Khilafah**] for two months. It was a battle of the Holy Roman Empire in league with the Polish–Lithuanian Commonwealth (Holy League) versus the Ottoman / Turkish Empire and chiefdoms of the Ottoman / Turkish Empire at the Kahlenberg Mountain near Vienna. The battle marked the end of the Islamic 2nd jihad (see **Auwal and Tani** for 1st & 2nd jihads). Note the date. It was not by accident that **Usama bin Laden** picked that date to attack the U.S. It was a clarion call to the Followers around the world that the **3rd Jihad** [see: **Thaaleth Jihad**] was on us, and this time Islam would not be stopped from conquering the West as it had been in 732 (**Battle of Poitiers**) and again here, in 1683.

Battle of Badr, *Qitaal Badr*: Place of the first full military confrontation between the Muslims and the **Meccans**. Even though the Muslims were outnumbered, they were victorious over the Quraish of Mecca (624 AD. Year 2 of the Islamic calendar, see: **Hijra**).

Battle of Constantinople, *Qitaal Constantinople* (now Istanbul), 1453. Marked the end of the Roman Empire. Strengthened the Islamic Ottoman / Turkish Empire which had begun in 1299 and lasted until 1925 (see **Khilafah**).

Battle of Karbala, *Qitaal Karbala*. 10th day of Muharram, 680. Hussain ibn Ali (Muhammad's grandson) was killed that day, fighting against the first of the Umayyad sultans, which began the **Sunni** sect of Islam, and took the leadership from Muhammad's line away and began a dynasty. Hussain's followers claimed that only Muhammad's direct descendant had the right to be caliph [**Khalif**]; Hussain's father was Ali ibn Abni Talib, Muhammad's cousin. Hussain's mother was Fatimah, Muhammad's daughter. Those who followed Hussain became known as the **Shi'a** ["Followers"]. Hussain's death is com-

memorated every year in a ritual known as **Ashura**, the Day of Mourning.
http://en.wikipedia.org/wiki/Family_tree_of_Ali

Battle of Lepanto, *Qitaal Lepanto*. October 7, 1571. A coalition of southern European Catholic maritime states (the Holy League) decisively defeated the main fleet of the Ottoman / Turkish Empire [see **Khilafah**] in five hours of fighting on the northern edge of the Gulf of Patras, off western Greece. The Ottoman / Turkish forces sailed westward from their naval station in Lepanto and met the Holy League forces, which had come from Messina. The victory of the Holy League prevented the Mediterranean Sea from becoming an uncontested highway for Muslim forces and helped to prevent the Ottomans/Turks from advancing farther along the Mediterranean flank of Europe.

Battle of Poitiers, *Ma'arakat Balat ash-Shuhada*: Battle of the Court of the Martyrs. Poitiers, France. October, 732. The battle pitted Charles Martel and his French forces against an army of the Umayyad **Khilafah** [caliphate)[see **Battle of Karbala**] led by Abdul Rahman Al Ghafiqi, Governor-General of al-Andalus (Spain). The Franks were victorious. Christian chroniclers and pre-20th century historians praised Charles Martel as the champion of Christianity, characterizing the battle as the decisive turning point in the struggle against Islam, a struggle which preserved Christianity as the religion of Europe.

Bayah: Rule/ruling from Sharia. The more popular term is **Fatwa.**

Bayt al-mal: State treasury in an Islamic nation. Receives and handles **zakat, jizya**, and **kharaj**, as well as other sources of income [like oil drilling payments].

Behead/Decapitation. http://www.meforum.org/713/beheading-in-the-name-of-islam. There is no question that Islam directs its adherents to behead its enemies to keep that enemy from fighting you again.

Q8:12 reads: "I will cast dread into the hearts of the unbelievers. Strike off their heads, then, and strike off all of their fingertips." In the original text, the relevant phrase is *adrabu fawq al-'anaq*, "strike over their necks."

Q47:4*: "When you meet the unbelievers, smite their necks, then, when you have made wide slaughter among them, tie fast the bonds; then set them free, either by grace or ransom, till the war lays down its loads. So it shall be; and if Allah had willed, He would have avenged Himself upon them; but that He may try some of you by means of others. And those who are slain in the way of Allah, He will not send their works astray."

The Qur'anic Arabic terms are generally straightforward: *kafaru* means "those who blaspheme/are irreligious," although *Darb ar-riqab* is less clear. *Darb* can mean "striking or hitting" while *ar-riqab* translates to "necks, slaves, persons." With little variation, scholars have translated the verse as, "When you meet the unbelievers, smite their necks."

----

*Q47.4 has been abrogated (**al-Nasikh wal-Mansukh**) in its entirety in favor of the Verse of the Sword [**Ayah al-saif** *]*, Q9:5, which just says kill all **kafir** until every last one has submitted to Allah; it doesn't mention the how of doing it. It is clear that Michael Adebolajo, who murdered British soldier Lee Rigby on a street in London in May, 2013, by beheading him and then saying Allah said it was what he was supposed to do, wasn't concerned with the how, but with the do.

Bi'dah (**Sayyi'ah**, bad; and **Hananah**, good): Religious innovation (renaissance, enlightenment, new ideas). Frowned on in Islam. BUT, maybe not, or at least not in England. When trying to ascertain the difference between the two *bi'dat*, I happened across this ages-old thread on the 'Net: http://www.therevival.co.uk/comment/181375

Bin: Son of. High or classic Arabic. "**Usama bin Laden**" is an example of high or classic Arabic, wherein bin means son of.

Bint: Daughter of (the father's name). Women simply disappear in Islam.

Bishmillah [pro: *bismellah*]: "In the name of Allah."

Bismillah rahmanir rahim [pro: *bismellah alrahman alraheem*]: "In the name of Allah, the Most Beneficent, the Most Merciful." A phrase from the Qur'an that is recited before reading the Qur'an and immediately after the phrase: "*A'uzu Billahi Minashaitanir Rajim.*" A phrase also recited before doing daily activities.

Bi'thah: 610; beginning of Muhammad's mission. The year the Angel Gabriel (**Ji'bril**) appeared to Muhammad in the Cave of Hira in the mountains outside Mecca.

The Black Flag of Islam: *ar-Raya or al-Uqab*. Carried into battle from the early days of the Islamic conquest. The script is the **Shahada,** the Testimony [See: **Setta Kalimat** (6 Fundamentals)]: "There is no god but Allah and Muhammad is his prophet." According to Islamic history and tradition, Muhammad, the "prophet" and founder of Islam, carried a large black banner known as *ar-Raya* into battle. The first black banner was said to be made from a large piece of cloth once wrapped around the head of his child-bride, Aisha. Another name for the flag in Arabic is *al-Uqab*, and is sometimes referred to as "the Eagle" or alternately as "the Punishment."

The Black Stone, *Al Hajar al Aswad*: a meteorite embedded in one of the walls of the **Ka'aba**, which is surrounded by the **Masjid al Haram** in **Mecca**. Muhammad claimed that Abraham and Ishmael found the shining white stone (it later turned black because it was handled by women having their menses) while in the area that would become Mecca 2600 years before Muhammad was born. The idolaters of the time used it as the cornerstone of what was to become the Ka'aba. The Ka'aba has been rebuilt several times since Abraham's time, and the Black Stone has been re-embedded every time. Muhammad stated that Allah's instructions to him in 610 were to rid the Ka'aba of the 360 pagan stone idols in the Ka'aba . . . and yet the Black Stone remains in the Ka'aba and is intensely holy. So idolatry still reigns: Pious Muslims (and even less pious) pray to a rock from outer space up to 5x a day.

Boko Haram: "Western Education Is Sin." **Jihad** organization located in Nigeria. Boko Haram has the dubious honor of killing more Christians during Christmas-time in 2010-2012 than any other Islamist organization, 42 in 2012 alone. The U.S. State Department put it on the terrorist list in November, 2013.

Burqa: Female full body-covering robe. The "canvas prison," *the* symbol of female oppression and servitude. See **Awrah/nakedness**. Women in the West say, "Oh, the *burqa* (or the **chador**, or the **abayah**)," without giving it much thought other than knowing it's not something we want to wear. I wondered how the women needing to eat or drink while wearing one accomplished that; how they could see out; did it itch? I came across this article by Alissa Rubin which answered most of my questions: http:// atwar.blogs.nytimes.com/2011/05/05/my-first-afghan-burqa/

CAIR: Council of American Islamic Relations. Palestinian. Muslim Brotherhood [**Ikhwan**] front/co-conspirator in the Holy Land Foundation trial [**HLF**}, Dallas, TX, 2008. CAIR has been called "Hamas doing business in the U.S." Founded as the U.S. branch of the International Association of Palestine (**IAP**, Muslim Brotherhood), it bills itself as an Islamic civil rights organization.

It is primarily the attack dog on Western businesses; it files lawsuits (the

term "lawfare" originated with CAIR's tactics against American companies) sometimes not for the money or the principle, but to show its mus-
cle: Do not say no to us, or say bad things about us, or we will sue you."

It is practically the only "voice" the media listens to whenever a Islam-re-
lated issue is in the news. Has infiltrated federal and state homeland
security, police, and counter-terrorism agencies, is consulted for Muslim
outreach by the FBI, and has forced police to close private events in hotels
under the "civil rights" guise of being offensive to Muslims. It was the de-
fendant in a Michigan, May, 2012, lawsuit for violating First Amendment
rights to free speech. CAIR lost its non-profit 501(c)3 status in 2010; there
has been no obvious indication by the IRS that it will demand CAIR cease
operating as a non-profit organization.

CAIR's lawfare against employers through employees for religious discrimination lawsuits is now its biggest trademark. It does not, however,
do the actual trial work (should it actually come to that); the cases are
filed with, and handled by the EEOC, so the U.S. government is suing the
companies. In other cases, CAIR might take the case to the ACLU, which
then takes the case to trial against a government entity.

The EEOC handled 91 cases for Muslim plaintiff's between 2002-2013.
The plaintiffs were awarded $12.2M for harassment, and/or discrimina-
tion against the hijab (and miscellaneous other charges) during that time.
Some of the plaintiffs filed for *not being hired* for reason of discrimination
and still won their cases.

The ACLU boasts here: https://www.aclu.org/protecting-religious-freedom-muslims
about how it's protecting freedom by demanding the Monster Mosque in
NY be allowed to be built, that the NY police should give Muslims a pass
on terrorism attention, that profiling at airports is wrong . . . . Yes, they
are a "civil liberties" organization. What is hard to understand is that they
don't get it that Islam *isn't* a civil liberties organization and it will be as
happy to take the ACLU down as it will the NYC police department.

Chador: Female full-body-covering robe. See **Awrah/nakedness**.

CMCU. Center for Muslim Christian Understanding. Saudi-funded
Muslim Brotherhood [**Ikhwan**] front group. Works to rewrite the training manuals used to teach law enforcement personnel about the Islamist
threat to America. New training manuals are to be "culturally sensitive."

Sometimes these people leave one breathless with their chutzpah. "Muslim Christian understanding? Look up **Seyyid Qutb** for the facts on how much understanding one can expect from the Islamic leadership.

COPAA: Council on Pakistani American Affairs. Muslim Brotherhood [**Ikhwan**] front. Considerable collusion with CAIR, particularly.

CSID: Center for the Study of Islam and Democracy. Muslim Brotherhood [**Ikhwan**] front.

Da'ee (var. sp.: Da'iy): Muslim proselytizer involved in **Da'wah**. One who invites others to Islam. See **Tarbiya** for how they're supposed to do this inviting.

Dajjal: Liar, cheat—between Muslims only—unless the liar and cheat is employing **taqiyya**, approved lying and cheating to advance the cause of Islam in non-Muslim nations when the Muslim is outnumbered. There are also interpretations that say this means "the anti-Christ."

Dar ad Da'wah: House of Preaching.

Dar al Harb: House of War; every country not governed by Sharia. The people of those countries are Harbi.

Dar al Islam [pro: *dar aleslam*]: House of Islam (the Islamic **ummah**).

Dar al Kuffar [pro: *daralkoffar*]: Domain of disbelief; the term originally referred to the Quraish-dominated society of **Mecca** between Muhammad's flight to **Medina** (the **Hijra**) and the city's conquest.

Dar al Sohl (Farsi): House of Peace.

Dar ul Aman: House of refuge; non-Islamic nations. Wow! Think about that! They have a name for where the **kuffar** can go to get away from them! Well, no. It means countries that are designated Islam-friendly, where **jihad** is unnecessary. Might be Europe and America soon, way things are going.

Daruriyat Al Khams (Al) [pro: *daroreyyat alkhams*] (var sp.: daruee, daruri): The five fundamental needs of every Muslim: protection of life, religion (**deen**), reason (**aql**), progeny, and property. They have also been termed as *Maqasid al-Shari'ah*, i.e., the main objectives of the Sharia. An Islamic state is supposed to take care of these basic needs of all its inhabitants, should the individual, the family, or his community be unable to do it. From **zakat** collection, maybe?

Da'wah (var. sp.: dawa; da'wa, dawah): The invitation to join Islam; proselytizing. It is incumbent on all Muslims to act as *du'at* [plural for **da'ee**] for Islam. Some Muslims are better suited for this than others, of course, and are recruited into groups such as the Muslim Students Association [**MSA**], and others given formal training, called **tarbiya**.

A formal invitation to revert [**awdah**] to/accept Islam is made in three steps : 1) an explanation of what Islam is, and why a person (or nation) should revert; an offer to accept the reversion will be accepted immediately by the revertee saying the **shahada**. 2) If that invitation is rejected, an offer will be made that the person (or nation) may take **dhimmi** status and pay the **jizya** and **kharaj** (if appropriate) taxes. If accepted, the new dhimmi will be protected by the state. 3) If that position is also rejected, the person can be killed immediately (if in a Muslim-dominant nation), or a nation attacked immediately.

It is said that **Usama bin Laden** was rebuked by the **ulema** when he devised and carried out the attack on the Twin Towers in NYC on 9/11/01— not for the attack, but because he had not followed Sharia law by issuing the proper invitation to the U.S. head of state (President George W. Bush) prior to the attack and allowing the president the opportunity to accept in the name of the American people.

Ibn Khaldun (1332-1406; an early sociologist) said it this way: "It is the duty of every Muslim to induce Christians [to come to Islam] in three ways: by violence, extortion, or enslavement." More simply put, it's: "Da'wah, dhimmi, or die."

There are a limited number of things a **da'ee** can say to thinking Westerners to revert them, before they begin getting too close to the truth of Islam. A big handful:
1: We are all children/people of the Book. [Allah says Christians and Jews are dogs and pigs.]
2: We all pray to the same god. [Allah says he is not begotten nor would he beget. The Bible clearly states that Jesus is the son of God, so right there is cause for pause.]
3: Islam is a religion of peace. [If you don't believe your lyin' eyes, can't read, don't know anything about honor killings, hanging gays, the practice of dhimmis, or the disappearance of the Armenians, maybe you can buy into this.]
4: There is no compulsion in religion. [Even if you believe this, the

imams know it isn't true. Q2:256 clearly states: "There is no compulsion in religion." However, **surah** (chapter) 9:5, the Verse of the Sword [**Ayah al-saif**], has abrogated (annulled: **al-Nasikh wal-Mansukh**) that verse completely.]

5: Islam regrets the death of all innocent people. [True! But only Muslims are innocent [**Barii**].]

6: Islam is simply misunderstood. True! But it's them spreading the misunderstanding deliberately, so it's kind of cheeky of them to whine about it. Actually, it's worse than that. This is victimology. This is criminal use of the language to immediately make the listener feel guilty (when there's nothing to feel guilty about) and *stop thinking*. See: **IIIT**.

Interfaith dialogues are da'wah. Since da'wah is just another Islamic tactic for **jihad**, no one should participate in these. But Christian, Catholic, Jewish, Buddhist, and Hindu clergy, not to mention Leftists, Democrats, members of Parliament, and other political groups and associations the world over are falling all over themselves to get in the dialogue game, led, directed, and orchestrated primarily by **ISNA** in the U.S. It's a phenomena that needs to die.

(And in case you think this is just all spontaneous missionary work, you should read this about another da'wah movement afoot in the U.S.: The Hired Muslim Missionaries who are being paid to get in your face with the word of Allah: http://www.faithfreedom.org/confronting-the-hired-muslim-missionaries/.)

The Middle East Quarterly had this report in 1999 (http://www.meforum.org/448/we-will-dominate-you) titled: "We Will Dominate You" from a Catholic priest who sent a letter regarding an interfaith dialogue he'd attended with Muslims to higher ups in Catholic officialdom. "One: During an official meeting on Islamic-Christian dialogue, an authoritative Muslim person, speaking to the Christians participating, at one point said very calmly and assuredly: "Thanks to your democratic laws we will invade you; thanks to our religious laws **we will dominate you**. . . . Two: During another Islamic-Christian meeting, always organized by Christians, a Christian participant publicly asked the Muslims present why they did not organize, at least once, a meeting of this kind? The Muslim authority present answered with the following words: "**Why should we? You have nothing to teach us and we have nothing to learn**. . . . Three: In a Catholic monastery in Jerusalem there was and perhaps still is a Muslim Arab servant. One day, he sadly told his employers: "Our chiefs have met and have decided that all the 'infidels' must be killed, but do not fear because **I will kill you without making you suffer**." The priest begged in his closing: Please do not ever hold interfaith dialogues in Catholic churches.

U.S. News, 6/20/2002: "Presbyterian Church (USA) Urges Muslim Dialogue: http://old.post-gazette.com/nation/20020620presby0620p4.asp "The paper emphasized that dialogue is neither for the purpose of trying to convert the other party nor to water down either party's beliefs to make them compatible." So what is the point? Why spend thousands of dollars and hours of time on big or little events where Christians, Jews, and Muslims all get together to agree that they can get along, without ever discussing why there is no way that can be true? There is certainly no question why the purveyors of Islam do it, but what can the other sides' goal be, if they aren't even going to *try* to save souls?

On 10/13/2007, 138 Muslim scholars and clerics of the Royal al-Bayt Institute of Islamic Thought of Jordan, including top leaders from around the world "representing every major school of Islamic thought" (that would be five. See **Sharia**) sent an open letter "to leaders of Christian churches (which mostly weren't, as it turned out; the recipients were major U.S. university divinity schools, and evangelical businesses, or very liberal religion-ishy operations), everywhere." The document and movement became known as A Common Word Between Us and You. The open letter was essentially Islamic da'wah to the U.S. (http://www.acommonword. com/the-acw-document/), telling these leader that there would be hell to pay if they didn't get on board asap now that the offer to come to Islam had been made. No. Not in those words, of course.

A Common Word was followed immediately on 10/13/2007 (do you think maybe that was planned?) by Yale Divinity School's Center for Faith and Culture: "Loving God and Neighbor Together" with 150 endorsers and 150 signatories, one of whom was Rick Warren of the Saddleback Church in California [http://www.yale.edu/divinity/news/071118_news_nytimes. pdf]. This document essentially said, "Yes, we accept our **dhimmi** status. We don't have a clue that's what we're doing, but we're foolish enough to believe that we all believe in the same god, and that means you can't be bad, so we'll accept you on the face of what you say without looking any deeper into your creed." [Yes, I prefer thinking that way. To think they *knew* what they were agreeing to is . . . unthinkable.]

Then came Chrislam (http://www.nowtheendbegins.com/blog/?p=1366). 2/4/2011: Rick Warren's Chrislam Starts To Spread In America: "In 2009, Rick Warren, founder and pastor of Saddleback Community Church in Orange County California, addressed the convention of the Islamic Society of North America [**ISNA**]. Warren stated that Muslims and Christians must work together to combat stereotypes, promote peace and freedom, and solve global problems. Warren went on to announce: "This weekend, the Memorial Drive Presbyterian Church in Houston along with Christian communities in Atlanta, Seattle, and Detroit will initiate a series of sermons that have been designed to produce an ecumenical reconciliation between Christianity and Islam." Reconciliation? Of what? For what?

This has been followed by far too many others, including the Catholic church, in the person of His Holiness, Pope Francis (November, 2013): "Apostolic Exhortation *Evangelii Gaudium* of the Holy Father Francis to the Bishops, Clergy, Consecrated Persons and the Lay Faithful On the Proclamation of the Gospel In Today's World," from Vatican.va, November 24: #253. In order to sustain dialogue with Islam, suitable training is essential for all involved, not only so that they can be solidly and joyfully grounded in their own identity, but so that they can also acknowledge the values of others, appreciate the concerns underlying their demands and shed light on shared beliefs. We Christians should embrace with affection and respect Muslim immigrants to our countries in the same way that we hope and ask to be received and respected in countries of Islamic tradition. I ask and I humbly entreat those countries to grant Christians freedom to worship and to practice their faith, in light of the freedom which followers of Islam enjoy in Western countries. Faced with disconcerting episodes of violent fundamentalism, our respect for true followers of Islam should lead us to avoid hateful generalisations, for authentic Islam and the proper reading of the Koran are opposed to every form of violence." Now this is really awful. He's the *Pope*. He *should* know better.

As an example of how da'wah works in an interfaith setting there is this: There was an article on the ISNA website in 2013 that had this paragraph: ". . . During his time in the Twin Cities, Dr. Said Syeed also delivered the **khutbah** at the Islamic Center of Minnesota and spoke at the University of St. Thomas' Muslim-Christian Dialogue Center. He spoke about pluralism and interfaith cooperation at each event, citing the prophetic model in the early community of Madinah." This is a **kitman** alert because: *He* *did not say anything* at the "Muslim-Christian Dialogue Center" about the fact that the "prophetic model" applied only to Arabs and Muslims, nor add that the Prophet *disposed* of the three Jewish tribes of **Medina**. He did so by beheading all Quraish [see: **Mecca**] males over the age of puberty and enslaved the women and children. The second tribe he drove out of town with only the possessions they could carry. He conquered the third, the Khaybar, an agricultural community near Mecca, and reduced them to **dhimmis**, for 50% annual produce as tribute.

Dialogue only works if the whole story is being told. Muslim speakers will never tell non-Muslims the whole story. Islam is at war with non-Muslims; da'wah's interfaith dialogue is **jihad**.

For a perfect example of "lying interfaith da'wah dialogue" check out: http://www.youtube.com/watch?v=mU-uwgLWqmc, brought to you by the intrepid United West.

Prison Da'wah/Prislam. "An unusually high number of convicts are being converted to Islam [in U.S. prisons]. [Blacks] especially . . . are converting in large numbers. According to estimates, up to 20% of prisoners in the U.S. are Muslims. This figure is approximately 20 times higher than the national Muslim population [overall]."—Ryan Mauro, the Clarion Project. http://www.clarionproject.org/threat/homegrown-threat/us-prisons. According to a Wiki report, nearly 7M adults were in some form of incarceration at year end 2011, or ~7% of the U.S. population; 20% of 7M = ~1.4M Muslims. http://en.wikipedia.org/wiki/Incarceration_in_the_United_States. The most common number given for the U.S. Muslim population is 3M. Are nearly half former prisoners?

Why is this a problem? Because studies show that once black men (though certainly not all, and not only) come out of the prisons, they don't try to integrate back into society. They head for Islamic compounds, or "no-go-zones" as heavily Sharia-compliant areas are coming to be called. There they will meet like-minded, turned-on-against-the-U.S. thinkers. They will help build **mosques**, marry, and raise children in Islam. They could become the conduits between the radical organizations both within and without the U.S., such as **Al-Shabaab**, and recruit more black youth to fight and die for Islam. Once taught in the prison system how to think like a jihadist, some could become jihadists themselves, such as:

Malcolm X - A Civil Rights activist
Abdul Alim Musa - Muslim-American activist
H. Rap Brown - former Black Panther; currently in prison for murdering a police officer
Jeff Fort - former Chicago gang leader; convicted in 1987 of conspiring with Libya to perform acts of domestic terrorism
José Padilla - convicted of aiding terrorists in the "Dirty Bomb" plot
Kevin James - ringleader of the 2005 Los Angeles bomb plot

The point of incarceration and penal service is to break the cycle of crime. Make sure the criminal doesn't go out with the same mindset as when s/he went in, with the intent of making these rehabilitated people productive members of society. With Islamic *du'at* lurking there now, that long-term goal seems further away from success than ever before, but with even worse ramifications for U.S. society.

Dawla: State, as in nation.

Dawlat al Islam [pro: *dawlat aleslam*]: State of Islam. This title might tend to make one think that Islam is not, strictly speaking, a simple religion of peace.

Deen [pro: *din*]: the Faith. The ALL of what Islam is; the totality of the life in Islam. Values and perspective of Islam as a perfect and complete way of life; the way of honor, justice [**adl** and Sharia], and true equality because no man-made laws are used for justice and all men are free [**hourria**] from new man-made laws.

Deobandi. An Islamist study group named after the town in India where a group of Islamic scholars built a school to teach 10th century Sharia Islam to oppose Western thought. It was revived in the 20th century by Abul A'la **Maududi**. Its practitioners eventually became second in importance only to Al Azhar University in Cairo, Egypt, and the Muslim Brothers [**Ikhwan**]. Al Azhar spawned al-Qaeda; the Deobandi spawned **Jamaat-e-Islami, Tablighi Jamaat** (Pakistani), and the **Taliban** (Afghanistan). The group is also known as the **National Ummah Movement**. The Muslim Brotherhood and the Deobandi are not enemies.

Dharura: Lying/deceit because of necessity, such as times when Muslims are far outnumbered in a non-Sharia-compliant environment.

Dhikr [pro: *theker*] (var sp.: Zikr): Remembrance of Allah.

Dhimmi: Identifies a non-Muslim living under the protection of a

Muslim state. He is exempt from duties of Islam, such as serving in the military or the **zakat** tax, instead pays a tax called **jizya**, and sometimes the **kharaj**, the land tax. If the non-Muslim fails to pay the jizya or kharaj, his protected status is revoked and it is then permissible for a Muslim to kill him and his family. *Dhimmah*: Structure for Protected Persons: Christians, Jews, Hindus, and Zoroastrians allowed to live as subjugated citizens in a Muslim state and required to pay a poll tax, jizya. This began with the **Pact of Umar**, 627AD. Turkey rescinded this practice in 1850; reinstated it under another name in 1942.

Many people think this is nothing but ancient history, right? How many of you reading this might've been born in 1942, or have fathers, mothers, grandparents (who could've been fighting in WWII) still living who were born around that time? Anybody remember that *Casablanca* came out in 1942 and won the Oscar in 1943? Turkey's most important business was re-enslaving Jews . . . and yet Turkey was supposed to be secular at the time. See **Khilafah** for more information on Turkey.

Diyya: Compensation paid to the heirs of a victim, both blood money and ransom. For instance: if a Muslim "accidentally" kills another Muslim, his family can pay this as compensation.

Djinn: (or Jinn): Supernatural creature. The Qur'an is loaded with the occult.

Du'a: Prayer; supplication to Allah.

Dunya: Worldly affairs. Meaning to be too concerned with the earthly world or life (being alive), as opposed to the Hereafter, which is the **Akhirah**. A True Believer's total focus should be on getting to Paradise [**Jannah**], where the rewards for not enjoying the pleasures of the earthly world will be given to him. Besides other shortcomings, Muslims see Christians and Jews as entirely too focused on earthly pleasures, keeping open the unclosable rift between Islam and the rest of the world forever.

Ebaadah: Total obedience to Allah. Total obedience to Allah has been called the "perfect slavery." Can also mean worship of Allah.

Eid al Adha [pro: *eed aladha*]: Festival of the Sacrifice, Abraham's [**Ibrahim**] willingness to kill Ishmael, until Allah stopped him, and thus prepared the way for Muhammad to born in Abraham's line 2600 years later and fulfilling the biblical promise that God would make of Ishmael a great nation. Not that that hasn't been excellently refuted by Sam Shamoun: http://www.answering-islam.org/Shamoun/ishmael2.htm.

Eid al Fitr [pro: *eed alfetter*]: Festival of breaking the fast at the end of the month of **Ramadan**.

Eid Mubarak [pro: *eed mobarak*]: "May you enjoy a blessed festival." Said for **Eid al Adha**.

Emir [pro: *ameer*] (var. sp.: ameer, amir): Leader, ruler, commander, chief, nobleman.

Fajir [pro: *fajer*]: Wicked evil-doer.

Fajr: Dawn (1st) prayers of the five daily prayers.

Falah: Success (as in being a successful **da'ee** who reverts [**awdah**] people out of other beliefs into Islam). Also: Deliverance (as in delivering the world to Allah).

Faq'tuluhum [pro: *Foktuhlooum*]: "Kill them all," or, "Then kill them." A slice of the philosophy of **fitna**.

Fard: A religious duty, or an obligatory action: Praying five times a day is fard. (The Sharia stipulates when a Muslim can forgo praying, and when the time can be made up.) Neglecting a fard will result in a punishment in the hereafter.

Fard ayn: Obligatory on every individual Muslim to aid in any way he can (i.e., **jihad**).

Fard kifayah: An obligation on the Muslim community as a whole from which some are freed if others take it up for them, such as physical jihad.

Fashal Altasallal: "10 Infiltration Failures by the U.S. Government on the Domestic Islamist Threat" by Patrick Poole: Islamist operatives and one full organization successful at passing all U.S. security screening: Abdurahman Alamoudi, Ali Mohamed, Anwar Al-Awlaki, Operation Greenquest, Faisal Gill, Hesham Islam, Weiss Rasool, Louay Safi, Omar Alomari, Kifah Mustapha. http://www.centerforsecuritypolicy.org/upload/wysiwyg/article%20pdfs/10_Failures_Patrick_Poole_1115.pdf

Fasiq: Disobedient or rebellious to Allah.

FATAH/Harakat al-tahrīr al-watanī al-filastīnī, which can mean "conquering" or "victory": Palestinian National Liberation Movement, the largest faction of the Palestine Liberation Organization (PLO), a multi-party confederation. Their goals included removal of Israel, establishment of an Islamic state, and Islamism. Fatah became the dominant force in Palestinian politics after the Six-Day War in 1967. The word, Fatah, was used in religious discourse to signify the Islamic expansion in the first centuries of Islamic history—as in *Fath al-Sham*, the "conquering of the Levant"—and so has positive connotations for Muslims and a highly negative connotation for Jews. The term "Fatah" also has religious significance in that it is the name of the 48th **surah** (chapter) of the Qur'an, which, according to major Muslim commentators, details the story of the **Treaty of Hudaibiya**. During the peaceful two years after the Hudaibiya treaty, many reverted [**awdah**] to Islam, increasing the strength of the Muslim side. It was the breach of this treaty by the Quraish [false flag here!] that triggered the conquest of Mecca. This Islamic precedent [of not honoring treaties] was cited by [Fatah founder] Yasser Arafat as justification for his signing the Oslo Accords with Israel.

Fatah is generally considered to have had a strong involvement in the "revolutionary struggle" [struggle *means* **jihad**] in the past and has maintained a number of militant groups. Since Arafat's death in 2004, factionalism within the ideologically diverse movement has become more apparent.

In the January 25, 2006 parliamentary election, the party lost its majority in the Palestinian parliament to Hamas, and resigned all cabinet positions, instead of assuming the role as the main opposition party. Fatah's size is estimated at 6,000–8,000 fighters with 45–300 politicians. However, the Hamas legislative victory led to a split between the two main Palestinian political parties, with Fatah retaining control of the Palestinian National Authority in the West Bank. In April 2011, officials from Hamas and Fatah announced that both parties had reached an initial deal to unify into one government, with plans for elections, held in 2012.

Now, that led to this (and yes, yes, this is mostly all from Wiki, but it's about as much time as it's worth to me and my brain needed a break from trying to translate): The Fatah–Hamas conflict (Arabic: *an-Nizāh bayna Fatah wa-hamās*), also referred to as the Palestinian Civil War (Arabic: *al Harb al-'Ahliyyah al-Filistīnīyyah*), and the Conflict of Brothers (Arabic: *Sirāh al-'Ikhwah*), i.e., fratricidal war (the conflict is called *Wakseh* among Palestinians, meaning humiliation, ruin, and collapse as a result of self-inflicted damage), began in 2006, after Hamas' legislative victories and has continued, politically and sometimes militarily, up to this day. The conflict, which erupted between the two main Palestinian parties, Fatah and Hamas, resulted in the split of Palestinian Authority into two polities, both seeing themselves the true representatives of the Palestinian people—Fatah ruled Palestinian National Authority and Hamas the government in Gaza.

The Cairo reconciliation agreement between the parties was signed in May 2011, bringing hopes of reuniting the Fatah-ruled Palestinian National Authority and the Hamas government in Gaza. The implementation of the agreement, however, was not executed up until the withdrawal of the Hamas external office from Damascus, due to the 2011-2012 Syrian uprising. As a result, the Doha deal was signed by Mahmud Abbas and Haled Mashaal in 2012. On April 1, the Doha implementation was described as "stalling," with no progress on the joint elections scheme. In addition, Fatah blamed Hamas that its security forces had set up roadblocks and arrested dozens of Fatah members and individuals in Gaza, whom they accused of "spreading rumors."

Fath: Conquest. See: *Futuh*

Fatiha: See *Al-Fatiha*

Fatteh: Invasion. Used mostly in Muhammad's day before the words "crusade" and "colonialism" began to be used to soften the actuality of Islamic invasions and conquests.

Fatwa (var. sp.: fatwah): A legal opinion or ruling by a Sharia scholar (or one of the **shura ulema**). Fatwas are often death sentences, but can also be rulings on lesser offenses against Islam per Sharia law.

FEMYSO: Forum of European Muslim Youth & Student Organization.

Fi Amanillah [pro: *fee amanallah*]: "May Allah protect you." Similar to "May God go with you." Common Islamic expression for performing acts such as charity or **jihad** and **qatlu**.

Fikir ejramy: "Thoughts dangerous," was as close as any interpreters could come to "critical thinking," or freedom of thought." Freedom of thought is clearly not allowed, and to engage in reasoning thought is discouraged with the highest of punishments.

FIOE: Federation of Islamic Organizations in Europe.

Fiqh [pro: *fickah*]: Fiqh Council or Shura Council. The learned scholars who have a deep understanding of Islamic jurisprudence/Sharia law. Sharia was set by Allah; fiqh is the human comprehension of Sharia. The fiqh council can determine if something is or is not the Islamic way of doing things. The original Fiqh Councils determined what was and was not Islamic jurisprudence in the 9th-11th centuries.

Fiqh al-aqaliyyat [pro: *fick alakaleyyat*]: Islamic jurisprudence for minorities, i.e., **dhimmis**.

Fiqh as-Sunna [pro: *fick esonna*]: Islamic jurisprudence by Ibn Abbas. Fiqh as-Sunna does not call for **jihad** as violently and unequivocally as other **tafsir** works, such as Tafsir **Ibn Kathir**, but is still faithful to the Qur'anic stipulation that it is incumbent on all Muslims to fight against the non-Believer until Islam reigns supreme in the world.

Fiqra [pro: *fickrah*] (var. sp.: fikra): Ideology.

Fi sabil Allah [pro: *fee sabeelallah*]: "In the way of Allah"; also, "In the path of Allah": which means to be Islamic, to follow Allah in all things.

Fitna: Oppression, tumult (discord), opposition, temptation, interference, dissension, disbelief, and/or "making mischief in Dar al-Islam" and especially in Dar al Harb. *Elimination of fitna is the basis for Islamists' "right to protect Islam," which includes killing non-Muslims.* Fitna is explained in **surat** two and five (Q2.191, Q5.51, and Q5.82.) of the Qur'an, thus making it the direct, revealed word of God, as opposed to having come from, say, just Muhammad in a **hadith** or two. This is the crucible of Islam. If you understand this, and the **deen** of Allah, you will never be tricked into twisty arguments/debates in which Islam comes out sounding like a "religion just like everybody else's, only a little different."

This is the reason for the two swords in logos of organizations like the Muslim Brotherhood: one sword for prevention of fitna within the Islamic community, and the other sword for fighting against fitna outside the Islamic community (i.e., offensive jihad). Oppression, et. al., is caused by man made laws (including the U.S. Constitution). *The reason for **jihad** is to remove fitna from the world by replacing it with Sharia law, which is from Allah alone, and thus the only just law on earth.*

Oppression for Muslims is intolerable, as they are supposed to be the best of men. Anyone, or any nation fighting them and Islam, and their purpose of submitting the world to Islam is oppressing them and thereby causing tumult, which they have to throw off by jihad (which becomes defensive jihad then, not just holy jihad). If everyone were Sharia-compliant, there would be no oppression in the land (everywhere would be Dar al Islam) and thus there would be no oppression or tumult to fight . . . . And hence: [ta-daaaah!] Islam *would* mean peace.

However, don't forget the second sword for fitna within the Islamic community. "Mischief in the land" becomes heresy-speak and can be the **Shi'a** v. the **Sunni**. The Sunni v. the **Salafi**s, the Salafis v. **Sufi**, and every sect against the **Ahmadiyya**. There will never be peace in Islam.

Fitra: The *natural religion*; innate to human nature as *created* by Allah. Hm.

Fukaha'a [pro: *fokaha*]: Islamic jurists or scholars specializing in Sharia.

Futuh/Fath: Conquest. Note that, to Muslims, the Islamic conquests are seen as acts of altruism and they are referred to as *futuh*, which literally means "opening," because the countries conquered were "opened" for the light of Islam to enter and guide its infidel inhabitants. Thus to Muslims, there is nothing to regret or apologize for concerning the conquests; they are seen as done for the good of those who were conquered, i.e., the ancestors of today's Muslims. There are many who are furious that Muslims don't apologize for (or stop!) the atrocities they commit, but really, why should they? They do *not* see anything they do as atrocious; it is the non-Muslims who are committing the atrocity of not accepting Allah.

So, what do you think the chances are that those "interfaith dialogue" meetings are going to work? See: **Da'wah**.

Fuwaysiqah [pro: *fawasick*]: Vermin, evil to deviate from the right way. [Back to the interfaith dialogues. You're sitting across the table from an imam who sees you as vermin . . . .]

Ghanimah: Spoils of war, booty. See **Khums** and **Ghazwat**

Ghazwat: Raids/raiding. Muhammad's source of income and his followers' (**jihad**is) source of income during the 10 years between leaving Mecca and his death in 632. He is reported to have carried out 19 successful major raids during that time, plus he fought **7 major battles**.

Ghiba [pro: *gheebah*]: Slander (literally: backbiting). Slander means to mention, or say, or state anything concerning a person or Islamic community that that person or community doesn't like. It is not important that it be true or not; the point is that it is offensive to the Muslim and therefore slanderous.

Hadd; plural **Hudud** [pro: *hodood*] (var sp.: hadud, hudood): Fixed punishments. Also: Limits or restrictions. The bounds of acceptable behavior and the punishments for serious crimes. In Sharia, hudud refers to the class of punishments that are fixed for certain crimes that are considered to be "claims of God." They include theft, fornication, drinking alcohol, and apostasy [**ridda** or **murtad**].

Hadith [pro: *hadeeth*]: Traditions. Report. Speech. Collections of Prophet Muhammad on what he witnessed and approved. Explanations, interpretations, and the living example of the Messenger for teaching the Qur'an. Another explanation: What Muhammad said during his 22 years as the first caliph [**Khalif**] of Islam. There are only a few **sahih**—authoritative—hadith, primarily al-Bukhari and Muslim. *Hadith Mashhoor* is a well-known, fully documented, reliable statement or story by Muhammad. *Hadith Hasan* is a category of hadith which are "acceptable."

Examples of three sahih hadith on the subject of Jesus (**Isa**):
Sahih Bukhari (Volume 3, Book 34, Number 425): Allah's Apostle [Muhammad] said, "By Him in Whose Hands my soul is, son of Mary (Jesus) will shortly descend amongst you people [Muslims] as a just ruler and will break the Cross [kill the Christians] and kill the pig [the Jews] and abolish the **jizya**. Then there will be abundance of money and nobody will accept charitable gifts."

Sahih Muslim, Book 1, Number 287: It is narrated on the authority of Abu Huraira that the . . . Messenger observed: "I swear by God [Allah] that the son of Mary will certainly descend as a just judge and he would definitely break the cross [kill the Christians], and kill swine [the Jews] and abolish jizya and would leave the young she-camel, and no one would endeavor to (collect **zakat** on it). Spite, mutual hatred, and jealousy against one another will certainly disappear and when he [Allah] summons people to accept wealth, not even one would do so. [Peace will reign on Earth.]"

Sunan Abu Dawud: Book 37, Number 4310: The Prophet (PBUH) said: "There is no prophet between me and him, that is, Jesus. He will descend [to the earth]. When you see him, recognize him: A man of medium height, reddish hair, wearing two light yellow garments, looking as if drops were falling down from his head though it will not be wet. He will fight the people for the cause of Islam. He will break the cross, kill swine, and abolish jizya. Allah will perish all religions except Islam. He will destroy the Antichrist and will live on the earth for forty years and then he will die. The Muslims will pray over him."

Hadr. Void. As in "to void a life." Any Muslim has the right to kill anyone who insults Islam through fitna [with an act like burning the Qur'an, for instance, or drawing a cartoon of Muhammad], be they Muslim or non-Muslim. That Muslim does not have to wait for the state or the caliph [**Khalif**] to decide, he can and should do it himself.

Hafiz: One who has memorized the Qur'an.

Hajj: Pilgrimage: One of the 5 pillars of Islam [**Arkan al-Islam al-Khamsat**]. The Hajj is the pilgrimage to the **Masjid al-Haram** in **Mecca**, which recreates the last pilgrimage that Muhammad made before he died; the object and reward of hajj is to get to Paradise [**Jannah**], but that won't happen if the Muslim comes for that purpose. If the Muslim comes just for that, and not solely to worship Allah, he will fail and probably go to hell (as the Qur'an repeats *ad nauseam* "Allah knows all"). Muslims the world over are required [**fard**] to make the Hajj at least once in their lifetimes *if* they can afford to. The Hajj predates Muhammad. Early Arabs made the trip to Mecca to worship their pagan stone idols in the **Ka'aba**. See: **Hijra**.

Hajj Mabrur [pro: *hahj mabroor*] (var. sp.: Mabrour): The "reward" of Hajj, which is Paradise [**Jannah**].

Halal: Lawful, permitted, good, beneficial, praiseworthy, honorable. Generally and most universally recognized today with "halal food." Halal are meals that are made with food from meat that comes from an animal that's been killed in the proscribed way: Facing **Mecca**. Halal is another copy of the Jewish way of life that Muhammad tried to use to show that, really, Allah was just like Yahweh. Halal = Kosher. Allah = Kosher. When the Jews of Mecca, then **Medina**, then Mecca again, turned their backs (or worse, laughed at Muhammad) on Islam, Allah got even by murdering them. There is no record that it was done in the halal way. No non-Muslim is allowed in Mecca or Medina to this day. See: **IFANCA**.

Hamas/Harakat al-Muqawama al-Islamiyya: Palestinian Islamic Resistance Movement that governs the Gaza Strip. It was founded in 1987 by the Muslim Brotherhood [**Ikhwan**] during the Second **Intifada**, along with its military cadre, Izz ad-Din al-Qassam Brigades. Totally, fiercely anti-"Zionist" Israel. It's favorite saying is: "From the river to the sea, Palestine will be free." Clearly a call to destroy Israel. It chartered the Council on American Islamic Relations in 1994, making CAIR effectively "Hamas doing business in the U.S." Palestine was recognized on 11/29/12 as a "non-member observer state" by the UN largely because of Hamas' lout-like behavior. Study Hamas; there are probably 30 pages in Google alone on this subject. Ridding the mid-east of Hamas would go far to lower the world's temperature and lessen the need for anti-global warming efforts.

Hamas leadership would likely completely disagree with this exegesis by Shaikh Professor Abdul Hadi Palazzi: "The Qur'an says that Allah gave the land of Israel to the Jews and will restore them to it at the End of Days," @ http://www.templemount.org/quranland.html, that explains these Qur'anic verses: Q17:101: And indeed We gave to Musa (Moses) nine clear signs. Ask then the Children of Israel, when he came to them, then Fir'aun (Pharaoh) said to him: "O Musa (Moses)! I think you are indeed bewitched." 17:102: [Musa (Moses)] said: "Verily, you know that these signs have been sent down by none but the Lord of the heavens and the earth as clear (evidences i.e. proofs of Allah's Oneness and His Omnipo-tence, etc.). And I think you are, indeed, O Fir'aun (Pharaoh) doomed to destruction (away from all good)!" 17:103: So he resolved to turn them out of the land (of Egypt). But We drowned him and all who were with him. 17:104: ***And We said to the Children of Israel after him: "Dwell in the land, then, [and] when the final and the last promise comes near*** [i.e. the Day of Resurrection or the descent of Christ ['Isa (Jesus), son of Maryam (Mary) on the earth], ***we shall bring you altogether as mixed crowd (gathered out of various nations).***[Tafsir Al-Qurtubi, Vol. 10, Page 338.]

Hamdellah [pro: *hamdolellah*]: "Praise be to Allah." Also, Al-Hamdu Lillah [pro: *alhamdolella*] (var. sp.: Alhamdulillahl; Alhamdulla).

Hanif [pro: *haneef*]: Non-Christian or non-Jewish Monotheists; *Hanifiya*: Monotheism. It is likely that Muhammad's first wife, **Khadija**, was a Hanif (to some degree a Christian); her cousin, Waraqa was, and the two of them had considerable influence on Muhammad prior to Allah's sud-den appearance in his life and command that he, Muhammad, clear the **Ka'aba** of all the pagan stone idols in that site.

Haq (var. sp.: *haqq*): Truth, justice, inevitable, the word of Allah. All reli-gions are false except the **deen** of Allah, which is the True Religion.

Harãm: Forbidden. An individual is rewarded for keeping away from anything forbidden done out of obedience (rather than out of fear, shyness, or the inability to do it).

Haram: Sanctuary, holy, or sacred. The **Masjid al Haram** in **Mecca** is the most sacred mosque in the world.

Harem (var. sp.: *Haram, Harim*): House for Muslim concubines (who were forbidden to any but the Muslim "husband"). Muhammad had 22-28 wives (11-12 at the same time) altogether; Islamic law says a Muslim man may only have up to 4 wives. The Ottoman/Turkish sultans took the harem to whole new levels until as recently as after the mid-1800s when the Turkish palace harems occupied 400 rooms, and the women who controlled the harems (primarily the Queen Mother; she who gave birth to the Sultan) held great power over the sultanate. The concubines were captured in wars, bought, or recruited to work in the harems.

Hassan al-Banna: (1906-1949) Egyptian Sunni. First Supreme Guide of the "Muslim Brothers" (**Ikhwan al Muslimin**). One of his most famous statements in forming the now-world-wide organization was: "It is the nature of Islam to dominate, not to be dominated, to impose its laws on all nations, and extend its power to the entire planet." Al-Banna was assassinated in 1949 for denouncing the assassination of Prime Minister Pasha, who had disbanded the Ikhwan as a seditious organization against Egypt.

Hawwa: Eve (as in Adam and Eve). The concept of original sin does not exist in Islam. Eve is not blamed for leading Adam astray and eating the apple, but she is blamed for all women who are unfaithful to or betray their husbands, hence the development of varying forms of layered clothing, leading to the **burqa/abayah** to hide women in suffocating material prisons, I suppose. Men are never to be held to any standard of behavior, of course.

Hifz al-Qur'an [pro: *hefz alqora'aan*]: Memorize the Qur'an.

Hijab [pro: *heejab*]: Female head-cover only. See: **Awrah/nakedness**

Hijra [pro: *hihjrah*]: Literally, migration; can be emigration. Historically, "flight from danger," or to leave a bad place for another; specifically when Muhammad left **Mecca** to go to **Medina** in 622 to relocate himself and his 150 followers in Medina, approximately 150 miles north of Mecca. 622 is the beginning of Islamic calendar, and the end of Islam being only a religion and the beginning of a nation and **jihad** became the arm of Islam to force **Sharia** law on all others. Emigration also became fixed as both

da'wah and **jihad** as Islam's tools of conquest. Be sure to read Sam Solomon and E. Al Maqdisi's book *The Modern Day Trojan Horse* for a complete understanding of how the hijra is in use today, all over the world.

The Islamic calendar wasn't set to begin in 622 until Umar's time of rule in 638, seventeen years after the Hijra. Up to that point, correspondence or reference to years had been done by event, i.e., The Year of the Elephant. When Umar and his scholars set the first day of the first month of the Islamic calendar (so the new year), 1 Muharram 1 AH, it was Friday, 16 July 622 AD on the Julian calendar. The Hijra calendar was based on when the first crescent moon of each month was *seen* in the sky after the end of the previous month (it could be the 29th or the 30th day), and was calculated on 354-355 nights of the year. The Hijra calendar shows 2013 as year 1435; simple subtraction shows only 1391 years have passed on the Gregorian calendar.

The jurists Ahmad Muhammad Shakir and **Yusuf al-Qaradawi** both endorsed the use of astronomical calculations to determine the beginning of all months of the Islamic calendar, in 1939 and 2004 respectively. So did the Fiqh Council of North America (**FCNA**) in 2006, and the European Council for Fatwa and Research (ECFR) in 2007.

It is hard to imagine that anyone ever thought Islam was going to be less than a full-on empire. Its rulers even set up its own way of keeping a calendar!

The months:

1.Muharram—Shi'a Day of Mourning [**Ashura**]; *Islamic New Year* [note that in 2013, that was 11/4, and in 2014, it will be 10/25, eight days earlier than the year before]; and a "forbidden" month, meaning no fighting between tribes could happen then. The four forbidden months predate Islam; the proscription probably centered around the fair weather for trading, and pilgrimage to **Mecca** and the **Ka'aba.**

2. Safar

3. Rabi' al-awwal—Muhammad's birthday

4. Rabi' al-thani

5. Jumada al-awwal

6. Jumada al-thani

7. Rajab—A forbidden month, and Muhammad's Night Journey [**Isra'a**]

8. Sha'aban—Night of Deliverance/Forgiveness [**Lailatul al-Baraat**]

9. **Ramadan**—Month of fasting [**Sawm**], and Night of Power [**Lailatul Qadr**]

10. Shawwal—Festival of Breaking the Fast [**Eid al Fitr**]

11. Dhu al-Qi'dah—a forbidden month

12. Zhu-l-Hijjah—A forbidden month and the month of **Hajj** and Festival of Sacrifice [**Eid al Adha**]

Hikmah: Wisdom. *Methodology of Dawah*: ". . . We have to proceed patiently, cautiously, and with *hikmah* in the presentation of the message of Islam to the American People . . . ." Note: *The Methodology of Dawah* (1989) is a step-by-step how-to book by Muslim Brother [**Ikhwan**] Shamim Siddiqi, on how to turn the United States into a Muslim country within 20-25 years by using stealth jihad (successful **da'wah** efforts). It underestimated the American spirit of freedom and liberty, and the strength of Christianity, but many of the steps it laid out have been successfully implemented.

Hisbah: Keeping everything in order within the laws of Allah: "Enjoin what is good and forbid what is wrong." [*Amr bi 'l-ma'ruf wa nahy an al-munkar* (enjoining the good and forbidding the evil) seeks to convey the Message of Islam to all human beings in the world and to establish a model Islamic community—a caliphate [**Khilafah**]—on a world-wide basis." (See more at: http://thehayride.com/2013/12/holton-maybe-now-theyll-pay-attention-to-the-gulen-schools/#sthash.Pe2saaPJ.dpuf).] Note that this is part of the creed of the Muslim Students Association [**MSA**], a Muslim Brotherhood organization. Also, **Minhaj.**

Hizb [pro: *hezeb*]: Party. As in political party, i.e.: Hizballah.

Hizb al-Hori'at wa ladalat [pro: *hizeb alhoreyyah wal adallah*]: Muslim Brotherhood [**Ikhwan**] Freedom and Justice Party of Egypt, led by Chairman Mohamed Mursi, who became president of Egypt in June, 2012. He was removed from office by the largest mass uprising of people (2 million) in history of the world in June, 2013. The Egyptian people did not like his rigid Ikhwan rules and Sharia enforcements.

Hizballah [pro: *hizbal lah*] (var. sp.: Hesballah, Hezbollah): Party of Allah. A Lebanese **Shi'a** terrorist organization founded in the early 1980s with the assistance and backing of Iran for the purpose of fighting Israel. The current Hizballah leader, Hassan Nasrallah, has pledged *bayat* [oath of loyalty, from **bai'a**] officially to the Iranian Supreme Leader Khamenei, meaning he publicly acknowledges his spiritual as well as political authority. In a landmark 2011 legal decision by Judge George Daniels of the

Southern District of New York Federal Court, Hizballah and the Iranian regime were found directly responsible, together with **al-Qaeda**, for the 9/11 attacks.

Hizb al Tagammu al Watani al Taqadomi al Wahdawi: National Progressive Unionist Party. Egyptian Socialist Party.

Hizb ut-Tahrir [pro: *hizbut tahreer*]: Party of Freedom, or Party of Liberation. Its goals are the same as the Muslim Brotherhood's: [**Ikhwan**]restore the caliphate [**Khilafah**] and install and implement Sharia law as the sole source of law. Hizb ut-Tahrir's various groups have caused a variety of security concerns (they are exceptionally anti-semitic, anti-capitalism, and anti-democratic), leading to an outright ban of the organization from operating in several countries. The U.S. is not yet one of them.

HLF/Holy Land Foundation Trial: *Moasesset al'arazi al-Moghadaseh*: A **Sunni** Palestinian organization located in Richardson, Texas, pre-1995. Its officers were found guilty of funneling money illegally to **Hamas** (a federally ID'd terrorist organization) in 2008. It is still the largest successful trial in the U.S. for aiding and abetting a terrorist organization. It was not only an important trial for stopping internal enemies, it also produced documents that revealed the existence of the Muslim Brotherhood [**Ikhwan**] at work in the U.S., and also its goals (to destroy the U.S. by any means possible, but based on **civilizational jihad**), as revealed by the "Explanatory Memorandum," written by Mohamed Akram, a Muslim Brotherhood operative in the U.S., in 1991: "The Muslim Brotherhood . . . must understand that their work in America is a kind of grand jihad in eliminating and destroying the Western civilization from within and sabotaging its miserable house by their hands and the hands of the believers so that it is eliminated and Allah's religion is made victorious over all other religions."

The importance of the discovery of the Explanatory Memorandum cannot be understated, though it is often deliberately overlooked, ignored, denied, and otherwise made to *look* unimportant by the members of the U.S. government, the U.S. media, and certainly by the Muslim Brotherhood mouthpieces. What it is, is a Declaration of Independence FROM the U.S. Constitution. It is a document that defines strategic goals for how to achieve that and how to install Sharia law in its place. It is a shocking malfeasance of intelligence/military/and elected government that this information, a virtual step-by-step process for war against the U.S., which is being used and implemented, has been all but dust-binned.

Another important revelation found within the Explanatory Memorandum is the roots of the term "al-Qaeda," which means "the base." It is part of a larger phrase: *"Al-Qaeda al-Muslimina al-Moltzmena"*: "the observant Muslim base." Without this, essentially the turned-on **ummah**, the Muslim Brotherhood cannot win.

For more information on the trial and the Memorandum, see: http://www.discoverthenetworks.org/viewSubCategory.asp?id=1235

Equally revealing was a memo written by Omar Ahmad, then President of **CAIR** (Hamas doing business in the U.S.) in 1998: "Islam isn't in America to be equal to any other faith, but to become dominant. The Qur'an should be the highest authority in America and Islam the only accepted religion on Earth."

The Muslim Brotherhood fronts, i.e., ISNA—invited to the White House (White Mosque?) in March, 2013, for a confab on how to handle Israel prior to President Obama's first trip there—**ICNA**, CAIR, the **MSA**, etc., were found to be co-conspirators with the Foundation officers. None of these front leaders have stood trial yet (and have therefore never paid the penalty for working illegally in the U.S.) because Barack Hussein Obama's Justice Department ordered there be no further prosecutions resulting from the HLF trial.

Judge: U.S. District Federal Judge Jorge J. Solis. Prosecuting attorneys: U.S. Attorney James T. Jacks of the Northern District of Texas, and David Kris, Assistant Attorney General for National Security. Sentences: Shukri Abu Baker, 50, of Garland, Texas: 65 years. Ghassan Elashi, 55, of Richardson, Texas: 65 years. Mufid Abdulqader, 49, of Richardson, Texas: 20 years. Mohammad El-Mezain, 55, of San Diego, California, and Abdulrahman Odeh, 49, of Patterson, New Jersey: 15 years each.

Homegrown Jihad Camps: See: **MOA / Jamaat al-Fuqra.**

Honor killing / Qatl al Sharf (Arabic). *Karo-Kari* (Urdu/Pakistani). The regulation of female behavior is integral to Islamic perceptions of honor (known as *maryada* in many Indian languages and as *ghairat* in Urdu and Pashtu). It is the women who carry the honor in Islam, and the men are there to guard it. The "guarding" becomes more like punishment prisoner-guarding than body guards to Western eyes; it's almost inconceivable to Westerners that a man can think of "honor" in this manner. In contrast to other forms of domestic violence, honor killings are frequently performed out in the open, and the perpetrators rarely act alone. These murders are legal in (and therefore motivated by) Sharia (note *Reliance of the Traveller*, Section O, 1.4, and 1.5). See: **AHada-'Ashar Imra'a Maiyit Qatl al-Sharf** for more information and for actual honor killings in the U.S.

Non-Muslim ladies! See 11 Women Victims of Honor Killing": **AHada-'Ashar Imra'a Maiyit Qatl al-Sharf.** Understand that Islam is *not* your way out of poverty. Yes, the Qur'an says that the man has to take care of all your needs—but it also says in the Sharia that he can take other wives and relegate you to second, third, or fourth place, beat you half to death (in practice, even if it's not strictly speaking in the Qur'an) or, by the way, kill you and your daughter(s) because you've embarrassed him, and/or just dump you by giving you the old **talaq** divorce. He can have sex with your daughter(s), or your son(s) will have sex with them. . . . And maybe none of that will happen. But think: It *can*, because this is *Islam* you're entering into. "Here be demons" is something you should seriously consider before marrying that nice Arab guy because once you're in, it's viciously difficult to get out.

Hourria [pro: *horreyyah*] (var. sp.: Hurriyya): Freedom. Islamic freedom is "the recognition of the essential relationship between Allah the master and his human slaves who are completely dependent on him." Ibn Arabi, a Sufi scholar, is cited for having defined freedom as "being perfect slavery to Allah." To put it another way, Islamic-style "freedom" is freedom from the unbelief (**kafir**) loose in Dar al Harb. It has nothing to do with personal choice, decisions, speech, thought.

Hourris: Companions of pleasure waiting in Paradise (72 virgins); can be both boys and women.

Huda [pro: *hoda*]: Guidance.

Hudna [pro: *hodnah*]: Truce. Ceasefire. A time of waiting for conditions to change that would be more beneficial for an Islamic victory.

Hudna min Hudaibiya (var. sp.: Hudaybiyya). The Treaty of Hudaibiya. Muhammad wanted to visit the **Ka'aba** on a "small **hajj**" in 628. The **Meccans** refused to allow him inside the city unless he agreed to cease all hostilities with the Meccans for 10 years. He did, but went on to attack the Kaybar, and continued to nibble at the edges of the treaty, never completely upholding the tenets, until 630 when he broke it by attacking Mecca, destroying the city. Holding to two-year truces (not treaties, because there is no caliph [**Khalif**], and only a caliph can make treaties) are the standard now for Islamic agreements. Ongoing examples of that are truces Israel makes with Palestine. The Palestinians never truly cease hostilities and withdraw from them almost fully within two years.

HuJI/Islamic Jihad in Motion, Pakistani. *Harkat-ul-Jihad-al Islami*. Also, "The Islamic Struggle Movement." HuJI-B works in Bangladesh.

Hukumat [pro: *hokomaat*]: Rule, as in: Islam will rule the world.

Huquq al Insan: "Rights the man." [As close as translators could come to "Human Rights."] In Islam you have one human right: The right to follow the Sharia.

Hurr Khalam: Free speech. [As close as translators could come to "freedom of speech."] Islam's apologists have to torture their reasoning to make the absence of freedom sound like freedom. You can say whatever you like about Islam, as long as you realize there are limits to what it is you can say, especially if it crosses over into criticism of Islam (often called "factual truths" outside of Islam). These limits are good for the world, because the unlimited use of words can hurt the peace and goodwill that Islam in its core values wishes to spread. "Rather than focusing on privileges, Islam focuses on the principle to avoid speech that causes separation and conflict[i.e.: **fitna**]."—Harris Zafar http://www.washingtonpost.com/blogs/guest-voices/post/making-islamic-sense-of-free-speech/2013/01/14/95fc0b5a-5ec0-11e2-90a0-73c8343c6d61_blog.html. Limited free speech. Kind of like being a little bit pregnant.

IANA: Islamic Assembly of North America. Muslim Brotherhood [**Ikhwan**] front.

IAP: Islamic Association for Palestine. Now-defunct Illinois-based front group for the terrorist organization **Hamas**. It was established in 1981 by Hamas operative Mousa Abu Marzook. It called itself "a not-for-profit, public-awareness, educational, political, social, and civic, national grassroots organization, and was largely known for its "factual articles" that the "Zionist-controlled" Western media allegedly failed to report.

Iblis [pro: *eblees*]: Devil.

Ibn: Son of. In high-class Arabic, "son of" is "bin," hence, **Usama bin Laden**, rather than Usama ibn Laden.

Ibn Ishaq. Wrote Sirat Rasul Allah: The Biography (Life) of the Messenger of Allah (Muhammad), the most respected of all the histories on Muhammad, and thus the time frames used when deciphering the Qur'an. Is the third of the tripod of Islam's canon: The Qur'an and the Sunnah (the Hadith, and the Sira).

Ibn Kathir. (1301-1373) Full name: Abu Al-Fida, 'Imad Ad-Din, Isma'il bin 'Umar bin Kathir Ibn Daw' Ibn Kathir Ibn Dir. Professor at the Great Mosque of Damascus in 1366. Wrote the **Tafsir** ibn Kathir, which is famous all over the Muslim world, and among Muslims in the Western world is one of the most widely used explanations of the Qur'an today.

Ibn Khaldun (1332-1406), was of the Maliki school of law. Khaldun pioneering historian and philosopher, was also a Maliki legal theorist. In his "Muqaddimah," the first work of historical theory, he notes that "in the Muslim community, the holy war is a religious duty, because of the universalism of the Muslim mission and (the obligation to) convert everybody to Islam either by persuasion or by force." In Islam, the person in charge of religious affairs is concerned with "power politics," because Islam is "under obligation to gain power over other nations."

Ibn Rushd, aka **Averroes**. Full name: Abu al-Walid Muhammad ibn Ahmad ibn Rushd (1126-1198). Spanish Islamic philosopher (during the Islamic "Golden Age") postulated that Muslims have the right and duty to interpret the Qur'an in order to understand it. Primarily known for his interpretations of Aristotelian philosophy, however.

Ibn Sina, aka **Avicenna**. Full name: Abu Ali Al-Husayn ibn Ad Allah ibn Sina (930-1037). Considered the premier Islamic Persian philosopher during the Islamic "Golden Age."

Ibn Taymiyya (1263-1328): Taqi al-Din Ahmad Ibn Taymiyya. Hanbali school: Medieval theorist; Hanbali jurist. He directed that "since lawful warfare is essentially jihad and since its aim is that the religion is God's entirely and God's word is uppermost, therefore according to all Muslims, those who stand in the way of this aim must be fought."

Ibrahim: Abraham. Abraham became the Father of Islam at the same time Muhammad became the Messenger of Allah. The Qur'an states that Abraham and his son, Ismael (mother, Hagar, Sarah's servant), built the first **Ka'aba** (to worship Allah, which was eventually engulfed by the **Masjid al Haram**, the Most Sacred Mosque) in the area that was to become **Mecca**. The Qur'an also tells the story of Abraham agreeing to kill his son, Ismael, because Allah asked him to. Allah replaced Ismael with an animal at the last moment. Today, two animals are sacrificed in remembrance of that event during the annual **Hajj**. Muhammad states [in a manner copied by followers today: without empirical proof] he is a direct descendant of Abraham's (from **surah** 3:33 [chapter 3:33]) thus sealing the deal on making Islam the world's third Abrahamic religion. See **Eid al-Adha**.

ICNA: the Islamic Circle of North America. Muslim Brotherhood [**Ikhwan**] front/co-conspirator in the Holy Land Foundation [**HLF**] trial, Dallas, TX, 2008. Founding organization is **Jamaat-e-Islami** (which makes this organization doubly dangerous; it's roots are in the **Deobandi** organization, too). Is the "advertiser" for Islam, i.e.: the "Got Islam?" marketing program. It also hosts days for Muslims at amusement parks across the U.S., such as Muslim Day at 6 Flags Over Texas. Worked with the Muslim American Society (MAS) on "Sharia Campaign" to influence lawmakers and even school teachers that Sharia is not what it is. It produced and is using the "**Tarbiya** Guide" to teach the best and brightest of the new American Muslim generations aged 18 and over how to eliminate and destroy the U.S. civilization from within so that Allah's religion will be victorious over all other religions.

ICNA works closely with **Jamaat-e-Islami** (JEI) with regards to charitable collections. Its ICNA Relief USA, and ICNA Relief Canada sends the money it collects to JEI, which in turn sends it to Hamas in Palestine, which in turn uses it to fund jihad against Israel. There is/was some justifiable concern over the money being collected for the victims of "Sandy" in New Jersey (late 2012) by ICNA Relief USA; it's doubtful that the money made it to Sandy's victims.

For the full scope of ICNA's activities, see: http://publicpolicyalliance. org/2013/03/muslim-brotherhood-propaganda-comes-to-tallahassee-florida/ AND http:// www.clarionproject.org/analysis/powerful-us-islamist-group-shows-true-colors#

I'dad Al-'oda [pro: *ledad aloddah*]: Prep for battle according to the Qur'an.

Iftar [pro: *eftar*]: Meal. The meal after sunset on any night during Ramadan.

IIIT ("Triple I-T"): International Institute of Islamic Thought. An Islamic think tank, working on educational, academic, and societal issues. Muslim Brotherhood [**Ikhwan**] front/co-conspirator in the Holy Land Foundation trial, [**HLF**] Dallas, TX, 2008. The IIIT is responsible for the invention of the word "Islamophobia," which is designed to muzzle anyone who speaks the truth about Islam, the tool Muslim Brotherhood fronts use to cry "Victim!" when someone does manage to get the truth out loud enough to make a difference. Islamophobia brands someone as a bigot, a racist, a hater. It is such a successful word, all by itself, that the Organization of Islamic Cooperation (OIC) has built an entire effort for a call for world tolerance for all religions based on stamping it out. The real aim of this effort is to stop all true discussion or exposure of Islam—bottom line: Stop the freedom of speech.

Ijaz [pro: *ejaaz*]: Miracle of the Qur'an in content and form.

Ijma: Consensus on Islamic law among the **ulema**. The consensus on and the basis for the four **Sunni** schools of Islamic law, and about which there can never be any dispute, ever. Shi'a substitute obedience to the Imam, not the law, which is a considerable difference.

Ijtihad: Reform in Islamic law. During the early times of Islam, the possibility of finding a new solution to a juridical problem. Has not been allowed in Conservative Islam since the Middle Ages. However, Liberal movements within Islam generally argue that any Muslim can perform ijtihad, given that Islam has no generally accepted clerical hierarchy or bureaucratic organization, especially in this time (and only time) without a **khalif** for the **ummah**. Note, though, that settled Islamic law, **ijma**, *cannot* be changed through ijtihad, so there's not a lot of room for any reform. The opposite of ijtihad is **taqlid**, Arabic for "imitation," understood as blind acceptance of Sharia law.

Ikhtilaf [pro: *ikhtelafaat*]: Non-consensus of Islamic scholars.

Ikhwan al Muslimin [pro: *alekhwan almoslemeen*]: Muslim Brothers (aka Muslim Brotherhood). Begun in Egypt in 1928, it is now a world-wide organization dedicated to re-establishing the caliphate [**khilafah**] (the Islamic world governed by a caliph [**Khalif**]) that disappeared when Mustafa Kemal Ataturk turned Turkey into a secular state, ridding it of the last shreds of the last caliphate, the Ottoman / Turkish Empire. Its creed is: "Allah is our objective; the Qur'an is our law; the prophet is our leader; jihad is our way; and death for Allah our highest aspiration." Its first goal is to have Sharia-compliant nation-states with titular heads of state until a caliph can be found to rule the entire **ummah**/caliphate. Once that objective is reached, it can continue its ultimate goal: rid the world of Jews and Christians.

Mohammed Mursi's election as the President of Egypt in 2012 and his getting its decidedly pro-Sharia constitution ratified over considerable Egyptian opposition had been the Muslim Brotherhood's greatest achievements. The Ikhwan's goal of Sharia-compliant nation-states was progressing nicely with the fall of Mubarak, Libya's Qaddafi, and the on-going battle with Syria. However, Mursi was removed from office by the largest mass uprising of people (2 million) in history of the world in June, 2013. The Egyptian people did not like his rigid Ikhwan rules and Sharia enforcements. That does not mean the MB is out of the game (though in Egypt, it could be; see below).

Mursi's supporters have formed up behind a symbol: R4BIA: a four-fingered hand sign by pro-Mursi protesters during demonstrations in Egypt's Rabia al-Adawiya Square. The hand gesture is an image of the hand commonly depicted in black on a bright yellow background. In English it is officially spelled in capital letters and the letter "A" is replaced with the number 4. It has become the symbol of the massacre of pro-Mursi supporters in Rabia al-Adawiya Square on August 14, 2013. This new sign already has its own history, legend, and mysticism, and it contains all the attributes that Islamists favor in their symbology, particularly martyrdom.

"Egypt Buries the Brotherhood: Protest against President Mohamed Mursi in Cairo, Egypt." It's not unusual for the United States and a Muslim country to be on the opposite sides of the War on Terror. It is unusual for a Muslim country to take a stand against terrorism while the United States backs the right of a terrorist group to burn churches, torture opposition members, and maintain control of a country with its own nuclear program. . . . http://www.frontpagemag.com/2013/dgreenfield/egypt-buries-the-brotherhood/?utm_source=FrontPage+Magazine&utm_medium=email&utm_campaign=ae4053f27f-Mailchimp_FrontPageMag&utm_term=0_57e32c-1dad-ae4053f27f-156518973

"Egypt Declares Muslim Brotherhood a Terrorist Group": The Egyptian government formally labeled the Muslim Brotherhood a terrorist group on Christmas, banning all its activities, including protests. The Obama Administration, advised by Brotherhood-friendly groups in the U.S., is unlikely to follow in Egypt's footsteps in calling a spade a spade. http://www.frontpagemag.com/2013/ryan-mauro/egypt-declares-muslim-brotherhood-a-terrorist-group/?utm_source=FrontPage+Magazine&utm_medium=email&utm_campaign=469efb6def-Mailchimp_FrontPageMag&utm_term=0_57e32c1dad-469efb-6def-156513926

The Muslim Brotherhood adopted as its international icon crossed swords beneath the Qur'an and below that some Arabic wording. Most of us don't know what that says. It is "*Waidu*" (pro: *why-I-do*): "Prepare (you). Or: "Prepare yourself." This comes from Q8:60: "And prepare against them whatever you are able of power and of steeds of war by which you may terrify the enemy of Allah and your enemy and others besides them whom you do not know [but] whom Allah knows. And whatever you spend in the cause of Allah will be fully repaid to you, and you will not be wronged." For those who cannot understand what crossed swords could mean (not peace), maybe these words will do it.

The first Muslim Brotherhood members came to the U.S. in the early 1960s and steadily built hundreds of front organizations which have grown to have shocking influence in politics/government (some say U.S. foreign policy is driven by the Ikhwan), the education system, the religious establishment (see **Da'wah**/Interfaith dialogues), the spread of **mosques**, and civil rights/legal arenas, always pushing for more Muslim appeasement in one way or another. The major Ikhwan fronts in the U.S. are **ISNA, ICNA, CAIR, the MSA, MANA, MPAC, NAIT, IIIT, MPAC,** and **MAS**. The leaders of these organizations, all interchangeable, will have even more strength as they act perforce more independently of the worldwide Ikhwan, but certainly the Egyptian base.

There are many good books on the shelves that detail the Muslim Brotherhood. Three recent ones I'd recommend: *The Brotherhood*, by Erick Stakelbeck; the *Muslim Mafia*, by Gaubatz and Sperry; and, *Raising A Jihadi Generation*, by John Guandolo.

Ilah: a deity, a god, as in the gods (stone idols) in the **Ka'aba** pre-Islam. See *La ilaha illah Allah* to understand the importance of this word.

Illiyoun: A place in Paradise where the righteous' actions are recorded. Opposite: **Sidjin**: A place in hell [**Jahannam**] where sinners' records are kept.

Imaan: To have faith and to proclaim it.

Imam: Cleric or teacher.

Imamate: (**Shi'a**): A Muslim leader of the line of Ali held by Shiites to be the divinely appointed, sinless, infallible successors of Muhammad. Also, the land held by Islamic-dominant nations. **Ummah**, to Sunnis.

IMMA: Institute for Muslim Minority Affairs. Founded by Syed Z. Abedin, an Indian-born Islamic academic. The institute is backed by the

Muslim World League [**MWL**]; a Saudi Arabian/Muslim Brotherhood organization dedicated to spreading the Brotherhood.

IFANCA: Islamic Food and Nutrition Council of America. World's largest **halal** food certification company, based in Park Ridge, Illinois, a suburb of Chicago. IFANCA's symbol, a crescent alongside an "M," can be found on different baby formulas, including ones made by leading brands Similac and Gerber, their Crescent-M dwarfing the O-U kosher *hechsher* sitting next to it.

IFANCA is working with the Islamic Society of North America (**ISNA**) to create a national halal standards and accreditation body. IFANCA is an active member of the Council of Islamic Organizations of Greater Chicago (CIOGC). Other members include: the Mosque Foundation (MF), which has held fundraisers for individuals and groups associated with **PIJ** and **Hamas** Islamic Relief (IR), which has been associated with al-Qaeda financing and that was named by the Israeli government a front for Hamas; Helping Hand (HH), which partnered with a Pakistani charity at the same time that charity delivered close to $100,000 to the residence of the head of Hamas, Khaled Meshaal; and the Muslim American Society (**MAS**), which has used the Internet to propagate materials degrading women, cursing Christians, and calling for the murder of Jews and homosexuals. http://www.frontpagemag.com/2013/joe-kaufman/baby-food-jihad/print/ Also see for more halal icons: http://www.barenakedislam.com/2013/03/29/are-you-inadvertently-supporting-islamic-terrorism-by-unwittingly-buying-halal-food/#comment-163571?utm_source=twitterfeed&utm_medium=twitter

Insh'allah: "By the Grace of Allah"; "If it be the will of Allah."

Intifada: Shaking off. Popular translation is "uprising." Used primarily in the context of the Palestinian-Israeli conflict: "to shake off from Israeli oppression." There have been two Palestinian outbreaks against Israel in 1987 and 2000. See: **Al-Quds** Day.

Iqal [pro: *ikaal*]: Rope that holds the male head-covering (**keffiyeh**) in place.

Iqamat-ud-deen [pro: *ikamat addeen*]: Establishment of the Islamic system of life.

Iqraa: Read! The entity in the Cave of Hira [**Kahef Hira**] (later identified as the Angel Gabriel [**Ji'bril**]) in 610, told Muhammad that Allah wanted him to read the Qur'an to the people. Muhammad said he could not read, so the entity told him to recite after him as he (Ji'bril) spoke the words.

There are many arguments as to whether Muhammad could or could not read. Some say the Qur'an is proof of its being a miracle: No man who was illiterate could have brought forth such a document without divine help. Others say that Muhammad was illiterate in the sense that he had not yet been introduced to Allah and Islam and was still in the time of **jahiliyah**: ignorance.

IRCV: Institute on Religious and Civic Values. Formerly CIE, Council on Islamic Education, "founded in 1991 to provide academic support and scholarly resources about Islam and Muslim history to K-12 textbook publishers, educators, and others. We went on to cultivate expertise in world history and teaching about world religions, producing assessments of national and history-social studies state standards, . . . and reviewing numerous social studies textbooks." Muslim Brotherhood [**Ikhwan**] front for Islamic indoctrination through U.S. textbooks. It is without doubt one of its most successful **Da'wah** tools in the U.S. to date. Prominent organizations, such as ACT! for America, have devoted teams of volunteers in many states dedicated to exposing the bias toward Islam in middle school social studies and geography textbooks, with the intent to garner enough adverse public opinion to get the states' Boards of Education to demand they only buy from publishers who are even-handed with the data.

Irhabi: Terrorist. Anyone who is *keeping a Believer* from fulfilling (through **fitna**) Allah's command to submit the world to Allah. Muslims do not consider themselves terrorists; only **kuffar** can be "real" terrorists. Jihad is not terror; it is legally sanctioned tactic of war to establish Sharia law in **Dar al Harb**. Sectarian fighting is **fitna**, not terrorism, but wars of heresy.

IRIB: Islamic Republic of Iran Broadcasting. Located in Tehran, Iran.

IRUSA: Islamic Relief USA. Muslim Brotherhood [**Ikhwan**] front: Most prominent U.S. Muslim "charity"; distributes millions of dollars per year to an international partner immersed in **jihad**: Islamic Relief Worldwide (IRW), which helped launch the Union of Good, designated by the U.S. Department of the Treasury as a Hamas-financing coalition.

Isa [pro: *eesa*]: Jesus. Isa is a prime subject in the Qur'an. Muhammad called him one of Allah's prophets, and says that Isa announced Muhammad's coming. Muhammad said that Isa started out life as a Muslim (based on Allah's claims that he, Allah, existed before God, so everyone is born Muslim [hence the idea that people revert [**awdah**] to Islam, not convert]). Muhammad claimed that Isa would come back and stand with

Muhammad (as the **Mahdi [Shi'a]**) in the Last Days. The Islamic Isa is not the son of God; his mother was a lovely virgin because Allah made her pregnant by saying "'Be,' and he was." Allah never came to earth. Ever. He does not mingle with people.

Isa did not die on the cross to give man ever-lasting life. Q4:157: "That they [**kuffar**] said (in boast) 'We killed Christ Jesus the son of Mary, the Messenger of Allah' but they killed him not, nor crucified him, but so it was made to appear to them, and those who differ therein are full of doubts, with no (certain) knowledge, but only conjecture to follow, for of a surety they killed him not." The Islamic theory is that Allah tricked the people and put a fake Isa on the cross so he never died, let alone crucified, and took Isa up to Paradise fully alive, where he is today and from whence he will return on the End of Days when he stands at the right hand of Muhammad (as the **Mahdi**) to judge all of mankind whether each soul will go to **Jannah** (Paradise) **Jahannam** (hell).

Isa is extremely important to Islam as a **Da'wah** tool. Muslims claim the Bible is distorted and the Qur'an's version of it is the only accurate one, so Muhammad's version of Isa *has* to be true or Islam isn't true. Islam requires Isa to exist in order to "own" parts of Christianity. Without that linkage, Islam has no original source, is based upon lies, and lacks credibility. Organized Islam, i.e., the **Ikhwan**, needs Christians to be passive and buy into to the "same God" for Islam to be successful the world over. Christianity has no need of Islam. See: **Da'wah/Interfaith Dialogues**.

Ishha: The fifth and last of the daily prayers. Late night.

ISI: Inter-Securities Intelligence. Pakistani Intelligence (Secret) Service. Headquartered in Islamabad. Believed by American CIA to be completely sympathetic to the Afghanistan **Taliban** to the point of sending money and men, plus working against American diplomatic efforts to break it up. Thought to have known where **Usama bin Laden** had been hiding for years before the Americans located him in Abottabad. The ISI has also been connected to the Mumbai massacre in November, 2008.

Islam Hadhari: Civilizational Islam. Indonesian group that purports to be a moderate brand of Islam.

Islam: "To submit." Submission to Allah. The exact opposite of freedom = slavery. Islam cannot be compatible with democracy or the U.S. Constitution or English Common Law. You cannot "submit" and still hold the principles of natural law of born free.

Islam is also defined as a "complete way of life." A **deen**. It encompasses all aspects of life: social, legal, military, financial/economics, governmental, and religious.

Islamophobia: Islamic invented word. See IIIT.

Ismaili: Manifestation of ancient Persian religion, though it associates with the **Shi'a** sect of Islam. It parallels with Gnosticism; could be called Islam-light. Is led by a hereditary Aga Khan. The last two Khans have been world-wide philanthropists.

ISNA: Islamic Society of North America. The umbrella organization for the Muslim Brotherhood [**Ikhwan**] (in other words, the leading Muslim Brotherhood front organization) and co-founded by Palestinian Islamic Jihad (**PIJ**) leader Sami al-Arian. Co-conspirator in the Holy Land Foundation trial [**HLF**], Dallas, TX, 2008. September, 2013, the Canadian government stripped ISNA of its tax status in Canada for the financing of a Pakistani terrorist group. Best known publicly for its "interfaith dialogue" symposiums. [See: **Da'wah**/Interfaith dialogues.] These dialogues are another of the brilliant concepts the Muslim Brotherhood has come up with, based on their knowledge of the Western mind, to which strife and disagreement are uncomfortable. We would all like to get along, and believe in our flower-child way that so does everyone else. So ISNA provides a forum for everybody to get along and swap "good" stories and all the Liberal/Socialists evangelical preachers and pastors feel good and never ever trouble themselves to read any books about Islam, by Islam, of Islam, and trample the true story/meaning of Bible to fit current "opinion." And the imam at the "dialogue" smiles, nods, agrees to everything, greets the ladies nicely, without ever once coming close to telling a true word about the **Qur'an, jihad, fitna**, Jesus (**Isa**), or Sharia law. See **Da'wah**/Interfaith Dialogues.

Isra'a: Night Journey to Paradise. Muhammad related a dream in which he flew to Paradise on a white horse named Buraq, which had the face of a boy and wings of an angel. Muhammad met Allah in Paradise in this dream and the two discussed/negotiated how many times a day the Followers should pray. Allah started out with 50x; Muhammad eventually got him down to five. Muhammad did, after all, make his early living in the world of trading, bartering, and negotiating for goods.

Istidlaal: Human ability to reason. Unnecessary in Islam; Allah's already done all that's needed in this field. Only used by Muslims to find the "signs" Allah has set around a person for enlightenment to what Allah wants of his Followers.

Istishhad: Martyrdom. **Istishhadi**: One who martyrs himself (suicide bomber/attacker), particularly in the Palestinian fight against Israel. See **Shahid**.

Ithna Ashariyya: The Twelvers are the largest **Shi'a** sect. They believe that there are twelve imams descended from Hussain ibn Ali, Muhammad's grandson, and the martyred First Imam (Muhammad's *First* rightful caliph [**Khalif**] to the Shi'a), whose death at the **Battle of Karbala** was the cause of the epic split between what became the Shi'a and the **Sunni**. Eleven of the imams have made their appearance on earth, though the last one died in 874. According to Twelver doctrine, the twelfth one, Muhammad ibn al-Hasan al-Mahdi, is the current Imam, born in 869, hidden by Allah in 941, and will return with Christ [**Isa**] to reestablish the rightful governance of Islam and govern the earth with justice and peace. He is waiting to make his appearance in Tehran, Iran, where he is hiding in a well. His appearance is dependent on chaos in the world, which the Shi'a see as their duty to create by destroying Israel and the United States with the use of nuclear bombs. See: **Ashura** and **Battle of Karbala**, and the **Mahdi**.

Ja'afari [pro: *jafari*]: Shi'a school of Islamic jurisprudence.

Jaa'iz [pro: *jaaiza*]: Allowed, permissible.

Jahannam: Hell.

Jahiliyah [pro: *jaheleyyah*]: Age of Ignorance of religious truths before Allah. Also: All time/history before Islam. Once Islamist forces have conquered a nation, there is a marked effort to destroy that nation's monuments, etc., in order to wipe out all evidence of its culture, historical "memory," and beliefs. This serves to demoralize and divert the present population from persisting in believing in its previous religious or governmental system and leaders and gives the future population nothing to believe in but Islam. There is also *Jahl*: arrogance. *Jadid Jahiliyah*: modern ignorance. *Jahl-i-Basit*: simple ignorance. *Jahl-murakkab*: complicated ignorance or confirmed error.

Jakim: Indonesian Islamic Religious Police.

Jalabiya [pro: *jahlebeyya*]: Flowing robe (most often white) sometimes with a hood, worn both by men and women, but more commonly worn by the men as it does not cover enough of the body to be suitable for outdoor wear by Muslim women.

Jamaat [pro: *jhamott*] (var. sp.: jama'at, jami'ah): Gathering, group, society, organization, community. *Jamaat Khana*: literally, a "congregational place." The Persian word *khana* (house, place) is used by various South Asian Muslim communities to denote a place of worship or gathering, as opposed to the more familiar **masjid** or **mosque**.

Jamaat-e-Islami [pro: *jhamott eleslam*]: Pakistani Islamic Group, the southeast director of Hamas. Islamic Revivalist Party. Works closely with **ICNA**, the Al-Khidmat Foundation (AKF, founded by **Usama bin Laden**), Hamas working out of Qatar, receives ICNA's charitable money from the ICNA Relief USA and Canada), **Tablighi Jamaat**, and **MOA**. Started by **Maududi**.

Jannah: Paradise, the Garden. "And their recompense shall be Paradise, and silken garments, because they were patient. Reclining on raised thrones, they will see there neither the excessive heat of the sun, nor the excessive bitter cold (as in Paradise there is no sun and no moon). The shade will be close upon them, and bunches of fruit will hang low within their reach. Vessels of silver and cups of crystal will be passed around amongst them, crystal-clear. They will determine the measure of them according to their wishes. They will be given a cup (of wine) mixed with Zanjabeel, and a fountain called Salsabeel. Around them will (serve) boys of perpetual youth. If you see them, you would think they are scattered pearls. When you look there (in Paradise) you will see a delight (that can not be imagined), and a Great Dominion. Their garments will be of fine green silk and gold embroidery. They will be adorned with bracelets of silver, and their Lord will give them a pure drink." [76:12-21]

"And those foremost (In **tawhid** and obedience to Allah and His Messenger in this life) will be foremost (in Paradise). They will be those nearest to Allah in the Gardens of Delight. A multitude of those (the foremost) will be from the first generation (who embraced Islam) and a few of those (the foremost) will be from the later (generations). They will be reclining, face to face, on thrones woven with gold and precious stones. They will be served by immortal boys, with cups and jugs, and a glass from the flowing wine, from which they will have neither any headache, nor any intoxication. They will have fruit from which they may choose, and the flesh of fowls that they desire. There will be Houris with wide, lovely eyes (as wives for the pious), like preserved pearls, a reward for deeds that they used to do. They will hear no vain or sinful speech (like backbiting, etc.) but only the saying of: Salam, Salam, (greetings of peace). And those on the Right Hand, who will be those on the Right Hand? They will be among thorn-less lote-trees among Talh (banana trees) with fruits piled one above another, in long-extended shade, by constantly flowing water, and fruit in plenty, whose season is not limited, and their supply will not be cut off. They will be on couches or thrones raised high. Verily, We have created for them (maidens) of equal age, loving (their husbands only). For those on the Right Hand." [56:10-38]

There are more **ayat** describing Paradise. All gloriously glorious. None, however, mention 72 virgins; sorry.

Jenseyyah: Literally, nationality. According to the **AMJA** site, a Muslim cannot hold citizenship in a non-Muslim country without becoming an apostate. Muslims are members of the **ummah**, not citizens of any one country and cannot owe loyalty to any but Allah *or follow any laws but the Sharia.* This brings into serious question the legality of any Muslim who is presently holding any elected or appointed or ratified public/political of-fice in the U.S. *Milestones*, Chapter 9: "A Muslim has no nationality except his belief." —Seyyid **Qutb.** It also, in our ever-shifting world where right seems right until it can be made wrong, makes the upcoming 2014 Egyp-tian constitution, and the people's right to vote on it, also a crime against Islam and the 2013 2,000,000-person Cairo revolution totally unIslamic.

Ji'bril. The Angel Gabriel. The spirit, or the Entity of Light, that appeared to Muhammad in the Cave of Hira [**Kahef Hira**] in **Mecca** in 610. Ji'bril was sent by Allah to tell Muhammad that Muhammad was the last and best prophet of all time, better than Moses and Joseph and Jesus [**Isa**] and all the rest. (His appearance to Muhammad in the Cave of Hira could be considered vaguely reminiscent of God's appearance on Mt. Sinai when He commanded Moses to inscribe the 10 Commandments on the Tablet of Stone.) The others had been placeholders, as it were, for Muhammad. Muhammad does not identify the spirit as the Angel Gabriel. His wife's cousin, Waraqa, does. On hearing Muhammad's story of the first visit in the cave, he said: "This is the same one who keeps the secrets (Angel Gabriel) whom Allah had sent to Moses." Waraqa was a Nestorian, a Christian sect in the Arabian peninsula; it is possible he did not have a clear understanding that, according to the Bible, God spoke to Moses, not an angel go-between who spoke to Moses.

Jibt: Idol mentioned in Qur'an; can also be the devil. Loosely, belief in anything that isn't from Allah.

Jihad [pro: *gheehaad*]: Literally: struggle. *Mein Kampf* means "My Struggle." Did anyone ever think that Hitler meant it to mean as inner soul-struggle against the vicissitudes of life? No. And neither did Muhammad. If you're not inclined to read the Qur'an (that's easy to understand, it's a toughy and you don't know much when you're done) you could try *The Qur'anic Concept of War*, by Brigadier S.K. Malik, 2008. It's probably on the library shelves right next to *The Christian Concept of War* and the *Jewish Concept of War*, you think? Maybe Buddha's got one out, too . . . .

The reason for jihad is to remove **fitna** from the world by replacing it with Sharia law, which is from Allah alone, and thus the only just law on earth. For those of you who want the legal definition of jihad, it's in *Reliance of the Traveller*, O9.0 (page 599) wherein the inner struggle is given one sentence and the war part goes on to page 606.

Jihad fi sabil Allah: Fighting in mortal combat for the sake of Allah;
Jihad bis saif: literally, "struggle by the sword": holy war;
Jihad al Saghir: Offensive jihad declared by caliph;
Jihad al talab: Offensive jihad;
Jihad al def'a: Defensive jihad;
Jihad bil mal: Financial jihad;
Jihad Akbar: the great jihad.

There are two Qur'anic **ayat** (verses) which succinctly sum up jihad as physical war, not inner struggle: Q9:5 (see **Ayah al Saif**) "When the sacred months are over, slay the idolaters wherever you find them. Arrest them, besiege them, and lie in ambush everywhere for them. If they repent and take to prayer and render the alms [**jizya**] levy, allow them to go their way." And Q9:29 "Fight those who do not believe in Allah or in the Last Day, and who do not consider unlawful what Allah and His Messenger have made unlawful, and who do not adopt the religion of truth [Islam] from those who were given the Scripture [Muslims]—[fight] until they give the jizya willingly while they are humbled."

Jihad is obligatory on all Muslims, but they may carry it out with time, treasure, or talent. As a last resort, jihad can be as simple as carrying hatred in the heart for the **kafir** while pretending friendship for them.

A note of interest: Islam calls itself a religion in only one country in the world: the United States, because the Constitution is unique in the world by guaranteeing freedom to all religions. Islam is a **deen** everywhere else, and no pretense is made to hide the meaning of jihad as anything but warfare to establish Sharia. Lesson 1, pp 2, 3rd para, *What Islam is All About* by Yahiya Emerick (a school book used in **madrassas** in the U.S.): "Islam is not a religion . . . it is a complete way of life. . . ." This is Sharia law, of course.

For a particularly good dissection of an Islamic website's attempt to spread confusion re: Jihad by **Da'wah** and **muruna/taqiyya**, see: http:// theinstituteforjihadiresearch.org/category/islamic-supreme-council-of-america/

Jilbab: Long, flowing scarf, less restrictive than the hijab. See: **Awrah/ nakedness**

Jinn (var. sp.: Djinn): Genies. Supernatural creatures that occupy a parallel world to that of mankind, but interact with and are important to Allah for keeping Muslims on the straight path through fear.

Jizya [pro: *gizzyah*]: Poll tax imposed on the dhimmis, the "protected" class of **kuffar** in Islam-dominant countries (see: **Pact of Umar**). Non-Muslims must accept this status from conquering Islamic invaders when offered, or the alternative is slavery or death. The thinking is: We did not kill you, so you owe us your life." There are several rules imposed on **dhimmis** (including constant humiliation); breaking any of them results in the dhimmi no longer being protected and he will again face slavery or death. The jizya has historically been the basis of the **khilafah**'s economy; the jizya can be as high as 70% of the dhimmis' income from production. Turkey abolished the jizya in 1850, then reinstated it with another name (the Wealth Tax [and what a misnomer that is]) in 1942; only non-Muslims have to pay the Wealth Tax. The jizya is called the Bumiputra System in Malaysia: Non-Muslims are taxed higher than Muslims = dhimmi status without the title.

The "entitlement" mindset flows from the practice of jizya. If you believe that the **kafir** exists to serve you because you "are the best of men," then the idea that the state *owes* you money is an easy jump. There is no guilt or misunderstanding in the Muslims' minds about why they apply for and take (or just accept) all city/county/state/country benefit/welfare funds with never a thought about getting self-reliant, so as to get off the gravy train. It's not even laziness. This is jizya: rightfully owed money to keep Muslim men and families taken care of.

Juhud [pro: *johood*]: To deny, reject Islam. Jaahid (the denier). Disbelief of Islam out of rejection. Juhud includes rejection (*kufr at-taktheeb*) and resistance (*kufr al-'inaad*). See **Murtad or Ridda** (apostasy).

Jummah salat: Friday prayers. There is no holy day, the day God rests, in Islam as there is in Christianity and Judaism. There are only two references in the Qur'an to Friday as being a designated "best" prayer day: 62:9: "O you who believe (Muslims)! When the call is proclaimed for the salat (prayer) on the day of Friday (Jummah prayer), come to the remembrance of Allah [Jummah religious talk (**khutbah**) and salat (prayer)] and leave off business (and every other thing), that is better for you if you did but know!" 62:10. "Then when the (Jummah) is finished, you may disperse through the land, and seek the Bounty of Allah (by working, etc.), and remember Allah much, that you may be successful." Other references to Jummah are all from the **Hadith**, so, from Muhammad. Friday was traditionally market day, so the remarks about leaving off business and then seeking the bounty of Allah would have held significance to the people of the time.

Friday is a dangerous day for non-Muslims in the **ummah**. It is traditionally the day within the **mosques/masjids** for incitement to riot, exhorting the faithful to acts of righteous **jihad**, sending the troops to battle full of blood-lust and thirst to kill . . . and the first victims are often the **dhimmis**; lately simply **kuffar** who have the misfortune to live near the mosque (think: Danish cartoon riots). The mosques are at the fullest on those days and when the imams or other leaders want to spread the word about something, that is the day to do it.

Jusur: Bridges. But, see: **Qutb**, Seyyid.

Ka'aba (var sp.: Kabah, Ka'bah): Walled temple/shrine, but specifically, the holiest site in Islam; it contains the **Black Stone**. The Ka'aba is centered in the **Masjid al Haram**, the first mosque of the world, located in **Mecca**. Muhammad claimed it was built by Abraham and Ismael. The Ka'aba at one time held the 360 pagan stone idols which the Arabs prayed to before Muhammad destroyed idolatry through Islam—the first order of business Allah sent down to Muhammad through the Angel Gabriel. The **Well of ZamZam**, the only fresh water within many miles of Mecca, is now located beneath the Ka'aba.

Kafir (var sp.: Kafr, Kaffur; pl.: Kufr, Khufr, Kuffar): Literally: The Cover-er. One who hides or ignores or covers up the truth of Allah. The unbeliever. Commonly: Non-Muslim/Infidel. "Infidel" is not found in the Qur'an. The story is that the first crusaders used "infidel" to describe the non-*Christians* occupying Jerusalem at the time, which would have meant the Mohammedans and Jews. Eventually, the Muslims adopted it to mean all non-*Muslims*, but "kafir" and "kuffar" permeate the Qur'an, which predates the Crusades.

Kahef Hira: Cave of Hira. Cave in mountains outside **Mecca** where the Angel Gabriel (**Ji'bril**) first appeared to Muhammad in 610.

Keffiyeh [pro: *kofeyyeh*] (var. sp.: kufiyyah) also known as a *ghutrah, mashadah shemagh*; in Persian: *chafiye*; Kurdish: *cemedan*; and Turkish, *pusi*): traditional Arab headdress for men, fashioned from a square, usually plain white, sometimes checkered, cotton scarf. The checkers can be black or red or dark green, depending on the clan or tribe. Wahhabi Saudis have adopted the red-checkered head-dressing almost exclusively. Palestinians have made the black-and-white checkers their colors.

Khadija bint Khuwaylid (555-619): Muhammad's first wife, the rich widow of a very successful trading merchant. She was 40 and he 20 (perhaps 25) when they married. She put him in charge of the caravan business and from all accounts, he did very well with it, which would seem to indicate that he was not illiterate as so many claim made it "impossible" for Muhammad to have written the Qur'an (and thus making Islam a false religion from the get-go), and it had to have been sent down from Paradise [**Jannah**] by Allah. (Note: the theory now is that "illiterate" does not mean that Muhammad could not read or write, but that he was illiterate because Allah had not taught him Islam yet.) Khadija was most likely a Hanif, one who believed in monotheism. She undoubtedly had great influence on his thoughts and actions and could have been the original impetus to find a viable method to energize the **Meccan** populace to turn away from polytheism and rid the **Ka'aba** of its pagan stone idols—which just happened to be one of the first of Allah's commandments to Muhammad.

That was significant if he were trying to sway Jews and Christians to his new "One God" (**Tawhid**) religion of Islam. (Very difficult for him from the beginning anyway, since Islam as royal tax-collection practice had been active in Mecca for many years: see **Mecca**.) They would surely back him up about getting rid of the idols, right? They didn't. It is possible, that beyond not believing what he was pitching, there was likely the problem that if Muhammad got rid of the idols, which brought people from far and wide to worship at the Ka'aba, the city would be looking at economic disaster. Closing the Ka'aba was a no-sale from the get-go.

Muhammad had four daughters (and two sons, but both died very young) with Khadija. After she died in 619, he immediately married Sawda bint Zam'a, who was reportedly old and heavy. Sawda sounds very much like she was a housekeeper rather than a wife, and a fill-in until **Aisha** (daughter of Muhammad's good buddy, Abu Bakr) could come of age to wed (at 6!) to be the "real" wife. Muhammad eventually had 11, possibly 12 wives living with him at the same time, and perhaps 28 in total. All other Muslim men are limited to 4.

Khafd (var. sp.: khifad): Female circumcision. There are arguments all over the place that Islam doesn't allow female circumcision, but as always, one look at Islamic law and the question is answered. *Reliance of the Traveller*, e4.3: "Circumcision is obligatory for both men and women. For men it consists of removing the prepuce from the penis, and for women, removing the prepuce . . . of the clitoris (n: not the clitoris itself, as some mistakenly assert). (A: Hanbalis hold that circumcision of women is not obligatory but sunnah [normal], while Hanafis consider it a mere courtesy [!] to the husband.)" Some courtesy.

At any rate, there is no mention of age, or how the operation is to be performed. There is a considerable body of evidence that shows it's being done to young girls in barbaric ways that could be described as torture that inflicts incredible pain, and without any decent medical attention at hand. These girls often die of the diseases they catch from the open wound, and if they live, are crippled with the pain all their lives.

There are organizations which have come together to stop FGM around the world. A quick search on Google brings up quite a few. Laws have been passed in roughly half of the U.S. states that criminalize the practice: Go here for a particularly interesting report: http://reproductiverights.org/sites/default/files/documents/pub_bp_fgmlawsusa.pdf. This does not mean that young Muslim girls are not being taken out of the country to have the procedure done in Third World countries.

Khalif: Caliph: Successor. Leader of the **ummah** as Muhammad's rightful successor. **Sunni** title for the one who governs the **khilafah** (those areas that are Islam dominant). He is a combination of a pastor and a president, or, **emir** and **imam**. "Render unto Caesar those things which are Caesar's, and unto God the things that are God's" is totally foreign to Islam. In Islam, there is no separation of church and state, so the caliph runs it all. Any Muslim male may take on all the duties of a caliph in the absence of a sitting caliph, as has been the case since 1925, except make treaties with foreign states. These duties, such as issuing **fatwas**, more often fall on the **ulema**, or specific **shura** councils, but if an individual Muslim, such as **Usama bin Laden**, wants to take on **jihad**, it is his duty (**fard**) to do so, since jihad is a universal Islamic duty at all times.

Khalwat [pro: *kholwat*] (Indonesian): Close proximity between non-related men and women who aren't married. Not allowed. Extremely important in Sharia law. Women who are seen too close to men they are not related or married to can be put to death.

Kharaj: Land tax placed on **dhimmis** exclusively.

Khatam al-nabiyyin: Seal of the Prophet: a title for Muhammad, meaning that he sealed forever any chance of any other prophet getting any traction as a "next" prophet. One wonders then how Joseph Smith and Brigham Young managed to bring life to Mormonism.

Khatib (var. sp.: khateeb): Lay sermon and prayer leader at mosques, not the imam.

Khatm (var. sp.: khatma): Complete recitation of the Qur'an during Ramadan nightly prayers, called **Tarawih Salah**.

Khilaf:(Urdu): Essentially, **fitna**: Controversy, dispute, discord.

Khilafah (Turkish: *Hilafet*): Islamic state (an ecclesiocracy, as there is no separation of church and state in Islam) led by a supreme religious/political leader known as a **khalif** ("successor to Muhammad") who governs through Sharia law. A caliphate is also a state which implements such a governmental system. The first khilafah was led by Muhammad's 4 Rightful Caliphs, Abu Bakr (632), then Omar, Uthman, and Ali, known as the Rashidun caliphates. From the end of the Rashidun period until 1924, caliphates, sometimes two at a single time, real and illusory, were ruled by dynasties. The first dynasty was the Umayyad. This was followed by the Abbasid, the Fatimid (not recognized by Muslims outside the Fatimid domain), and finally the Ottoman / Turkish Dynasty (with the caliph's HQ in Istanbul).

The Ottoman / Turkish Empire defeated the Mamluk Sultanate in 1517 and took control of most Arab lands until 1925 and even then, despite its degenerate weakness relative to Europe, represented the largest and most powerful independent Islamic political entity, controlling Muslim thought and action throughout the **ummah**, including Egypt, India, and Central Asia. The last, real, 35th Ottoman/Turk sultan, Mehmed V. Reshad, issued the last known jihad against the Allies of WWI. He died in 1918, ending 1,286 years of Muslim rule.

The Ottoman / Turkish Empire was defeated by Mustafa Kemal Ataturk ("Father of the Turks"), who led the Turkish national movement in the Turkish War of Independence until he won in 1925. He established a provisional government in Ankara and his military campaigns gained Turkey independence. Ataturk then embarked upon a program of political, economic, and cultural reforms, seeking to transform the former Ottoman / Turkish Empire into a modern, secular, and European nation-state. Under his leadership, thousands of new schools were built, primary education was made free and compulsory, and the burden of taxation on peasants was reduced ["peasants" is code for **dhimmis**, by and large]. He died in 1938.

Turkey's rulers have clearly been trying to get back to the good old days of **khalif** and **khilafah** ever since, rejecting democracy, independence, and secularism. As early as 1942, the Turkish government reestablish the **dhimmah** system of taxation, calling it the Wealth Tax. Turkey's rulers (i.e., Prime Minister Tayyip Recep Erdogan) appear to be helping any efforts against Israel. "Erdogan is a fanatical Islamist and a vile bigot who lavishes praise on the Muslim Brotherhood [**Ikhwan**], **Hamas**, and **Hizballah** and whose behavior is more reminiscent of an Ottoman/Turk sultan than a democratically elected leader." http://www.jpost.com/Opinion/Columnists/Candidly-Speaking-Turkeys-Erdogan-An-autocratic-Islamist-bigot-330005. There is also the matter of the 2010 *Mavi Marmara* incident, aka the Gaza Flotilla.

Khimar: Scarf. Female head-covering. See: **Awrah/nakedness**.

Khums [pro: *khoms*]: literally: "one-fifth." Originally, what was given to Muhammad from the booty taken in war and raids. It has evolved in **Shi'a Ja'afari** law to mean "charity" in the same way the Sharia calls **zakat** charity, i.e.: an income tax of a fixed rate. To Westerners, charity is something freely given, not set at a specific amount, given at a specific time, and divided up into specific recipient categories each year.

Khutbah [pro: *khotbah*]: The sermon at **Jummah** (Friday) noon prayers.

Kitaab (var. sp.: Kitab): Book.

Kitman (Farsi): Conceal, cover up, keep secret. This refers to knowledge about Islam that non-Muslims cannot know until they've reverted [**aw-dah**].

Kuffar: See: **Kafir.**

Kun [pro: *kon*] (also *kon va yakoon*—be and became): "Be." Allah commanded the world to "Be," and it was. Allah commanded Adam to "Be" and he was. Allah commanded **Isa** (Jesus) to "Be" in Mary's womb and he was.

Q3:45: (Remember) when the angels said: "O Maryam (Mary)! Verily, Allah gives you the glad tidings of a Word "Be!" —and he was! i.e.: "Isa (Jesus) the son of Maryam (Mary)] from Him, his name will be the Messiah 'Isa (Jesus), the son of Maryam (Mary), held in honour in this world and in the Hereafter, and will be one of those who are near to Allah." 3:46: "He will speak to the people in the cradle and in manhood, and he will be one of the righteous." 3:47: She said: "O my Lord! How shall I have a son when no man has touched me." He said: "So (it will be) for Allah creates what He wills. When He has decreed something, He says to it only: "Be!" and it is. 3:59: Verily, the likeness of 'Isa (Jesus) before Allah is the likeness of Adam. He created him from dust, then (He) said to him: "Be!" —and he was. Also see **Isa.**

La ilaha il Allah [pro: *la elaha el allah*]: "There is no god but Allah."

La ilaha illah Allah: "The name of god is Allah." Muhammad's great-great-great grandfather, King Qusayy of Mecca, who had control of the **Ka'aba**, had a favorite idol, the Moon God, Allah. Allah happened also to be the biggest rock in the Ka'aba. Muhammad's favorite rock was Ar-Rahman, a much smaller and less powerful deity than the Moon god, Allah. After 610 and **Ji'bril**'s appearance before Muhammad in the **Cave of Hira**, Muhammad first identified the god who spoke through **Ji'bril** as Ar-Rahman. The citizens of Mecca found this as incredulous as most everything else about Muhammad's claims and asked him why he didn't pick Allah as his god if he wanted a god that would put fear and respect into people. It wasn't long after that Muhammad announced: "*La ilaha illah Allah.*" [There are 15 supporting **ayat** in the Qur'an, plus two **hadith** for this info. Craig Winn's *Prophet of Doom* delves into the story the most heavily as part of his evidence that there is no Supreme Being in Islam, there is only Muhammad. Robert Spencer's book, *Did Muhammad Exist?*, posits the idea that there wasn't even a Muhammad.]

La ilaha illallah muhammad ur rasulullah [pro: *la elaha ella allah mohammad rahsoolallah*]: "There is no god but Allah and Muhammad is his messenger." Say these words in a mosque and you've reverted [**awdah**] to Islam. Opening to all Islamic prayer times.

Lailat al-Baraat: Night of Deliverance or Night of Assignment. Second holiest night in Islam (first is **Lailatul Qadr**), which falls mid-**Sha'aban**, the 8th month in the Islamic calendar. Muslims believe that Allah answers all prayers on that night and possibly forgives all sins, except a **mushrik** (idolater—which would include Christians) a Jew, an apostate, or a **mushahin** (a Muslim who hates another Muslim).

Lailatul Qadr: Holiest night of the Islamic year. Night of Power or Night of Destiny. The night Allah sent down the entire Qur'an to the Angel Gabriel. The Qur'an was later revealed to Muhammad verse by verse. Celebrated during Ramadan through recitation of the entire Qur'an.

Lan astaslem: "I will not submit to Islam." Also, "I will not surrender to Allah." This is a phrase for **kuffar** to say, of course.

LARIBA: "No Interest." A conglomerate of Islamic financial companies, pushing Sharia-compliant finance. Muslim Brotherhood [**Ikhwan**] front.

Lashkar-e-Taiba [pro: *lashcahry-tie-eeba*]: Army of the Righteous. Pakistani terrorist group responsible for the 2008 Mumbai massacre.

Lbadat: Special worship during **Lailatul Qadr** (Night of Power), during **Ramadan**, which is the celebration of the night when Allah first sent down the Qur'an to Muhammad.

Madrassa (var. sp.: mahdrasa, madrasse): Islamic school or university. Also referred to in the United States as Islamic academies, and sometimes, Islamic Centers. There is a mosque/masjid portion in any of these venues; the madrassa is just the school.

Maghrib: 4th daily prayer of the 5 daily prayers, sunset prayers.

Mahdi: (Shi'a): Guide; Lord of the Age: *Sahib-ul-Zaman*; a figure who will appear with **Isa** before the end of time, when Allah allows it, to bring world peace, order, and justice after it has been overcome with injustice and aggression. For interesting descriptions of the End Days from the

Islamic perspective, see: http://www.islaam.org/al_mahdi/who_is_imam_mahdi.htm AND http://www.al-islam.org/articles/signs-reappearance-twelfth-imam-ajtf. See: **Shi'a.**

Majlis al-Ifta' al-A'ala [pro: *majles alefta ala'a*]: Saudi Arabia's highest religious council.

Majlis Ash-Shura: Islamic law advisory group to the caliph [**Khalif**]. All **shura** councils are important because they're the rules guys. It doesn't look like it to the outsider, but no **jihad** organization or cell makes a move against **Dar al Harb** unless he/it has got approval from some level of shura council. Islamists (much less your average Bahrainian shopkeeper) don't just "wantonly kill"; there has to be a genuine rule of law for it. In this caliph-less time, the standing rule that it is obligatory (**fard**) on Muslims to do in the **kuffar** is sufficient in most cases, but approval from imams, mullahs, or other leading members of a shura council counts for a lot. It is important as a fall back, in a way: If an independent assault (or whatever) fails, it is considered an insult to Allah, but if various scholars have approved it and it fails, it was simply because Allah did not will it.

Makrooh (var sp.: makrah, mashbooh): Questionable or abhorrent: It is better not to do something than to do it. Generally used in reference to whether food or drink is halal or haram, not whether one should revert (if possible) or kill a non-Muslim if the opportunity is there.

MANA. Muslim Alliance in North America, an alliance of imams and presidents of the major **mosques** and organizations of mosques (such as the Islamic Society of Greater Houston, Texas) in the U.S. A council of the top Muslim Brotherhood [**Ikhwan**] councilmen, the **majlis ash-shura**, setting policy and agenda, the tone, attitude, rules, directions, etc., in the mosques across the nation. Militarily speaking, this is the Joint Chiefs of Staff sending its war plans to the mid-ranks, who send it to the troops along with the ROEs.

Mandub [pro: *mandob*]: commendable or recommended.

Maryam: Mary. Conceived Jesus (**Isa**) by a word from Allah, who said "Be" and he was. She is highly honored woman in Islam, but is not considered to be the Mother of God—it is clear in the Qur'an that Allah would never split his oneness as the followers of the corrupted New Testament believe he did. This confusion about Jesus being the son of Allah is one of the reasons Allah sent **Ji'bril** to Muhammad in 610: To set the record straight that the Jews and Christians had deliberately muddled up just to hide his (Allah's) existence. See **Isa** and **Kun.**

MAS: Muslim American Society. Muslim Brotherhood [**Ikhwan**] front founded in 1993 by high-ranking members of the MB to serve as the Muslim Brotherhood's educational and outreach arm. See: **Usra**.

Masha Allah: "Allah has willed it."

Masjid al-Haram [pro: *almasjed alharam*]: The Sacred Mosque, AKA the Grand Mosque. In **Mecca**. Largest in the world; holds the **Ka'aba**, Islam's most sacred shrine. All Muslims everywhere must know the exact latitude and longitude from where they live so they can pray in the direction [**qibla**] of the Ka'aba. This is where the annual **Hajj** is held; millions of Believers gather from all over the world here; if not each year, over successive years.

On November 20, 1979, this most sacred space in all of Islam was attacked, hundreds of the 50,000 Hajj attendees killed, and many hostages held captive for fourteen days while the terrorists fought off the best the Saudi forces had to offer. The "terrorists" (**irhabi**) were led by Juhayman al-Otaybi, who believed that he was the **Mahdi**, and that the Saudis had lost their way, gone too far West, and he had been sent to bring the "real" Islam back to the Believers. Whatever his aims, he failed. Juhayman was caught, and he and his followers were tried, convicted, and publicly **beheaded** in the squares of four Saudi cities after approval for that sentence was issued by **ulema**.

As a complete side note to this, the Prince Sultan appointed Turki bin Faisal Al Saud, then head of the *Al Mukhabaraat Al 'Aammah*, Saudi Intelligence, to run the forces against Juhayman, which he did with steadfast fierceness and resolve, by all reports. Fast-forward 34 years, and al Saud was participating in an **interfaith dialogue** event at the Northwood Church in Keller, TX. Like he was just your average imam chatting with other gentle people rooted in faith.

Back to the assault on the Sacred Mosque: In Iran, Ayatollah Khomeini told radio listeners, "It is not beyond guessing that this is the work of criminal American imperialism and international Zionism" which it clearly wasn't. This was shortly after the ayatollah had taken fifty-two Americans hostage in Teheran, and who were ultimately going to be held for 444 days from 11/4/79 to 1/20/81.

Never mind facts. Anti-American demonstrations followed the ayatollah's rabble-rousing in the Philippines, Turkey, Bangladesh, eastern Saudi Arabia, the United Arab Emirates, and Pakistan. On 11/21/79, the day following the takeover, the U.S. embassy in Islamabad was overrun by a mob that burned the embassy to the ground. A week later, this anger swept to the streets of Tripoli, Libya, where a mob attacked and burned the U.S. embassy there on 12/2.

But Islam is a religion of peace.

Masjid al-Nabawi [pro: *almasjed alnabawy*]: Medina "Mosque of the Prophet," where Muhammad, Abu Bakr, and Umar (the 1st and 2nd rightful caliphs [**Khalif**]) are buried. Second holiest site in Islam. First is the **Masjid al Haram** in Mecca. Third is the **Al-Aqsa Mosque** in Jerusalem.

Maududi, Abul A'la (var. sp.: Mawdudi) (1903-1979): Journalist, Muslim revivalist leader, political philosopher, and 20th century Islamist thinker in British India, and later Pakistan. Revived the **Deobandi** school of thought and founder of **Jamaat-e-Islami**.

Maut [pro: *mawt*]: Death. The word is used throughout the Qur'an to indicate real death, not emotional death, or figurative death. The "maut" count by jihad since 622 is presently about 270,000,000. See: http://www. politicalislam.com/tears/pages/tears-of-jihad/

Maw'lawi: Scholar; learned person.

Mazhab (var. sp.: Madhhab): Doctrine, mainly as a school of legal thought. There were many schools of jurisprudence after Muhammad's death in 632. All were resolved into 4 major schools, Hanafi, Hanbali, Maliki, and Shaf'i (Iranian is Ja'afari) when the **ulema** codified the Qur'an and Sunnah into Sharia law in the 850s.

MCA: Muslim Community Association. San Francisco, CA. One of the largest Muslim communities in the United States. Muslim Brotherhood [**Ikhwan**] front.

MCC/Muslim Canadian Congress, founder Tarek Fatah (retired, 2006). Uses the Canadian Charter of Rights and Freedoms, and the Canadian Constitution as its guiding principles. Pro-democracy Islamic organization.

Mecca (also Makkah): Arabic: "A place or goal around which an activity or interest is centered." Physically, city in Saudi Arabia. Muhammad was born there, 570. Is the location of the **Ka'aba**, in the **Masjid al-Haram**.

Home of the Quraish tribe of Jews. Muhammad's great-great-great-grand-father, Qusayy, came to Mecca circa mid-4th century. He married the richest man's daughter, fought off all the strongmen around, set himself up as king, took control of the Ka'aba and the **Well of ZamZam**, chose Allah, the moon god, as his personal/favorite god/deity, charged money for entry to the shrine and for the water, and said "submit to me" or don't see your god. He enforced the long-standing rules for the four months when tribes could and could not fight. Islam was born. [This story comes from Craig Winn's *Prophet of Doom*.]

Medina (also Madinah): Arabic: "Old city." Physically, city in Saudi Arabia, originally called Yathrib, approximately 150 miles north of **Mecca**. Muhammad fled from Mecca to Medina in 622; this flight is known as the **Hijra**. Muhammad was buried there, 632, in the 2nd holiest mosque, the **Masjid al-Nabawi**. See **Hijra** for information on Islamic calendar, which begins with the date Muhammad entered Medina.

Melk al-yamin: Sex slave or, "what your right hands possesses." The woman is a possession, not a human. According to Islamic jurisprudence, whereas the "free" (Muslim) woman is mandated to be hidden inside the canvas tent of the **burqa** (see **Awrah/nakedness**] sex-slaves are mandated only to be covered from the navel to the knees—with everything else exposed. Caliph Omar, the second Rightful Caliph [**Khalif**], would strip sex slaves of their garments whenever he saw them overly dressed in the marketplace. One of the reasons was so the men could tell the difference between the good Islamic women and the slave women, who were allowed to be raped at any time. http://www.meforum.org/3280/egypt-sex-slave-marriage

Mi'ad: The Resurrection, when Allah will resurrect all the people on the Earth and judge them to Hell (**Jahannam**) or Paradise (**Jannah**).

Minaret: Tower from which the **mu'adhin** (or **muezzin**, Turkish) call the faithful to prayer 5x a day.

Minhaj: Rules, systems, methodology, methods of the Qur'an, and thus Sharia law. Also, **Hisbah**, and Usul al-fiqh, which are essentially the same things.

Misaq: Covenant. Muhammad says that Allah called all the souls of mankind together and took a promise (*wa'dah*) and a covenant (*misaq*) *from* them. Not made a promise *to* or a covenant *with* them.

Misyar (Arabic): The traveler's marriage. **Mut'ah: (Shi'a)** Temporary marriage. A Muslim man cannot freely have sex with a woman not his wife, nor can he avail himself of a prostitute. But, he can "marry" a willing woman (prostitute, usually) for three days, have the sex, and then divorce her by stating three times "I divorce you." In fact, any male Muslim can divorce his wife by saying "I divorce you" three times (**talaq**).

MOA/Jamaat al Fuqra (Muslims of America): designs and runs the "homegrown jihad camps" in the U.S. Funded by **Tablighi Jamaat**; formed by Pakistani cleric, Shaikh Mubarak Ali Gilani in 1980 to "purify" Islam through violence. See: http://www.youtube.com/watch?v=IjML6FN8yjo
Molhid: Atheist. Not allowed to live in Islam-dominant nations.

Moslem. See: *Muslim.*

Mosques/masjids: Houses of Allah. Places of worship, seats of government, and fortresses in times of war. Note: There is no time that Islam does not consider itself at war, so one could correctly interpret that to mean that mosques are always considered fortresses/abodes of war no matter where they are. (Boise, Salt Lake City, Houston, Marseilles, Madrid, Rio de Janeiro, Moscow . . . name a place in **Dar al Harb** . . . .)

The very first building Muhammad built in **Medina** when he arrived in 622 was a mosque; he used it as an all-purpose building: spiritual, governmental, community, war, armory, treasury. Therefore, mosques/masjids now function in the same way: any time a mosque goes up, or an existing building is converted to use as a mosque, the uses will be the same as in Muhammad's time. Mosques are the spear points of "civilizational jihad" (from the 1991 Muslim Brotherhood's [**Ikhwan**] "**Explanatory Memorandum**" and exposed in the Holy Land Foundation Trial, see **HLF**) going on in the United States particularly, but in the Western world everywhere: to destroy Western culture.

The most respected Islamic religious authority in the Islamic world, **Yusuf Qaradawi,** had this to say: "The mosque at the time of the prophet was his propagation center, the headquarters of the State, as it was for his successors ... the mosque was their base for all their activities political as well as non-political .... As Muslims, [politics] is part of our religion, for it is doctrine and worship. A system for the whole of life ... and the mission of the mosque as required by correct Islam is not an isolation from ... politics .... The mosque must then have a role in guiding the nation and informing her about the critical issues and making her see her enemies. From ancient times, the mosque has had a role in jihad for the sake of Allah, . . . That blessed **Intifada** in the land of the prophets, Palestine, started from none other but the mosques; and its first call came from the minarets; and it was first known as the mosque revolution. The mosque's role in the Afghan jihad and every Islamic jihad … cannot be denied."

Turkey's Prime Minister Tayyip Recep Erdogan had this to say: "The mosques are our barracks, the domes our helmets, the minarets our bayonets, and the faithful our soldiers. . . ."

A 2011 study by Mordechai Kedar and David Yerushalmi, the American Freedom Law Center, found that 81% of 100 American mosques randomly surveyed contained materials promoting "moderate" (30%) or "severe" (51%) violence, while only 19% of the mosques contained no material promoting violence. Muslims attending the pro-violence mosques vastly outnumbered those attending the non-violent mosques. Non-violent mosques had a mean attendance of only 15 worshippers; violence-promoting mosques, whether falling in the "severe" or "moderate" category, had a mean attendance of 178 worshipers. It would appear that the Muslims themselves have chosen which form of Islam they prefer. See: **Jummah Salat** for more on violence from mosques.

In their most organized form, mosques (which themselves are often organized into such sets as the Islamic Society of Greater Houston, or The Council of Islamic Organizations of Greater Chicago with 65-75 mosques and centers and madrassas) are outposts for mobilization against a citizenry with commands sent from a centralized HQ, such as a **shura** council (see **MANA**) in Washington DC, or some other major city in the world.

Mosques can be found in small store fronts, shopping malls, on rural paths, on standalone lots, in houses in the suburbs, in community rooms inside churches, are made from renovated, conquered cathedrals, in city apartment buildings, or famously, in the Burlington Coat Factory in NYC. If the mosques have been built specifically as mosques, a Believer who's died will be buried somewhere within that building, making the land sacred Islamic territory, never to be ceded back to the home country (i.e., the U.S.). There is a pattern to how these mosques are set up in the major cities: They are built/bought/rented in circles around the cities (albeit rough circles). If you're thinking warfare strategy, isn't surrounding your enemy a classic movement?

Mosques have steadily become much larger edifices as the Muslim Brotherhood has gained more influence and control over city councils and federal officials/departments (by the public electing Muslim Brotherhood members to city councils, or council members appointing Muslim Brotherhood members to boards, even chairman of boards of powerful committees/departments, like planning, zoning, and the police). There are 2600 mosques in the U.S., up from 1200 or so pre-9/11 (not all where you'd think, like just major cities).

The larger mosques serve two purposes: one is to bring many hundreds more Muslims to the area to settle [the Muslim Brotherhood's "settlement process," i.e.: **civilizational jihad**]. Think: "If you build it, they will come." And two: to show sheer, overwhelming superiority to the **kafir**. Think: "Give up now." The largest mosque in the U.S. is located in Dearborn, MI. A 50,000 square foot mosque went up in Murfreesboro, TN, (2012) which has all of 150 Muslim families to care for. There's a mosque-a-building in Alaska on 70,000 square feet of land. Alaska, really?

Given what is known about classic Islam, and its almost unbroken 1400-year record of warfare against the world, which includes using mosques as redoubts, ribats, and arsenals, the question often comes up as to why the people in the West allow mosques in their communities. Partly ignorance, partly PC-ness, and partly fear. And obeying the law, of course, though there have of late been steep legal battles and popular protests against them. It is different outside the U.S., but here they are allowed because of the 1st Amendment, and freedom of religion: *The Supreme Court has interpreted religion to mean "a sincere and meaningful belief that occupies in the life of its possessor a place parallel to the place held by God in the lives of other persons. . . ."*

The Supreme Court has addressed this issue and (along with many other laws in the U.S.) mosques can be outlawed in the U.S.: In *Reynolds v. United States* (1878) the Supreme Court used these words to declare that "it may be accepted almost as an authoritative declaration of the scope and effect of the amendment thus secured. Congress was deprived of all legislative power over mere [religious] opinion, but was left free to reach [. . . *those religious] actions which were in violation of social duties or subversive of good order."* Quoting from Jefferson's Virginia Statute for Religious Freedom the court stated further in *Reynolds*: In the preamble of this act

. . . religious freedom is defined; and after a recital 'that to suffer the civil magistrate to intrude his powers into the field of opinion, and to restrain the profession or propagation of principles on supposition of their ill tendency, is a dangerous fallacy which at once destroys all religious liberty,' it is declared *'that it is time enough for the rightful purposes of civil government for its officers to interfere [only] when [religious] principles break out into overt acts against peace and good order.'* In these two sentences is found the true distinction between what properly belongs to the church and what to the State.

Keeping in mind that the Muslim Brotherhood intends that the people will rise up and demand the change in the Constitution that makes Islam the state religion, so, well, there simply won't be a Constitution anymore, its members are working hard to make sure mosques are exempt from *". . . [those religious] actions which [are] in violation of social duties or subversive of good order."*

There's a back-door entry called RLUIPA, to force city councils to accept a mosque in reluctant communities: The Religious Land Use/Incarcerated Prisoners Act; in shorthand, that equals: No city councils get to zone out religious houses out of just plain mean old discrimination. And the Muslim Brotherhood (**CAIR** through the **ACLU** is at the forefront) is using it for all it's worth, threatening lawsuits against small city councils to push mosques where none are wanted because of the high level of danger to the community they represent. The councils often simply have to give in given the burden of proof they have to show that they are not being discriminatory.

Yet there is another avenue to fight mosques, under the Free Exercise of Religion clause. The study above of 100 mosques in America showed that 81% of those had moderate to high support for *advocating jihad to advance Sharia law in the U.S.* The sole reason for jihad is to clear the field for Sharia to govern the world. So these mosques are teaching sedition, a clear danger to the communities in which they exist. Even if the imam isn't pounding hard on that simple premise at **Jummah** prayers, he can't help but be preaching out of Sharia (the Law of God) itself, and it doesn't take anyone long on a cursory reading of *Reliance of the Traveller* to see that Sharia is anti-Constitutional on many levels.

Mosque-expansion should be stopped; it's simply common survival sense.

MPAC: Muslim Public Affairs Council. Established in 1988 in Los Angeles, CA, by followers of the Muslim Brotherhood [**Ikhwan**] and admirers of Hizballah, they are Democratic-party activists and programmatic Leftists, who condemn post-9/11 national-security measures, Conservatives, and Jews. The leaders have significant ties to Los Angeles political figures, police hierarchy, and local sheriffs. They managed to stop the TSA from giving pat-downs to women wearing **burqas** (at the least, in public), because it's "un-Islamic." MPAC filed a lawsuit via the **ACLU** and **CAIR** against the FBI to keep FBI surveillance out of its **mosques**; a federal judge dismissed the case.

MQI: Minhaj-ul-Quran International. Reformist (**ijtihad**) Islamic organization headquartered in Lahore, Pakistan. Minhaj means "rules." This group is attempting to re-order the way the rules of the Qur'an work.

MSA: Muslim Students Association. First of the Muslim Brotherhood [**Ikhwan**] associations formed in the United States in the early 1960s. The MSA is almost militant in its approach to infiltrating schools, colleges, and universities to sow discord on the campuses, form Islamic-Sharia compliant groups, foster middle-eastern studies by "expert professors," and to belittle and debase Christianity, Judaism, and the American way of life; burning the American flag is a staple in their protests. The MSA has its own creed, slightly different from the **Ikhwan**'s: "Allah is my lord. Islam is my life. The Koran is my guide. The Sunnah is my practice. Jihad is my spirit. Righteousness is my character. Paradise is my goal. I enjoin what is right. I forbid what is wrong. I will fight against oppression. And I will die to establish Islam." Not your normal college campus civics group.

John Guandolo, former FBI agent, contributing author to *Sharia the Threat*, and author of *Raising a Jihadi Generation*, stated in an interview in frontpagemag. com, that: "the MSA's roots can be traced to the Muslim Brotherhood. The MSA serves as a recruitment tool to bring Muslims into the Brotherhood, which was its original purpose: to evaluate Muslims and to bring them into the Brotherhood and to recruit non-Muslims into Islam as a **da'wah** entity, giving them the call to Islam." He goes further. "Their goal, both from their senior leaders, presidents of MSAs around the country, national leadership, is to implement Islamic government here in the United States," he explained. "And they say that."

Despite their self-professed innocence, terrorism expert Patrick Poole [and also contributing author to *Sharia the Threat*], who has investigated them, explains who they are [in the same article]. "The Muslim Students Association has been a virtual terror factory. . . . Time after time after time again, we see these terrorists — and not just fringe members: these are MSA leaders, MSA presidents, MSA national presidents–who've been implicated, charged, and convicted in terrorist plots." http://frontpagemag.com/2013/arnold-ahlert/uc-irvines-islam-awareness-week-a-cair-convention/?utm_source=FrontPage+Magazine&utm_medium=email&utm_campaign=8fddf2e54f-Mailchimp_FrontPageMag

MSS: Muslim Student Society (UK). See **MSA**.

Mu'adhin [pro: *mooahdeen*] (Arabic); **Muezzin** (Turkish): Chosen person who calls [**Enchanting (Adhan)**] the Believers to prayer every day, five times a day.

Mu'ahadat [pro: *moa'hadat*]: Treaties. May only be committed to by the **khalif**. In the absence of a caliph (as has been the case since 1925), secondary officials in Islamic nations can only agree to truces: **Hudna**.

Muamalat [pro: *mow amalat*]: Islamic banking.

Mufassir [pro: *mofasser*]: Authors of a **tafsir**.

Mufti: **Sunni** Islamic scholar.

Muhajiroon: Immigrants. Specifically, those who "escaped" **Mecca** to go with Muhammad to **Medina**.

Muhammad. Full name (on his death) Abu al-Qasim Muhammad Ibn Abdullah Ibn Abd al-Muttalib Ibn Hashim Ibn (King) Qusayy. Born 570, in **Mecca**. Married **Khadija**, 590; perhaps 595. Visited by a spirit (aka "an entity of light") in the Cave of Hira [**Kahef Hira**] in 610. The entity claimed Muhammad was to be the final prophet of Allah, the One God. The spirit, later identified as the Angel Gabriel (**Ji'bril**) had been sent by Allah to tell Muhammad that Muhammad was the last person who was to transmit the word of Allah to mankind, and he corrected (meaning he uncorrupted it from what all the Jews and Christians had done to Allah's words over the years) and fulfilled all revelations (recited everything Ji'bril said Allah said), bringing the Qur'an to completion.

Muhammad's instructions from Allah, always through Ji'bril, were to rid the **Ka'aba** of the pagan idols, teach Allah's **deen**, Islam, to the Meccans, and install Allah's law in the land. He preached this message in Mecca until 622 when he left with his followers and moved to **Medina** (see: **Hijra**). He fought **seven major battles** (see the next entry) and many smaller ones, reverting [**awdah**] all men and women in the Arabian Peninsula to Islam between 622 and 632, when he was poisoned to death. He is called the Prophet of Allah, and the Messenger of Allah. No prophesies have yet been credited to him.

There are 26 variant spellings of this name, which means "praised one" or "praiseworthy," in Arabic.

Muhammad's Aljihad al-Akbar: Muhammad's 7 major battles: (624) Battle of Badr; (624) expedition to Banu Qainupa; (625) Battle of Uhud; (625) expedition of Banu Nadir; (627) expedition of Second Badr; (627) Battle of the Trench; and, (628) expedition to Khaybar.

Muharebeh [pro: *moharabah*]: Person who wages war against Allah; any non-Muslim.

Muharram: 1st month of the Islamic calendar. It is forbidden to fight during this month. **Ashura (Shi'a)** begins in this month.

Muhartiq [pro: *mohartek*]: Heretic. One should note that not only do all Islamic sects consider non-Muslims heretics, but pretty much each Islamic sect thinks all other Islamic sects are heretical, too. Leon Uris penned a classic paragraph in his novel *The Haj*: ". . . the basic canon of Arab [Islamic] life: It was me against my brother; me and my brother against our father; my family against my cousins and the clan; the clan against the tribe; and the tribe against the world. And all of us against the infidel." If you haven't already read the info on **Fatah** and **Hamas**, you might want to check it out now.

Mujahedeen [pro: *mojahedeen*]; plural for mujahid: "One who does jihad." Literally: Strivers. Commonly referred to as Holy Warriors for Allah.

Mujahedeen-e-Khalq: The People's Mujahedeen (Holy Warriors) for Iran. The oldest, most determined, and best organized of the Iranian opposition groups and the most feared by the mullahs' regime. The MeK (sometimes called PMOI, People's Mujahedeen of Iran) are committed to regime change in Iran and a political platform that states their support for a democratic, secular, free market society, gender equality, an end to the death penalty, and renunciation of all WMD programs and support for terrorism. Removed from the UK list of terrorist organizations in 2008, the EU followed suit in 2009, and the U.S. removed the group from its Foreign Terrorist Organizations list in 2012. Senior U.S. military, policy, and political leaders who have championed the MeK cause for many years include Andrew Card, Newt Gingrich, Rudy Giuliani, General Jim Jones, Patrick Kennedy, Tom Ridge, and Fran Townsend.

Mujtahid (Shi'a) [pro: *mojtahed*]: Learned interpreter of the law.

Mullah (Shi'a): Learned person, scholar.

Mu'minin: Faithful.

Munafiqun [pro: *monafik*]: Hypocrites. A hypocrite (faking loyalty to Allah) is an Islamic sin second only to apostasy [**Murtad or Ridda**]. If a hypocrite confesses and returns to Islam, the punishment may only be a whipping. A hypocrite can be executed if he persists in pretending.

Munkar [pro: *monkar*]: Evil doings (primarily behavior or habits of the non-Muslims). But certainly can be turned around and used this way: *Amr bi l-ma'ruf wa nahy an al-munkar*: Enjoining the good and forbidding the evil, which means to convey the Message of Islam to all human beings in the world and to establish an Islamic caliphate.

Murabaha [pro: *morabaha*]: Sharia-compliant mortgage.

Murshid: A **Sufi** teacher.

Murtad (can also be **murtad fitri**) [pro: *mortad*]: Apostate, natural; born genetically Muslim and formally renounces Islamic religion, rejects his gift of birth; punishable by death.

From: "A Shocking Interview with I. Q. Rassooli, Islam Expert" http://www.familysecuritymatters.org/publications/detail/a-shocking-interview-with-i-q-rassooli-is-lam-expert#ixzz2OByHcrhA: by Clare M. Lopez 3/21/13

Lopez: "Is there a significant number of Muslims in the world today who are willing to contradict, either publicly or within their own communities, Islamic teachings on things like the death penalty for adultery, apostasy [**ridda** or **murtad**], or homosexuality?"

Rassooli: "No Muslim can live more than a few seconds if he/she in any way, shape, or form contradicts anything in Muhammad's Qur'an or says anything against him. Only a handful of apostates from Islam can do so in our democracies. Please understand that the instant any follower of Muhammad criticizes anything about their cult belief system, that person becomes instantly an infidel worthy of death and destruction. . . .

"[T]o cite from the *Reliance of the Traveller*. . . : Acts That Entail Leaving Islam: 08.7 (3) to speak words that imply unbelief; (4) to revile Allah or His messenger; (7) to deny any verse of the Koran or anything which by scholarly consensus belongs to it; (14) to deny the obligatory character of something which by the consensus of Muslims . . . is part of Islam . . . ."

Murtad milli: Apostate after reverting [**awdah**] to Islam. A person who has turned his back to the **ummah** after having accepted Islam; punishable by death.

Muruna. Lying/deceit in a very big, national and/or international way. To throw total confusion and sow dissension and division wherever and whenever possible. There are no limits on this form of deception; fooling the **kafir** to Islamic intentions is paramount; they are at war with the **Dar al Harb**, after all. This is the *modus operandi* of the Muslim Brotherhood [**Ikhwan**].

Musa: Moses. Moses is referred to in the Qur'an more times than any other person, including Muhammad. He is described as a prophet and a messenger of Allah, meaning he wrote laws as well as brought scripture to the Israelites, per Allah's instructions. Allah saved Moses by having the Pharaoh's wife adopt him, thus opening the door in later years for Moses to try to bring the Pharaoh *to Islam*. **Ji'bril**'s appearance to Muhammad in the cave of Hira [**Kahef Hira**] could be considered vaguely reminiscent of God's appearance on Mt. Sinai when He commanded Moses to inscribe the 10 Commandments on the Tablet of Stone.

Musallah: Usually the vast open space where the men pray inside the mosque, but can also refer to open spaces for prayer outside the **mosque** or masjid.

Mushaf: Book. When the second rightful **khalif**, Umar, was putting the Qur'an together, he simply referred to it as a "book," not the Holy Qur'an.

Mushashin: A Muslim who hates another Muslim. These Muslims will not be forgiven on **Lailat al-Baraat**. Given the historic level of internecine wars in Islamic nations and wars between Islamic nations, it would seem that not many Muslims are given this pass on Lailat al-Baraat.

Mushrikoon [pro: *moshrekoon*]: Polytheists. Christians are considered polytheists because they believe in the Trinity of God, His Son, and the Holy Spirit, which to Muslims means Christians worship three gods, not one. This is intolerable to the Islamic doctrine, so it is incumbent on True Believers to rid the world of Christians, the idol worshippers.

Muslim: "Devoted to Allah." All adherents to the Islamic faith. According to the Center for Non-Proliferation Studies, a Muslim means "one who gives himself to God," and *Moslem* means "one who is evil and unjust." I do not agree. It's just a regional accent.

Mustahab: Commendable or recommended.

Mut'asibun [pro: *mota'asseb*]: Fanatic.

Mutawe'e [pro: *motawwe'een*]: Religious police: the Saudi Commission for Promotion of Virtue and Prevention of Vice.

Nabi: Noble person. Literally, prophet. Plural: Anbiyaah. In the Islamic context, a Nabi is a man sent by God to give guidance to man, but not given scripture, i.e., Jesus and Abraham were Nabi. Muhammad alone was given scripture through the Angel Gabriel (**Ji'bril**) from Allah. See: tp:// www.danielpipes.org/comments/27818.

Nafs: Carnal self or desires. [Or, the lower soul; the ego/id (which is not an Islamic concept).]

NAIF: North American Imam Federation. Muslim Brotherhood [**Ikhwan**]front.

NAIT: North American Islamic Trust. Muslim Brotherhood [**Ikhwan**] front/co-conspirator in the Holy Land Foundation trial [**HLF**], Dallas, TX, 2008. NAIT is the Saudi banker in the U.S., primarily funding **mosque**-building, the bigger the better, and only secondarily because of community need. The bigger the mosque, the more the projection of superiority. The Saudis are also a major benefactor to U.S. liberal universities and colleges, the result being in-your-eye atrocities such as that the Harvard Law School recently inflicted on America. See Introduction.

Najasa: Impurities.

Najisun: Filth. As in: the "People of the Book" (**ahl al-kitaab**) are filth. So, Secretary of State Hillary Clinton was sitting across from recently elected Egyptian president Mohammed Mursi and they're both all friendly-like and she's like saying: "We're all so happee to have Egypt in the democratic fold after that nasty time you poor people have had to put up with, with Mubarak," and do you suppose the word *najisun* popped into Mursi's head? Maybe *burqa*? American Leftist politicians are ideological partners with Islam, and they think they have the upper hand. I am considerably less convinced of that. See: **Hassan al-Banna**.

Namaz: "Making prayer." As separate from attending **mosque** services, generally, "in the field of the fight." One might correctly interpret that to be on the streets of Paris or New York City, or in airplane aisles, or airport terminals . . . .

Naqba (var. sp.: Nakba): Catastrophe; the Misery. How the Palestinians refer to Israel becoming a nation, specifically, in the PLO charter.

Naqis: Deficient. An imam cannot be an imam without having mastered the Doctrine of Abrogation or he would be considered deficient in his studies. One would be right then, to question any Islamic scholar who denies the Doctrine of Abrogation in the Qur'an. See **Al-Nasikh wal-Mansukh**.

Nawafil: Supererogatory prayers. "Extra credit" prayers, not to be confused with **Namaz** prayers. Over and above the normal number of obligatory prayers. This is still no guarantee to get to Paradise. The only guarantee for that is to kill one or more **kuffar** for Allah.

NIAC: National Iranian American Council is an advocacy and policy group founded in 2002 by Iranian-born Trita Parsi. Its agenda is strongly supportive of the Tehran regime despite its assertion to be non-partisan. NIAC lost a key defamation legal case in 2012 in which the presiding judge found that assertions that NIAC acted as an agent of influence for the Iranian regime were based in fact.

Nifaq: Falsehood, dishonesty, hypocrisy, ridicule, being "two-faced." NO Muslim should behave like this, and in fact, nifaq is divided into physical (behavior) and mental (voice) subsets. There is a **hadith** in which Muhammad says:" . . . the double-faced person will come on the Day of Resurrection in such a condition that one of his two tongues will protrude from the back of his head and the other from the front, and both the tongues will be aflame, making his entire body ablaze with fire. Thereupon, it will be announced that he was double-faced and double-tongued in the world." There is some evidence that this punishment could be for a Believer acting against another Believer, but it more likely pertains to the **kafir**, because Muhammad really really hated it when the Jews of **Mecca** said one thing to him and then (he believed) laughed at him and said other things behind his back (re: gossip, back-biting). As with all things Islam, Hypocrisy is covered in Islamic law, in *Reliance of the Traveller*, r16.1. See **Munafiqun**.

Nikah: Marriage ceremony. There are two official segments of an Islamic marriage, basically, before and after consummation: First: Mutual agreement (*Ijab-O-Qubul*) by the bride and the groom [though arguably sometimes not the bride if she's under 18]; two adult and sane witnesses [so not necessarily the bride's parents]; and, the *Mahr* (marriage-gift) to be paid by the groom to the bride either immediately (*muajjal*) or deferred (*muakhkhar*) after consummation, or a combination of both. [Half now, half later?] Then comes the party (*walima*) the next night: Legal guardian (*wakeel*) representing the bride; the written marriage contract (*aqd-Nikah*) signed by the bride and the groom and witnessed by two adult and sane witnesses; the **Qadi** (State appointed Muslim judge) or *Ma'zoon* (a responsible person officiating the marriage ceremony) who says the *Khutba-tun-Nikah* to solemnize the marriage.

\-\-\-\-\-\-\-

The Khutba-tun-Nikah is as close to saying vows like the **kuffar** do as it gets, though they are rarely required to say anything. The Qadi generally reads these three Qur'anic verses and then the marriage is done (so much for love, honor, and cherish):

\-\-\-\-\-\-\-

3:102: O you who believe! Fear Allah (by doing all that He has ordered and by abstaining from all that He has forbidden) as He should be feared. [Obey Him, be thankful to Him, and remember Him always], and die not except in a state of Islam (as Muslims) with complete submission to Allah.

\-\-\-\-\-\-\-

4:1: O mankind! Be dutiful to your Lord, Who created you from a single person (Adam), and from him He created his wife [**Hawwa** (Eve)], and from them both He created many men and women, and fear Allah through Whom you demand your mutual (rights), and (do not cut the relations of) the wombs (kinship). Surely, Allah is Ever an All-Watcher over you.

\-\-\-\-\-\-\-

33:70: O you who believe! Keep your duty to Allah and fear Him, and speak (always) the truth. 33:71: He will direct you to do righteous good deeds and will forgive you your sins. And whosoever obeys Allah and His Messenger he has indeed achieved a great achievement (i.e. he will be saved from the Hell-fire and made to enter Paradise [**Jannah**]).

Niqab: Female head-covering that covers the face except for the eyes. See **Awrah/nakedness**.

Nuh [pro: *Nooh*]: Noah. Nuh has a remarkably similar story (in the Qur'an and the **Hadith**) as that of Muhammad's. Nuh was in Adam's bloodline. No one believed that Nuh was Allah's prophet or took seriously Allah's promise of dire results if they did not change their wicked ways in worshipping idols. When Nuh had had enough of their disbelief, Allah revealed to him that he would be bringing a great flood upon the land, and Nuh asked that no one be left alive.

Nukra: A really big evil, prohibited, dreadful thing. Israel, for instance.

NUM: National Ummah Movement.

OIC/Moassesseh Ta-awon al-Islamiyya: Organization of the Islamic Co-operation, composed of 56 member states and Palestine and is, after the UN, the largest governing body in the world. It was started in 1969 as an independent political body to promote human rights in Islam and supersede the UN Universal Declaration of Human Rights. It passed the Cairo Declaration of Human Rights in Islam in 1990, and in 1993 served it to the UN as a legal document. Article 24 makes it absolutely clear that Sharia governs all human rights: "ARTICLE 24: All the rights and freedoms stipulated in this Declaration are subject to the Islamic Sharia." Today (2013), with the help of its Turkish Secretary General Ihsanoglu, and U.S. Secretary of State Clinton, it seeks to prevent all defamation of religion and racial bigotry and eliminate any criticism of Islam or Muslims for any reason. It calls critics "Islamophobes" [see **IIIT**] and has worked successfully in several European countries to criminalize free speech. Secretary Clinton stated at the OIC conference in Turkey in 2011 that she did not want to criminalize speech but merely to shame and embarrass critics to *force their silence*. See: **AHada-'Ashar Imra'a Maiyit Qatl al-Sharf** (honor killings), and **Huquq al Insan** (Islamic human rights). And **Sharia law.**

Om: [alt. sp.: Um]: Mother. Generally, once a woman has a son, her first name is suppressed and she's known as "the mother of the first born son," i.e.: Om Usama. See **Bint**.

PA/Palestinian Authority. As-Sultah Al-Wataniyyah Al-Filastiniyyah: An administrative organization established to govern the West Bank and Gaza Strip as a consequence of the 1994 Oslo Accords. Following elections in 2006 and the Gaza conflict between the Fatah and Hamas parties, its authority has extended only as far as the West Bank. It renamed itself the Palestinian National Authority after 1994, and in 2013 renamed itself the State of Palestine. For an excellent description of the outdated use of the PA, the PLO and the PIJ, see: http://www.gatestoneinstitute.org/4110/palestinians-is-abbas-being-asked-to-sign-his

----

The PA, the PLO, the PIJ and Hamas should also take a look at their Qur'ans and perhaps get a clue that their Allah is not condoning what they're doing. These verses have *not* been abrogated (**al-Nasikh wal-Man-sukh**):

Q17:102 [Musa (Moses)] said: "Verily, you know that these signs have been sent down by none but the Lord of the heavens and the earth as clear (evidences, i.e. proofs of Allah's Oneness and His Omnipotence, etc.). And I think you are, indeed, O Fir'aun (Pharaoh) doomed to destruction (away from all good)!" 17:103: So he resolved to turn them out of the land (of Egypt). But We drowned him and all who were with him. 17:104: And We said to the Children of Israel after him: *"Dwell in the land, then, [and] when the final and the last promise comes near* [i.e. the Day of Resurrection or the descent of Christ ['Iesa (Jesus), son of Maryam (Mary) on the earth], *we shall bring you altogether as a mixed crowd* (gathered out of various nations). [Tafsir Al-Qurtubi, Vol. 10, Page 338.]

This, I am sure, does not trump all the other "You-are-to-hate-Jews-and-run-them-out-of-the-world" verses, but there you are. Muhammad said that Musa said that Allah said . . . .

Pact of Umar. Al-Uhda Al-Uhmariyya. Essentially, this is the law of the **dhimmis**. It was originally a pact made by a defeated Christian population and the Muslim invaders led by Umar Ibn Al-Khattab, the second rightly-guided caliph in 627. These rules became codified into Sharia law in *Reliance of the Traveller* (*Umdat Al-Salik*) as o11.1-11 and w52.1(381-383) which apply to Jews and other non-Muslims. It is written as if the rules below were the Christians' ideas. The Christians had to (and still do), follow these rules or be eligible for death in Islamic-dominant nations (just check out Egypt, for instance):

1. We will neither erect in our areas a monastery, church, or a sanctuary for a monk, nor restore any place of worship that needs restoration nor use any of them for the purpose of enmity against Muslims.

2. We will not prevent any Muslim from resting in our churches whether they come by day or night, and we will open the doors [of our houses of worship] for the wayfarer and passerby. Those Muslims who come as guests, will enjoy boarding and food for three days.

3. We will not allow a spy against Muslims into our churches and homes or hide deceit [or betrayal] against Muslims.

4. We will not teach our children the Qur'an, publicize practices of Shirk, invite anyone to Shirk, or prevent any of our fellows from embracing Islam, if they choose to do so.

5. We will respect Muslims, move from the places we sit in if they

choose to sit in them. We will not imitate their clothing, caps, turbans, sandals, hairstyles, speech, nicknames and title names, or ride on saddles, hang swords on the shoulders, collect weapons of any kind or carry these weapons. We will not encrypt our stamps in Arabic, or sell liquor.

6. We will have the front of our hair cut, wear our customary clothes wherever we are, wear belts around our waist, refrain from erecting crosses on the outside of our churches and demonstrating them and our books in public in Muslim fairways and markets.

7. We will not sound the bells in our churches, except discreetly, or raise our voices while reciting our holy books inside our churches in the presence of Muslims, nor raise our voices [with prayer] at our funerals, or light torches in funeral processions in the fairways of Muslims, or their markets.

8. We will not bury our dead next to Muslim dead, or buy servants who were captured by Muslims.

9. We will be guides for Muslims and refrain from breaching their privacy in their homes.

10. We will not beat any Muslim.

Paradise: See **Jannah.**

PIJ/Palestinian Islamic Jihad. Harakat al-Jihad al-Islami fi Filastin, a Palestinian militant organization created after some members of the Egyptian Muslim Brotherhood [**Ikhwan**] believed that the organization did not commit enough effort to prevent Israel from occupying Palestinian territories. It's favorite saying is: "From the river to the sea, Palestine will be free." Clearly a call to destroy Israel, the same as Hamas. The PIJ continued its work in Gaza until it was exiled to Lebanon in 1987. In 1989, the PIJ moved to Damascus, where it remained until July 2012, when it relocated its headquarters to Iran.

Pir: Teacher of Islam.

PLO/Palestinian Liberation Organization. Munazzamat at-Tahrir al-Filastiniyyah, a political and paramilitary organization created in 1964. It is recognized as the "sole legitimate representative of the Palestinian people" by the United Nations and over 100 states with which it holds diplomatic relations, and has enjoyed observer status at the United Nations since 1974. [Hamas likely challenges that, now that the UN has granted it Observer Status.] The United States and Israel considered it to be a terrorist organization until the Madrid Conference in 1991. In 1993, the PLO recognized Israel's right to exist in peace, accepted UN Security

Council resolutions 242 and 338, and rejected "violence and terrorism";
in response, Israel officially recognized the PLO as the representative of
the Palestinian people.

Conceived by the Arab states at the first Arab summit meeting, the 1964
Arab League summit (Cairo), its stated goal was the "liberation of Palestine" through armed struggle. The organization was called the Palestinian
Liberation Organization. The original PLO charter (5/28/64) stated that
"Palestine with its boundaries that existed at the time of the British mandate is an integral regional unit" and sought to "prohibit . . . the existence
and activity" of Zionism. It also called for a right of return and self-deter-
mination for Palestinians. The group used multi-layered guerrilla tactics
to attack Israel from their bases in Jordan (including the West Bank),
Lebanon, Egypt (Gaza Strip), and Syria. Yasser Arafat was the Chairman
of the PLO Executive Committee from 1969 until his death in 2004. He
was succeeded by Mahmoud Abbas (also known as Abu Mazen).

PNA/Palestinian National Authority/Charter. See *Munazzamat at-Tahrir
al-Filastiniyyah:* PLO (just above).

Qabl Alhijra: Before Hijra. Used in Arabic calendar, which began in 622
AD. See **Hijra**.

Qadar: Predestination. Muslims believe that Allah has already written
their lives when they are born and that fate cannot be changed.

Qadi: Judge in Islamic law.

Qathf [pro: *qadhf*]: Accusing a person (generally a woman) of fornication
or adultery. It's the accusation that's the problem, not the truth of it. If
convicted (often on the accuser's word alone), the punishment is death by
stoning or whipping.

Qatl: Murder. There are 5 types of murders that are recognized in Sharia. All are only applicable to Muslim-on-Muslim murders. The killing
of non-Muslims is never considered murder. See **Adl**, or *Reliance of the
Traveller,* o1.0.

Qatlu [pro: *katlo*]: Killing in mortal combat for the sake of Allah. See
Jihad.

Qatlu nafsi-hi [pro: *katlo nafsehi*]: Suicide. Forbidden in Islam, except
when in the furtherance of the Way of Allah. This is a recent and particularly maleficent form of **jihad**, promoted by **Yusuf al-Qaradawi** [consid-

ered the "holiest" man in Sunni Islam at the time of this compilation] in 2001, claiming that no one could put limits on how a Muslim carried out **jihad**. Suicide bombers are considered martyrs [**shahid** or **istishhadia**] of Islam. First suicide attack was employed in Iraq in 1981, followed by Lebanon, 1983; Hamas, 1993; and al-Qaeda, mid-1990s. There have been 2000+ suicide attacks in the mid-east and Africa since 9/11/2001, as of 12/2013.

Qibla [pro: *kebla*]: Direction to **Mecca**. All Muslims must know where the **Ka'aba** is in relation to themselves, in order to pray correctly.

Qisas: Retribution; retaliation. Muslims are allowed personal retribution [but don't have to take it, depending on how the victim feels] against another in specific cases under Islamic law. Code of "get even," or perhaps vigilantism.

Qist: Justice. From Allah alone; Islamic justice. See: **Adl**.

Qitaal (pro: *keetall*): Mortal combat. See: **Jihad**.

Qitaal [pro: *keetall*]: To kill.

Qiyamah [pro: *kiyaamah*]: Judgment Day. **Isa** and Muhammad (or the **Mahdi if you're Shi'a**) determine who's going to go to **Jahannam** [hell] or **Jannah** [Paradise].

Qiyas: Analogy; foundation of Islamic legal reasoning. See *Reliance of the Traveller*, Justice, o22.1(d (III)) for explanation. Essentially, like things get like rulings (an eye for an eye), but yes, more complicated than that.

Qur'an (var. sp.: Koran): "Recitation"; Islamic holy book; believed by the followers to be the uncreated, "revealed" word of Allah. Revealed to Muhammad through the Angel Gabriel (**Ji'bril**) over a period of 22 years. It worked this way: Allah would send a message to Ji'bril, who recited it to Muhammad, who recited it to his followers. The **hafiz** set to memorizing the words; some scribes were allowed to write them down and gradually the record was built. Muslims believe that the original book resides in Paradise, and was already written prior to Ji'bril's appearance in the Cave of Hira [**Kahef Hira**] in 610. It is written in classic Arabic (the language of Allah) and is considered to be the perfect miracle. No Muslim can question it; no human can desecrate it without running the risk of losing his life.

Note that Arabic is the only "true" Islamic language and the only one in which the Qur'an can be understood. So, even though the best Arabic translators have turned the Qur'an into English, German, French, Swahili, whatever, no true Muslim ever recites, prays, or memorizes it in the indigenous language and (therefore) can't fully comprehend Islam without learning Arabic. The subconscious message reverted [**awdah**] Muslims receive is: You'll never be a "real" Muslim until you learn Arabic. This is another masterful stroke by Muhammad; it forces sameness.

Umar and Uthman (2nd and 3rd Rightful Caliphs) consecutively compiled the present version of the Qur'an (finished around 640), though the **ulema** is still in disagreement about it. There was the concern at the time when Abu Bakr was the first Rightful Caliph [**Khalif**] that there was a "risk of the Qur'an falling into the hands of less responsible, less knowledgeable people, who might not preserve it intact and who would almost certainly differ as to its true meaning. There was even the danger of its being entirely lost to posterity." http://www.quran4theworld.com/articles/Articles/ Preservation_of_the_Quran.htm.

It is said that Uthman destroyed "all other versions" in existence at the time (which might make one wonder about the singularity of that book up there in Paradise/**Jannah**) because Muhammad told him that Ji'bril had come to him (in 632) and twice repeated the order of the physical Qur'an; therefore, Uthman knew this way was the correct way. There is no good way to prove if what's being used now is authentic or not; it's simply all there is—except for the Qur'an found in Yemen in 1972 and taken to Germany for translation and compilation. It has been dated to 647. Apparently there are many discrepancies between it and the presently accepted Qur'an in use today.

There are only five approved English translations of the Umar/Uthman version: Ahmed Ali, Pikthal, Muhsin Khan, Yusuf Ali, and Shakir. [Note that for this book, I have consistently referred to the online translation, The Nobel Qur'an, for verses. It has the added value of filling in the blanks of meaning and who's talking to whom and/or about what that the printed versions do not have.]

The present version has 114 chapters which are largely based on verses and stories from the Torah and the Bible. The only entirely Arab inventions/concepts are **fitna** and **jihad**. The Qur'an is not in chronological order, meaning the two periods of Muhammad's reign—the nicer, more patient period in **Mecca**, and the jihad period in **Medina**—are inter-woven, and many **ayat** (verses) that are part of stories are started in one **surah** (chapter) and completed in different chapters. The original intro-duction of **Ji'bril**'s meeting with Muhammad [which started the whole Islam thing] is **surah** 96. The chronologically last chapter, Surah 9, is the most strident call for jihad/violence in the book against all **kafir** forever, a fitting ending for a treatise that goes from reasonable to despotic, an excuse for power and control hidden behind the cause of a god. Add the Doctrine of Abrogation (the nullifying verses, **al-Nasikh wal-Mansukh**—keep in mind that one has to completely believe that Allah had already figured out which verses he was going to change-up or nullify when he sent it down in order to accept Islam) to the mix and the Qur'an becomes a very difficult document for anyone to read.

Some believe that Uthman deliberately confused the text for reasons we will likely never know, though the consensus is that he did it to hide the true goal: Conquest of the world. It does not matter to the Muslims; they fully accept that the Qur'an is the revealed word of Allah and that is suffi-cient for faith and imitation: The Qur'an is Islam's map of conquest. This is the way Allah told Muhammad to lead the ignorant from **jahiliyah** to knowledge of the Path and Sharia in a step-by-step process, and that is the way it's done today when reverting [**awdah**] individuals or subjugating nations in three stages: mild and unassuming, to pushy and demanding while physically building strength, then to war for conquest. It's the way it was and the way it will always be.

Qutb, Seyyid: (1906-1966) Egyptian **Sunni**. Father of the modern Muslim Brotherhood [**Ikhwan**]. Author of *Milestones*, a rallying cry for Muslims of the world to fight **jihad** for Allah. Two examples of what he taught in *Milestones*: "The basis of the message is that one should accept the Sharia without any question and reject all other laws in any shape or form. This is Islam. There is no other meaning of Islam." ". . . the chasm between Islam [and the non-Muslims] is great, and a bridge is not to be built across it so that the people on the two sides may mix . . . but only so that the [non-Muslims] may come over to Islam . . ." Qutb was the influ-ence behind such jihadist eminences as Ayman al-Zawahiri, **Usama bin Laden**, and the "Blind Shaikh," Omar Abdel Rahman, behind the 1993 World Trade bombing.

"Qutb believed that the timeless message of the Koran included the sacred duty of faithful Muslims to wage jihad 'against the corrupt new Kingdom of Israel, its imperial American sponsor, any other Western influences, and corrupt Muslim rulers.' According to Qutb, a Muslim must wage war against any influences in opposition to traditional Islam, and especially against the 'Zionist Entity' in Dar al-Islam."—Gary Aminoff, http://www.americanthinker.com/2012/12/islamic_fascism_qutb_and_azzam.html#ixzz2FVwIXcNZ

Rabb: Allah/Lord

Rahim [pro: *raheem*]: Merciful.

Rahimuhu-Allah: "By the mercy of Allah."

Rajm (var. sp.: Rahm): Stoning. It is commonly used to refer to the **hadd** punishment wherein an organized group throws stones at a convicted individual until that person dies. Traditionally, it is called for in cases of adultery (for being raped) committed by a woman. It is applicable to rapists—if the woman raped can produce four witnesses in her defense, otherwise she is considered guilty and is stoned, and the man goes free—and prostitutes.

Rakat: Cycles of prayer, important specifically during **Ramadan**'s **Tarawih Salah,** the complete recitation of the Qur'an.

Raka'at Salah (var. sp.: raka'at salat): Kneeling down on the knees to pray.

Ramadan: Islamic holy month. Celebration of Angel Gabriel's (**Ji'bril**'s) first appearance to Muhammad. The word is derived from an Arabic word for intense heat, scorched ground, and shortness of food and drink.

Ramadan comes during (and is the name of) the ninth month of the Islamic calendar, which is a lunar calendar, which is shorter than the Gregorian calendar. The entire cycle of months takes about 35 years. Ramadan predates Islam. Originally, it was one of the four sacred months in the Arabian Peninsula during which the tribes could not fight. Ramadan fasting (**sawm**) is one of the 5 pillars of Islam, **Arkan al-Islam al-Khamsat**. Muslims are not allowed to eat or drink from dawn to dusk during the month. They may do whatever they like during the time before dawn (**suhur**) when Muslims are permitted the things they are forbidden in daylight, including eating, drinking, and having sex. Non-Muslims in Muslim-dominant areas or nations are also forced "to show respect for Islamic holy ways" with beatings or death if they, too, do not "celebrate" Ramadan by not eating or drinking in public during the month.

Rasulallah [pro: *rasoolallah*]: Messenger of Allah. Muhammad alone has this title.

Rayyis al-kuffar [pro: *rai'ees alkoffar*]: A leader of the infidels.

Riba: Usury. Interest payment. Not allowed by Sharia law.

Ribat: Barracks, stronghold, **mosque**: A small fortification built along a frontier during the first years of the Muslim conquest of the Maghreb to house military volunteers, called the *murabitun.*

Ridda (most commonly used word for): Apostasy, in which a person abandons Islam for another faith or no faith at all.

Ridda Wars: See **Auwal and Tani Jihads** (1st and 2nd Jihads).

Ruh [pro: *rooh*]: Spirit. The divine breath that Allah blew into Adam.

Sadaqqa (var. sp.: sadaqa, sadaqah): Charity, specifically for the poor. This is not part of official **zakat** collection.

Sa'ee: Going back and forth seven times between Safa and Marwah (two small mountains now within the **Masjid al Haram** in **Mecca** on opposite sides) that is done during the **Hajj** to symbolize Hajar's [Hagar's] search for water for her son, Ismael [she was alone and desperate after Ibrahim (Abraham) had sent her into the desert]. She found none on the first 6 trips, but when she came down from the mountains the 7th time, Ishmael was lying next to a spring of clear water (later named the **Well of Zam-Zam**), Allah's tribute to her for her faithfulness. And that seems to be all the recognition Hajar is afforded in Islamic history for the mother of the man who was destined to be "a great nation."

Genesis 16:11-12: And the angel of the Lord said to her, "Behold, you are pregnant and shall bear a son. You shall call his name Ishmael, because the Lord has listened to your affliction. He shall be a wild donkey of a man, his hand against everyone and everyone's hand against him, and he shall dwell over against all his kinsmen."

Genesis 17:20: As for Ishmael, I have heard you [Abraham]; behold, I have blessed him and will make him fruitful and multiply him greatly. He shall father twelve princes, and I will make him into a great nation.

Genesis 21:13: And I will make a nation of the son of the slave woman also, because he is your [Abraham] offspring."

Nowhere does God promise a new religion through Ishmael. Yet this tenuous connection was Muhammad's "proof" he was the world's prophet of Allah, the One God, and other people are still buying the connection today, that Islam is one of the world's "three great Abrahamic" [see **Eid al Adha**] religions. Muhammad further pounds home the link by putting Abraham and Ishmael in the Arabian desert together with the need to build the **Ka'aba** 2600 years before Muhammad came along. Since that did not happen, see: http://www.answering-islam.org/authors/toler/abraham_kaaba.html, is it perhaps not time for the world to accept that Muhammad was just taking advantage of what God *did* say?, and he made *not* a religion, but "the Nation of Islam," as the Believers will tell you at the drop of a **keffiyeh**: A Complete Way of Life. A **Deen**.

Sahabah: Muhammad's companions.

Sahih: Authentic/Authority. Most often used when referring to an interpretation (**tafsir**) or report on a **hadith**. i.e., Tafsir Ibn Kathir, or Sahih Bukhari.

Saif al-Islam: Sword of Islam.

Salat al-Yawmi al-Khamsat. 5 Daily Prayers. 1) pre-dawn: *Fajr*; 2) noon: *Zuhr*; 3) afternoon: *Asr*; 4) sunset: *Maghrib*; 5) late night: *Ishha*. See **Salah**, and **Arkan al-Islam al-Khamsat.**

Salafi/Salafis/Salafism: Pure Islam. The Purist of Muslims. Believe absolutely in every word of the Qur'an and the a**Hadith**, and follow Sharia law to the letter. Most orthodox of the orthodox sects. Are the "righteous predecessors/ancestors," the first three generations of Muslims. Anyone who died after this is one of the *khalaf*, or a "latter-day Muslim."

Salah (var. sp.: Salat, Salaah): Prayers. A spiritual relationship and communication between the creature and his Creator. Salah is one of the 5 pillars of Islam [**Arkan al-Islam al-Khamsat**]. There is a congregational prayer on Friday noon (**Jummah Salat**) with a sermon (**khutbah**) to be delivered by a religious leader called a **khatib**. To perform salah, a Muslim has to have first performed his ablutions (**wudhu**).

There are no specific Qur'anic rules in the Sharia regarding the timing of prayers. Nor is there a designated holy day, as in Saturday for the Jews (because they are to do no work of any kind on Sunday, the day God rested), and Sunday for the Christians because Allah did it in six days [see this interesting explanation of Allah's creation of earth: http://www.sunniforum.com/forum/showthread.php?56715-Tell-me-how-Allah-created-this-world], though Friday [**Jummah Salat**] has clearly come down through time as the most important day of prayer for Muslims. Westerners who have Muslim employees who demand special time considerations during **Ramadan** should take heed. Prayers can be made up, even during Ramadan. They may not be able to eat until after dusk, but that means less time off work, not more. See **Sawm**.

Salla Allahu alaihi wa salaam (SAWS): "Peace Be Upon Him" (PBUH). Used only for Muhammad.

Sawm: Fasting. Total abstinence of food and liquid from dawn to sunset for one whole lunar month (Ramadan). For those who are married, they are to abstain from sexual relations during that time, too. Sawm takes place during the ninth month of the Islamic lunar calendar. Total fasting is a training process to attain self-restraint, self-control, self-discipline, self-obedience, self-education, and self-evaluation. Few people are excused from fasting during Ramadan. Some are required to make up later for the days they did not fast such as the travelers (over 50 miles by any means), sick, pregnant women, women nursing babies, and women during their periods. Other excused people are required to feed a poor person one meal for each day they do not fast if they can afford it, such as the elderly, and the ones who have permanent diseases like ulcers.

SAWS: ***Sallallahu 'alaihi wa salaam***: "May the blessing and the peace of Allah be upon him" (Muhammad).

Seeghe: Temporary wife. A Muslim man cannot freely have sex with a woman not his wife, nor can he avail himself of a prostitute. But, he can "marry" a willing woman (prostitute, usually) for three days, have the sex, and then divorce her by stating three times "I divorce you." In fact, any male Muslim can divorce his wife by saying "I divorce you" three times (**talaq**).

Setta Kalimat: 6 fundamentals of Islamic belief:
The Word of **Purity** (*Tayyabah*): *La ilaha ill Allah Muhammadur-Rasul Allah*: "There is no God but Allah Muhammad is the Messenger of Allah."

The word of **Testimony** (*Shahaadat*): *Ash-hadu an-La illaha ill Allahu, Wahdahu La Sharika lah, wa ash-Hadu anna Muhammadan 'abduhu wa Rasoolu:* "I bear witness that no-one is worthy of worship but Allah, the One alone, without partner, and I bear witness that Muhammad is His

servant and Messenger."

The word of **Glorification** (*Tumjeed*): *Subhan Allahu, wal Hamdu lilla-hi, wa la illaha ilAllahu, wallahu Akbar. Wa la hawla wa la quwwata illa billah-al 'alii-al 'adheem*: "Glory be to Allah and Praise to Allah, and there is no God But Allah, and Allah is the Greatest. And there is no Might or Power except with Allah."

The word of **Unity** (*Tawhid*): *La ilaha illAllahu Wahdahu La Sharee-ka lahu, lahulmulk, wa lahulhamd, yuhyee wa yumeet, wa huwa hayy la yumoot abadan abada Dhul Jalaali waal Ikram beyadihi alkhayr, wa huwa 'ala kulli Shay'in Qadeer*: "There is none worthy of worship except Allah. He is only One. (There are) no partners for Him. For Him (is) the Kingdom. And for Him (is) the Praise. He gives life and accuses death. And He (is) Alive. He will not die, never, ever. Possessor of Majesty and Reverence. In His hand (is) the goodness. And He (is) the goodness. And He (is) on everything powerful."

The word of **Penitence** (*Astaghfar*): *Astaghfirullaha Rabbi min kul-li dhanbin adhnabtahu amadan aw khata'an, sirran aw alaniyatan, wa atubuhu ilayhi min adh-dhanb illadhi a'lamu, wa min adh-dhanb illadhi la a'lamu, innaka anta allamal ghuyub, wa sattar ul'uyoubi, wa ghaffarudh dhunub, wa la hawla wa la quwwatta illa billahil 'aliy-al 'adheem*: "I seek forgiveness from Allah, my Lord, from every sin I committed knowingly or unknowingly, secretly or openly, and I turn towards Him from the sin that I know and from the sin that I do not know. Certainly You, You (are) the knower of the hidden things and the Concealer (of) the mistakes and the Forgiver (of) the sins. And (there is) no power and no strength except from Allah, the Most High, the Most Great."

The words of **rejecting disbelie**f (*Rud-A-Kuffer*): *Allahumma innii a'udhu bika min an ushrika bika shai-anw- wa ana a'lamu bihii. Was tagh fi ru ka limaa laa alamu bihee. Tubtu anhu wa tabarra-tu min al-kufri wash-shirki wal-kizdhbi wal-ghiibati wal-bid'ati wan-namiimati wal fawaahishi wal-buhtani w-al-ma'aasii kulliha. Wa aslamtu wa aquulu La illaha illAllahu Muhammadur RasulAllah*: "O Allah! Certainly I seek protection with you from that I associate a partner with you anything and I know it. And I seek forgiveness from you for that I do not know it. I repented from it and I made myself free from disbelief and polytheism and the falsehood and the back-biting and the innovation and the tell-tales and the bad deeds and the blame and the disobedience, all of them. And I submit and I say (there is) none worthy of worship except Allah, Muhammad is the Messenger of Allah."

Seyyid: Venerated men accepted as Muhammad's descendants. Equivalent of "Mr." Muhammad's descendants are responsible for protecting and keeping the **Ka'aba** safe, and the water in the **Well of ZamZam** pure and clear.

Sha'aban: 8th month of the Islamic calendar. The month will fall between June and July, and then between May and June in the years 2014-2015. Sha'aban is important because the **Lailat al-Baraat**, the second holiest night in Islam, comes in Sha'aban. See **Hijra** for the Islamic calendar.

Shahada: One-sentence statement of testimony to faith: "I bear witness that there is no God but Allah and Muhammad is Allah's messenger." By so saying, one becomes Muslim for life and surrenders the right of ever leaving it. Anyone who leaves the Islamic fold is **murtad** or **ridda**: Apostate.

Shahid [pro: *shaheed*]: Martyr; one who dies while fighting in the way of Allah.

Shaikh [pro: *shaykh*] (var sp.: shaykh): Chief or leader. Can also refer to an elderly/wise person, or religious leader.

Shaitan [pro: *shaytan*]: Devil; evil. When Allah created Adam, he ordered the angels as well as Iblis to prostrate for Adam. They all obeyed Allah's order except Iblis. His argument was that Allah created Adam from clay [note: This is not particularly clear in the Qur'an; select the method of creation you prefer out of verses 22.5, 23.14, 32.8, 39.6, and 75.38] and Iblis from the flame of fire. Accordingly, Iblis thought that he was better than Adam.

Sharia-compliant Finance: "Jihad with Money." In Sharia-compliant banking, lenders may not charge interest and investors cannot make money from forbidden industries like gambling, alcohol, pork, and pornography. Selling debt, devising derivatives, and short selling are also prohibited, and investments must be closely tied to actual assets. http://www.ft.com/cms/s/0/8c9bc2fc-8845-11df-a4e7-00144feabdc0.html#axzz2onLxDXvD. SCF is called "ethical banking" in some circles since it's based on the "ethics" of Sharia law. If one does not ask—and in fact there's no requirement in the U.S. to report—where the profit goes, this sounds benign.

It is not. SCF is tied to **zakat**. One of the required zakat recipients are those who fight in the way of Allah: **jihad**is. Another recipient is Muslim charities, which are often just covers for jihad collection centers: "It is no wonder that the three largest Muslim charities (Holy Land Foundation, Benevolence International Foundation, and Global Relief Foundation) in the United States were shut down due to ties to terrorism. No one in the West knows for sure how widespread the use of Muslim charities for terrorism funding is, however, the U.S. Treasury Department has so far designated no fewer than 27 Muslim charities in the U.S. and worldwide as terrorism entities, due to their funding of terrorist groups like Al Qaeda, Hamas and others. Given the terrorist ties, background, and philosophy of Sharia authorities such as Shaikh Qaradawi, it is obvious that Wall Street and Washington ought to reject the insidious, seditious financial system known as sharia-compliant finance."—Christopher Holton, Family Security Matters http://www.familysecuritymatters.org/publications/detail/exclusive-sharia-compliant-finance-how-not-to-solve-the-financial-crisis#ixzz2onQvcugK.

SCF generates hundreds of millions, billions, perhaps trillions of dollars every year. No U.S. bank/banker is required to ask what the money is used for. Westerners as a whole, and Americans specifically, send billions of dollars a year to Iran and Saudi Arabia, etc., for oil. The Saudis (hardly alone, but a big player) put that money into **mosques** in U.S. through **NAIT** to create **jihad**is, and "Middle-Eastern Studies" professors (and all that that entails) to mindscrub our youth and media. Our dollars are also turned against us through financial deals which result in more money getting through to those who want to (and do) kill us . . . . And yet the favorite hobby horse of many Libertarians and Constitutionalists is the Fed.

Sharia Law/Islamic Jurisprudence (var sp.: shari'ah, shariah); also, *tashri* in Urdu: Islamic law, the canonical laws of Islam. Literally: "the way to the watering hole/well." Water equals life in the desert where the Sharia was developed—and that's what Sharia is to Islam. There are *only four* schools of Islamic jurisprudence, from four imams: Hanbali, Hanafi, Maliki, and Shaf'i. A fifth, practiced by the Shi'a, is Ja'afari.

First: The Big Lie: "There's really no such thing as just Sharia, it's not one monolithic continuum—Sharia is understood in thousands of different ways over the 1,500 years in which multiple and competing schools of law have tried to construct some kind of civic penal and family law code that would abide by Islamic values and principles, it's understood in many different ways . . . ." —Reza Aslan. "And yet whenever we see Sharia implemented, it looks the same. Now, why is that?"—Question posed in jest by Robert Spencer, JihadWatch, 12/22/12, http://www.jihadwatch.org/2012/12/sharia-in-action-in-modern-moderate-indonesia-house-mulling-total-ban-on-alcohol.html. Answer: With one notable exception, the expectation that the **Mahdi** will be coming to save the **Shi'a**, Sharia law *is* the same throughout the **ummah**, (**imamate** to the Shi'a) because it is Allah's Law, and that is unchangeable; it *cannot* be interpreted differently by anyone.

The Sharia concerns itself with all facets of life: cultural, social, sexual/marriage/family, financial/economics, military, legal, scholarly, and when needed, religious. Western psychologists and sociologists refer to the term "environment" as important in every single external factor that even minutely affects human lives. Sharia is the environment of Islam; it is all-encompassing in a Muslim's life. When you hear politicians or apologists claiming that Western civilization is "not at war with Islam," it is somewhat true. Western civilization is at war with the core of Islam: Sharia law, the scholarly distillation of the three major works in Islam: the **Qur'an**, the **ahadith**, and the **sirat**. The Sharia is believed to be the Law of God. Ipso facto, it is the only source of true justice [**Adl**] on earth.

Sharia law has been translated for English-speaking infidels (but is intended for the Believers in English-speaking nations) in the book *Reliance of the Traveller* (in Arabic, *Umdat al-Salik*) by Ahmad ibn Naqib al-Misri and translated by Nuh Ha Mim Keller. This handbook has several endorsements/certifications of its reliability as a true translation of the law, including one from Al Azhar University in Cairo, Egypt, the highest Islamic authority in the world. You can get the book from Amazon.com, but you will be increasing the Muslim Brotherhood's [**Ikhwan**] wealth that way. Perhaps buying a used copy off Amazon.com would make you feel better.

The book is divided into 24 sections, A-Z, that, if you read it like a book, will leave you with no doubt about what is and is not allowable to you as a Muslim, and in some cases, as a non-Muslim, or a second-class **dhimmi**. Every possible subject is covered, including such interesting bits as how to have sex with your wife and why your children can't retaliate if you kill her. (Section O2.0(5).) Read this RotT, and you'll know the minutest details about Islam.

Some standards for Sharia (there are hundreds you could find you might

dislike as much as I dislike these):
*Men are superior to women;
*A woman's testimony is valued at half that of a man's;
*A woman may be convicted of sexual misconduct (which is a death sentence) if she is raped, unless she produces four male witnesses to testify in her behalf [this is one of those I can't let pass. So, there are four guys standing around watching the poor lady get raped. What do you think her chances are that they're going to suddenly rush to condemn the rapist? Chances are better they're going to partake of the activity and then condemn her; it is her fault in their culture, after all];
*A woman's husband may freely divorce her without providing for her welfare, and she may be beaten for disobedience whenever he feels the need (the fear of being divorced with no way of supporting herself, and families who might kill her for the embarrassment of that divorce probably keep most women "in line"). We cannot discount, though, the women's absolute certainty that this is the correct way to live.

". . . . Islam is not merely about diet/fasting, devotion, prayer, worship, pilgrimage, and proselytizing (**da'wah**), which are completely 100% protected by the First Amendment to the U.S. Constitution. No, . . . Islam is also a 'complete way of life,' encompassing a legal, military, political, financial, and social system. The name of that 'complete way of life' is Sharia (Islamic law), which governs every aspect of a Muslim's life and actually forbids a separation between faith and governance. It is unlawful under Sharia for a devout, practicing Muslim to 'render unto Caesar what is Caesar's and unto God what is God's.'

" . . . . Islamic law must dominate all other laws on earth in every respect.
" . . . .[T]his sort of legal supremacism is not only in direct contravention of Article VI of the U.S. Constitution; if acted upon, it arguably also could be grounds for a charge of sedition, conspiracy to commit sedition, or misprision of sedition. See: **Mosques**.

"Aside from the obvious need to ensure that American law prevails in American courts, the specific nature of Islamic law is particularly problematic. . . . . [A]lthough Sharia . . . contains legal prescriptions about devotion and worship as well as many other aspects of life, there are also multiple elements of Sharia that are utterly antithetical to the U.S. Constitution and Declaration of Independence.

"Most important of all is that the Islam of Sharia mandates legal inequality between Muslims and non-Muslims [**kuffar**], and between men and women. Sharia . . . imposes barbaric, mutilating punishments for theft, flogging for 'fornication,' and the death penalty for adultery, apostasy [**ridda** or **murtad**], homosexuality and, in some cases, slander/blasphemy. For those who do not accept the rule of Islam, Sharia is a supremacist, violently expansionist doctrine that requires every Muslim to participate in jihad, which is 'warfare to spread the religion.'"—Clare Lopez of Radicalislam.com: http://www.radicalislam.org/analysis/cair-michigan-goes-after-us-constitution/#fm

----

All of that is coming into the U.S. on the sly, already. Sharia is pushing itself into our culture every day. It might be a demand, nicely put, of course, for footbaths at a state university, because it's part of the Islamic students' religious practice to wash before praying (5x a day), or they need special prayer rooms that separate the sexes (and nobody's eyebrows go right off the top of his or her head in the liberal university culture hierarchy?). Tuitions go up for all students.

Taxi drivers make a big noise about dogs being **haram** in Islam, so they can't carry passengers with dogs. At least one blind man has sued a taxi company for being left on the side of the street because the drivers refused to take him. Islamic prison inmates demand (not so nicely) their religious rights for **halal** food; instead of bearing the cost of making special meals for them, States just say "nobody gets to eat pork," and not only are the other prisoners' rights ignored but the suppliers are cut off, creating economic damage. Muslim imams demand the removal of crucifixes in hospitals (not just rooms) because they are offensive to Muslims who have the need to stay in the facilities.

Elementary and middle schools are getting pressure from **Ikhwan** front groups like **CAIR** to close schools on Islamic holy days like **Eid al Fitr** or **Eid al Adha,** and even give the Islamic children special time off for normal Friday (**Jummah Salat**) prayers, or not schedule tests on holy days. It doesn't matter that there might only be 20 Muslim students out of 800—the point is the continual push to make Islam dominant by making the **kuffar** appease and shift and move over/aside.

This push in and around educational facilities includes CAIR demanding that anti-MB-Sharia law-jihad speakers be refused "equal time" to speak to interested audiences in any public school space as a violation of separation of religion and state. That's so not right. They make the same demands of college boards of regents or alumni associations through pressure from the Muslim Students Associations [**MSA**] (implicit is the threat: We will make sure you get no more money if you don't cancel the speaker). The MSA comes close to being gangs of thugs—burning the U.S. flag, disrupting civil speech by such people as the ambassador to Israel, harassing Jewish students on campuses, forming protests with lovely chants like "Go back to the ovens, Jews!" Following Sharia all the time, everywhere through jihad even when it doesn't look like it.

When cases do come to court, (and there have been many in states, triggering the need for such successful legislation as American Law for American Courts) the problem with Muslims refusing to swear to tell the truth is popping up, and certainly refusing to recognize the judges right to judge them—only Allah can do that. In one memorable case when a **kafir** was attacked by a Muslim, the judge lectured the *victim* and said he "wouldn't get away with that under Sharia law," [**dhimmis** cannot fight with a Muslim; see **Pact of Umar**] or something similar. Well, no, but we don't have Sharia law here, sir.

The pernicious problem of police departments suffering under threat of religious discrimination lawsuits (see **CAIR**) have forced them into sending officers to "sensitivity training" or to Open Mosque Days to "understand Islam better." This also comes from **AMT**'s success at getting Muslims elected to city councils. Dearborn and Hamtramck, Michigan are test tube examples of what happens to American cities when Sharia becomes part of the legal mindset.

This kind of Sharia creep is everywhere, not just in the U.S. Muslims have to make a point of making Islam dominant. This article came from Turkey, with a Muslim punching Santa Claus in the nose, and saying: "Christmas and New Year's NO." http://www.bizpacreview.com/2013/12/26/poster-muslim-man-punches-santa-in-face-they-hate-him-too-90498.

On a lighter, but still serious note, Islamists go to these kind of extremes to make sure Islam is supreme by going to the trouble of putting the star and crescent moon on the top of the king for the chess games. I wonder how they missed swapping the bishops for imams? As an aside to this story, though, the Israeli contestants were not allowed to say they were from Israel: http://www.jihadwatch.org/2013/12/world-youth-chess-championships-in-uae-using-islamized-chess-sets.html

Shi'a (var. sp.: Shi'ite): Followers, as in: "the followers of Ali" (the 4th Rightful Caliph). Second largest Islamic sect, primarily headquartered in Iran, but spread out in the middle east in Iraq, Syria, Bahrain, and Lebanon. A branch of Islam which believes in Imam Ali and his sons (Hassan and Hussain) as custodians of Islam by the will of the Prophet Muhammad. They follow Ja'afari law, which is almost the same as Sharia law, except they believe in the return of the **Mahdi**, the Twelfth Imam (which makes them the **Twelvers**). The Mahdi will return when the Twelvers have thrown the world into utter chaos. There are other Shi'a elsewhere who follow the theory of the 5th or the 7th Imam who essentially do the same things the Twelfth Imam will.

Shirk: To put other gods on a par with Allah. Allah has no equals. Anyone who commits shirk is sinning and the person will go to hell. Shirk can mean that someone is assuming attributes that belong to Allah alone, e.g.: Pakistan forbade weather prediction in the '90s because only Allah could create any weather he wanted at any time. [Note: Pakistan is the world's second largest producer of buffalo milk; probably not highly dependent on weather forecasts. http://en.wikipedia.org/wiki/Economy_of_Pakistan. How convenient.] "The concept of *shirk* delegitimizes all religious traditions except Islam."—Robert Spencer, *The Complete Infidel's Guide to the Koran.*

Shura: Consultation/Counsel/Guidance. **Majlis ash-Shura**: Advisory council in a caliphate [**khilafah**]; can be a Board of Directors in an Islamic association in the U.S. In U.S.: Command center for the Muslim Brotherhood. See **MANA** and **Fiqh Council**.

Sidjin: A place in hell [**Jahannam**) where sinners' records are kept. Opposite: the register of the righteous in **Illiyoun** in Paradise [**Jannah**].

Sin al bulugh [pro: *sin alboloogh*]: Age of responsibility to Islam, the age of maturity and puberty. It is the age at which Muslim children are considered adults and become accountable for their duties to Islam (take up jihad). There is no fixed age for that in terms of years. It is decided by three signs: menstruation or pregnancy for girls, and being physically mature or having a wet dream for boys, growing pubic hair, or reaching the age of fifteen, whichever comes first.

Sira (var. sp.: sirah, pl: sirat): The writings of Muhammad's companions about him, his personality, his life story, and his ways of handling different situations is called the Sira. It's his biography. The famous collections of the Sira are At-Tabari, Ibn Ishaq, and Ibn Hisham. Ishaq's biography of Muhammad is one of the three sources [the other two being the Qur'an and the **ahadith**] that are the basis of Islamic Law (Sharia).

Siyasa: Rule/ruling from Sharia.

Solh: Peace ("Islam" means "to submit," not "peace.")

Sufi: (derived perhaps from the Arabic word for "purity" or the name of the tribe that served the **Mecca**n Temple). Sufis are Islamic mystics in which Muslims seek to find the truth of divine love and knowledge through direct personal experience of God; their tenets come closest to Hindu philosophy. Align most comfortably with the **Shi'a**, because they believe that Ali was the last rightful caliph [**khalif**]. A Sufi follower is called a Darwis. Also, Dervish; hence the expression "Whirling Devishes" after a religious dance they perform. **Al-Ghazali** became a Sufi and called for at least one good **jihad** a year, so being Sufi does not rule out being a jihadi.

Suhur: A small meal eaten just before sunrise to make the long day from sunrise to sunset easier to handle without food during the fasting month of **Ramadan**.

Sukuk [pro: *sokook*]: Bond that generates revenue from sales, profits, or leases, rather than interest. See: **Riba**.

Sunnah: Two of the three portions that make up the canon of Islam. The **sirat**, the biographies of Muhammad (most reliable by Ibn Ishaq), and the **ahadith**, compilations of the thousands of things Muhammad is supposed to have said (most reliable by Bukhari) that are not attributable to Allah, during his 22-year reign as **Rasulallah**. The third portion is the Qur'an, the uncreated, revealed word of Allah. The Qur'an cannot be understood without the biographies to confirm time-lines, and the ahadith to understand the various stories/histories that weave in and out of the Qur'an.

Sunni: Largest Islamic sect (75%-90% of all Muslims in the world); means "One of the Path." "The Path," is the Way of Allah. The Way of Allah is jihad and Sharia law. Those who supported the Umayyad side in the Battle of Karbala against Muhammad's grandson Hussain ibn Ali, which created the **Shi'a** branch of Islam. See: **Battle of Karbala** and **Ashura**.

Supreme Guide / Morshed-al-ala (or simply **Murshid**). Iranian (**Shi'a**) term for leader. Also, highest position in the International Muslim Brotherhood [**Ikhwan**].

Surah [pro: *soorah*]: A chapter in the Qur'an.

Surat Al-Ikhlas: Sincerity; genuine in religious belief. In order to verify that someone truly wants to revert [**awdah**] to Islam and is not doing it under force, imams can demand the revertee repeat Surah 112:1-4, "Say: He is Allah, the One and Only; Allah, the Eternal, Absolute; He begetteth not, nor is He begotten; And there is none like unto Him." This would be surety for those who simply say the **shahada** to revert: "I bear witness that there is no God but Allah and Muhammad is Allah's messenger."

SWT (see: **Subhanahu wa Ta'ala**): "Glorified and exalted be He; May he be glorified and exalted."

Ta'aa [pro: *taa-ah*] (var sp.: ta'ah) Obedience to Allah. This would be Muslims doing what they should; **Usama bin Laden** was one who was giving *total obedience* to Allah = **ebaadah**. See: **Abd**.

Tablighi Jamaat [pro: *tableeki jamott*], Pakistani. Society for Spreading the Faith, or, *Congregation for Religious Propaganda*. They tell us and tell us exactly who they are and what they want to do, but do we listen? This is the largest group of Islamic proselytizers in the world. See **Deobandi** and **Jamaat-e-Islami, MOA**.

Tafsir [pro: *tafseer*]: Interpretation, or exegesis, or commentary on the Qur'an.

Taghut [pro: *taghoot*]: Loosely, any belief in anything (a false god) that isn't from Allah. Has been interpreted to mean voting in democratic elections—a Muslim living in Western nations should not vote. The idea of democratic elections in Muslim dominant nations is considered un-Islamic. Also, an idol (**Jibt**) mentioned in Qur'an; can also be the devil, devil-worship, idolatry, idolatrous, impurity.

Tahrif [pro: *tahreef*]: Corruption, forgery, fake, as in: Muslims believe the Torah and the Bible scriptures were corrupted because man hid Allah from the people; but the Qur'an is in its original form, the uncreated word of Allah (man created the words in the Bible; it is irrelevant that God inspired the writers), and thus perfect. See **Qur'an**.

Tahrir [pro: *tahreer*]: Freedom (from man made laws).

Tajdid: To purify society; to make new. [To make it Islamic.]

Tajdif [pro: *tajdeed*]: Blasphemy, saying anything against Islam, an indignity to Allah.

Takaful [pro: *takafol*]: Mutual, cooperative insurance plans for Muslims with other Muslims.

Takbir [pro: *takbeer*]: Call for the crowd to shout "Allahu Akbar!" The number of times "Allahu Akbar" is to be shouted out by a crowd is usually included, i.e.: *"Al-khamsat takbir!"*= "Shout Allahu Akbar five times!"

Takfir [pro: *takfeer*]: The practice of naming (calling out, identifying, denouncing, whistle-blowing) a Muslim as a non-Muslim, thereby making him an apostate and eligible for death.

Takfir wal-Hijra: "Excommunication and Exodus" or "excommunication and emigration" or "anathema and exile." Islamist group founded by Shukri Mustafa in Egypt in the 1960s as an offshoot of Muslim Brotherhood. Group was stopped by Egyptian security forces in 1977; it is not dead, however, and has members or supporters in several other countries allied to Al-Qaeda.

Taliban: Students. Fundamentalist **Sunni** Muslims, mostly from Afghanistan's Pashtun tribes. There was no such thing as the Taliban until Afghanistan's civil war in the wake of Soviet troops' withdrawal in 1989, after a 10-year occupation. Most of the fighters were part-time or full-time students at **madrassa**s, hence the name. A *taleb* is an Islamic student, one who seeks knowledge, compared to the mullah who is one who gives knowledge. By choosing such a name, the Taliban (plural of *taleb*) distanced themselves from the party politics of the **mujahedeen** and signaled that they were a movement for cleansing society rather than a party trying to grab power. The Taliban turned to Mohammed Omar for their leader, an itinerant preacher born in 1959 in Nodeh village near Kandahar, in southeastern Afghanistan. Mullah Omar is considered to still be alive.

The Taliban dominates large swaths of Afghanistan and a large part of Pakistan's Federally Administered Tribal Areas. The Taliban seek to establish a puritanical caliphate [**khilafah**] that neither recognizes nor tolerates forms of Islam divergent from their own. They scorn democracy or any secular or pluralistic political process as an offense against

Islam. The Taliban's Islam is a close kin of Saudi Arabian Wahhabism. The Taliban's original aims were, as Ahmed Rashid, the Pakistani journalist and author of *Taliban* (2000), wrote, to "restore peace, disarm the population, enforce Sharia law, and defend the integrity and Islamic character of Afghanistan."

Talaq [pro: *talak*]: Divorce. A Muslim man may divorce his wife by saying "I divorce you" three times (aka "Triple Talaq"). In intensely fundamental Islamic nations she has no recourse to law or from family; she simply has to go. If they have children over seven, they go with him. She is entitled to nothing, unless she had a decent dowry [*mahr*] that she can demand to have returned, and in some countries, such as Afghanistan, where she cannot work or be seen with men she's not related to, she is essentially facing death. If the husband really wants to do her harm, he can accuse her of adultery, which can be punishable by death by stoning in Muslim-dominant nations. It is possibly more merciful than starving to death alone in the dark of the canvas prison of the **burqa**.

A woman *can* initiate a divorce; it's called Khula or Khul'a. She puts a monetary offer on the table, essentially. If there was a mahr that can be turned into money, or it was money to begin with, she can give it up to her husband to buy him out. She has to have a way to support herself and sometimes the mahr is all she has, so giving it up is a huge step. And then he still has to agree to the divorce, and say the words of divorce, "talaq," or it's a no-go. A divorce is a terrible insult to the Muslim man's pride; even if he could care less about the woman, he'd often rather say no than allow her to publicly humiliate him. See **Honor Killings**.

Talawa: Recitation. It is a rule that the Qur'an must be recited in Arabic during **Ramadan**, on **lailatul qadr**, for instance, though many Muslims have no idea what they are saying.

Tamarod: Rebel/Rebellion. This is best known for the grassroots movement under that name that was largely responsible for removing Mohamed Mursi (and thus the **Ikhwan**) from the Egyptian presidency in the summer of 2013. There were at least six other popular organizations involved in this extraordinary uprising. The leader of the Egyptian armed forces, General Abdul Fattah al-Sisi, called for mass demonstrations on 26 July 2013 to grant his forces a "mandate" to crack down on "terrorism." Tamarod agreed to put its 22M followers behind this request, while other groups did not. Mohamed Khamis, a leading Tamarod activist, said: "We support it, we will go out on the streets on Friday [see **Jummah salat**], and ask the army and the police to go and end this terrorism." Hundreds of protesters were killed on 14 August 2013, following a violent crackdown by security forces on supporters of deposed president Mohamed Mursi. Tamarod is called "a battalion of the Egyptian army," and like al-Sisi, is an enemy of the U.S. government for supporting the Ikhwan against the Egyptian people.

Taqdir [pro: *takdeer*]: Predestination, fate. Muslims believe that Allah has already written their lives when they are born and that fate cannot be changed. (This might stem from the acceptance that the Qur'an was already fully written before **Ji'bril** appeared to Muhammad in 610 and Allah then began to reveal bits of it to Muhammad over time.)

Taqiyya [pro: *takeyyah*] (var. sp.: takeya, tageyyeh): Lying, deceit. Muslims are allowed to lie under three circumstances: to save one's life if captured by non-believers during jihad; to advance the cause of Islam [which leaves the door wide open to mean "always," you think?, since it's worldwide conquest]; and to keep peace in the home between a husband and wife.

For a perfect example of "lying interfaith dialogue da'wah taqiyya-in-action" check out: http://www.youtube.com/watch?v=mU-uwgLWqmc, brought to you by the intrepid United West.

Taqlid [pro: *takleed*]: Total, unthinking acceptance and imitation of one of the four schools of Islamic jurisprudence: Hanafi, Hanbali, Maliki, Shaf'i. There is a fifth school: Ja'afari (Shi'a). Allah said these were the rules; if you break them, you pay for it by never seeing Allah.

Tarawih Salah [pro: *taraweeh*]: Special prayers held during **Ramadan**, during which there is a complete recitation of the Qur'an.

Tarbiya [pro: *tarbeya*]: Systematic training of members and possible members in Islamic texts and in the methodologies of political activism. In other words, **da'wah** training, or training in concealing the facts about the real goal of Islam: To submit the world to Allah. Da'wah training certainly includes the Doctrine of Abrogation and which verses the **da'ee** can and cannot use when enticing a candidate into Islam.

For a good example of how specific tarbiya gets, there is a pdf copy of *The Methodology of Dawah Elallah in American Perspective* at http://www.dawahinamericas.com/bookspdf/MethodologyofDawah.pdf, if you can't find the actual book. Check out Chapter VI, sections 4-7 for sure, but the whole book is an eye-opener as to how to manipulate Americans' minds.

Tasamuh (var. sp.: tasamouh, tahommol): "As far as one can handle things." As close a translation of "tolerance" as there is in Arabic. There is *no* concept of tolerance in Islam. Islam does not allow for other people's belief, legal, or cultural systems. It's all Islam all the time all over.

Tashri (Urdu): Islamic law. See **Sharia**.

Taslim: Submission, or surrender; root word for "Islam."

Tawagheet [pro: *tawagheet*]: Idolatry. See **Mushrikoon**.

Tawhid [pro: *tawheed*]: The idea of One God; the unity of the Godhead— fundamental basis of the religion of Muhammad.* (*This description of the "religion of Muhammad," not Allah, comes from *A Dictionary of Islam*, by T.P. Hughes, 1885.) See: **Da'wah**. It is critical to da'wah efforts that the kuffar buy into tawhid, and deny Christ's legitimacy and Yahweh's position. Also, see **Shirk**.

Ta'wil [pro: *taweel*]: Mystical or esoteric interpretation of the Qur'an. Also: to lead back or to bring something back to its origin or archetype, as in explaining/understanding the Qur'an as it was originally revealed to Muhammad. There are dozens of arguments on the meaning of ta'wil, as this shows: "Not a single verse of the Qur'an descended upon (was revealed to) the Messenger of God, which he did not proceed to dictate to me and make me recite. I would write it with my own hand, and he would instruct me as to its **tafsir** (the literal explanation) and the **ta'wil** (the spiritual exegesis), the **nasikh** (the verse that abrogates [it]) and the **mansukh** (the abrogated verse), the *muhkam* (without ambiguity) and the *mutashabih* (ambiguous), the particular and the general. . . ."—Imam Ali, 4th Rightful Caliph, and Muhammad's son-in-law.

Tawriya. Hiding, concealment; dissemblance, dissimulation, hypocrisy; equivocation, ambiguity, double-*entendre*, allusion. "As a doctrine, 'double-*entendre*' best describes tawriya's function. According to past and present Muslim scholars, tawriya is when a speaker says something that means one thing to the listener, though the speaker means something else, and his words technically support this alternate meaning [as in 'freedom' and 'justice']."—Raymond Ibrahim, JihadWatch, 2/29/12.

Taysir (var. sp.: tay'seer, tay'asur). Allows for Muslims living in non-Islamic countries to relax Sharia compliance until the country becomes Islamic. This practice is also called **taqiyya** and **kitman**.

Tazir [pro: *tazeer*]: Sharia punishment, usually corporal (i.e. beating, whipping), administered at the discretion of an imam.

Tazkiyah [pro: *tazkeyah*]: Purification of the soul through charity. Not the same as **zakat**.

Thaaleth Jihad: The Third Jihad. Commonly considered the time we are in now in relationship to Islam's present war and expansion (**hijra**) on (and into) the West, or **Dar al Harb**. Since this is not an "official" jihad, as are the book-ended **Auwal and Tani** [1st and 2nd] **Jihads**, it's difficult to pinpoint a date that it began, but it's not unreasonable to put it at the formation of the **Muslim Brothers, the Ikhwan**, in Egypt, in 1928, under Hassan al-Banna's guidance. The first "modern" (though unsuccessful) Islamic assassination (if one discounts al-Banna's death, likely by Ikhwan hands, in 1948) was planned for Gamal Abdel Nasser in 1954. The Ikhwan was successful in 1970 with the assassination of Anwar Sadat.

Twelvers: See **Ithna Ashariyya.**

Udhiyah: Sacrifice. Refers to the animal (camel, cattle, or sheep) that is/ are sacrificed as an act of worship to Allah during **Eid al-Adha,** until the last day of *Tashreeq* (the 13th day of Zhu-l-Hijjah, which is the 12th month of the lunar calendar), with the intention of offering sacrifice. The sacrifice is to honor, and maybe thank, Allah for supplying them with food throughout the year.

Ulema [pro: *ooo-lah-maw, u-lem-ah*] (var. sp.: olama'a): Islamic scholars trained in Islamic law; leaders in Islamic society. Scholars are allowed to issue fatwas in the absence of a caliph.

Umdat-al-Salik: "Wayfarer on the path toward Allah." *Reliance of the Traveller*; English desk reference of Sharia/Islamic law.

Umm al Kitaab: Claimed by Muslims to be the version of the Qur'an that the Angel Gabriel (**Ji'bril**) gave to Muhammad. Muslims believe the original Qur'an sits on a table in Paradise.

Ummah [pro: *ommah*]: the Islamic world.

Ummi (pl: Ummiyyun): Illiterate. People who do not "know" Allah are considered to be illiterate, not that they can't read. Thus the story that Muhammad was illiterate when **Ji'bril** first visited him in the Cave of Hira [**Kahef Hira**] in 610.

Usama bin Laden: Usamah bin Muhammad bin Awa bin Ladin (1957

2011). Founder of **al Qaeda**, the jihadist organization that claimed responsibility for the September 11 attacks on the United States, along with numerous other mass-casualty attacks against civilian and military targets. His father was billionaire Mohammed bin Awad bin Laden in Saudi Arabia and raised as a Wahhabi Muslim. He attended college in Saudi Arabia until 1979, when he joined the **mujahedeen** forces in Pakistan against the Soviets in Afghanistan, helping to fund them by funneling arms, money, and fighters from the Arab world into Afghanistan. Went to Sudan, until U.S. pressure forced him to leave there. Bin Laden and Ayman al-Zawahiri found safe haven in Sudan from about 1990-May 1996, when they were expelled, and returned to Afghanistan as guests of the Taliban's Mullah Omar. The ideology of Islamic Jihad made al-Qaeda and the Taliban perfect partners. Formed al Qaeda in 1996. In 1998 he declared war against the USA. On May 2, 2011, bin Laden was shot and killed inside a private residential compound in Abbottabad, Pakistan by American forces by order of President Obama.

Bin Laden was banished from Saudi Arabia in 1992. According to Wiki: The Iraqi invasion of Kuwait under Saddam Hussein on August 2, 1990, put the Saudi kingdom and the House of Saud at risk. With Iraqi forces on the Saudi border, Saddam's appeal to pan-Arabism was potentially inciting internal dissent. Bin Laden met with King Fahd, and Saudi Defense Minister Sultan, telling them not to depend on non-Muslim assistance from the United States and others, and offered to help defend Saudi Arabia with his Arab legion. Bin Laden's offer was rebuffed, and the Saudi monarchy invited the deployment of U.S. forces in Saudi territory. Bin Laden publicly denounced Saudi dependence on the U.S. military, arguing the two holiest shrines of Islam, **Mecca** and **Medina**, should only be defended by Muslims. Bin Laden's criticism of the Saudi monarchy led them to try to silence him.

Usra: Literally, "family." **Hassan al-Banna** [see: **Ikhwan**] used usrati for small, intimate prayer meetings with a chosen few, to plan out the next steps in the organization. This is still how it works in the American Muslim Brotherhood, most notably in recruitment for just the right people to join leadership. The Muslim American Society [**MAS**] scouts Muslims and then invites them to an usra without telling them what the agenda is. The chosen were told to focus on fundamentals during the usra meetings, including "the primary goal of the Brotherhood: setting up the rule of God upon the Earth."

Usul al-Fiqh. See: **Minhaj**.

Wa'ed [pro: *wa'ada*]: Promise.

Wahhabism: "The particular creed of Islam practiced in Saudi Arabia, which is known in the West as Wahhabism, emerged in the mid-18th century in Central Arabia from the teachings of Muhammad ibn Abdul Wahhab. This Arabian religious reformer sought to rid Islam of foreign innovations that compromised its monotheistic foundations and to restore what he believed were the religious practices of the 7th century at the time of the Prophet Muhammad and his immediate successors. He established a political covenant in 1744 with Muhammad bin Saud, according to which he received bin Saud's protection and in exchange legitimized the spread of Saudi rule over a widening circle of Arabian tribes. This covenant between the Saudi royal family and Wahhabism is at the root of modern Saudi Arabia."—Dore Gold. http://www.militantislammonitor.org/article/id/242

Waidu: [pro: *Why-I-do*] Prepare (You). Words on Muslim Brotherhood icon. See: **Ikhwan al Muslimin.**

Wajib [pro: *wajeb*]: Obligatory or mandatory, as in, jihad is an obligation on all Muslims.

Wala wa bara: Loyalty *and* enmity. Loyalty to Allah means enmity to non-Muslims. A Muslim American soldier, for instance, cannot serve two masters; if there's a conflict, the Muslim cannot go against the Sharia law that enforces the enmity. Nidal Malik Hasan is the poster boy for this conflict of interest, having murdered 13 people and injured 32 others (attempted murder) at Ft. Hood, Texas, November, 2009. It was his own **jihad** against being sent into war against his brothers . . . so he shot up his American "brothers."

WAMY: World Association of Muslim Youth. Very militant. Publishes pro-armed **jihad**, anti-Semitic, anti-Christian, and anti-**Shi'a** literature. Is part of the national Muslim Brotherhood [the **Ikhwan**] organization.

Waqf: Literally, "Confinement and prohibition" or causing a thing to stop or stand still." The legal meaning of Waqf according to Imam Abu Hanifa (scholar), is the detention of a specific thing in the ownership of *waqif* and the devoting of its profit or products . . . ." Another definition: A religious endowment or trust/a bestowal from Allah—and that's the one that fits the reality on the ground: It's more the meaning of never ever giving ground or ceding ground to non-Muslims. Once land or title or domicile is considered Islamic, it is always Islamic and can never go back to non-Muslim hands, such as the Dome of the Rock in Jerusalem, or the lands of Palestine, or the land a **mosque** is built on, no matter the real country the mosque is built in. *Allah* gave this land (or whatever) to Islam; therefore, it can't go back to any not Muslim.

Wars of Apostasy: See **Auwal** and **Tani Jihads** (1st and 2nd Jihads).

Wasat: Just and noble. As in: Muslims are superior to other people for they alone are just and noble.

Well of ZamZam: "Abundance." "Stay in one place." "Collect in one place." Sacred well under the **Ka'aba** in **Mecca** in the **Masjid al Haram**. The ZamZam water is said to have appeared when Hajar (Hagar) had to leave Ishmael alone to search for water. She traversed the hills around what was to be Mecca seven times, each time coming back from one or the other hill to check on Ishmael. When she returned the seventh time, the well was miraculously there. See: **Sa'ee**.

Wudhu: Ablution pre-prayers. See: **Sharia Law**.

Yusuf al-Qaradawi. (1926-) Egyptian Sunni. Presently the Spiritual Guide of the Sunni/Muslim Brotherhood Islamic world. Possibly the most influential of all Sunni Muslims alive today. Started IslamOnline, and has a regular show on Al-Jazeera news [now airing on American TV]. Mubarak banned him from Egypt possibly as long ago as 1963; he was invited to come back during the "Arab Spring" uprising in Feb., 2011. [See: **Ikhwan**] Al-Qaradawi put his stamp of approval on suicide bombing by saying that no one had a right to stop a Muslim from carrying out **jihad** in any way he or she saw fit.

Zabiha [pro: *thabeehah*] (var. sp.: Dhabiha) Ritual slaughter. Islamic approved method of slaughtering an animal. Cut the animal's windpipe, throat, and blood vessels of the neck with a sharp knife without cutting the spinal cord, to ensure that the blood is thoroughly drained before removing the head. The animal must be facing **Mecca**, so the food produced will be **halal**.

Zakat (var. sp.: zakah, zakaat): Tax. One of the 5 pillars of Islam [**Arkan al-Islam al-Khamsat**]. There is an entire chapter (H) on zakat in *Reliance of the Traveller*, the handbook of Islamic jurisprudence. The important point for this handbook is that all Muslims everywhere are required to pay zakat, and that zakat is divided into eight categories, one of which is "those fighting for Allah, meaning people engaged in Islamic military operations . . . ." So, 12.5¢ of every zakat dollar collected in the U.S. goes to support a jihadist somewhere in the world who could conceivably be using it to kill Americans (or any Western nation military person) fighting him. It seems reasonable to suggest that zakat should not be allowed to be collected in non-Muslim-dominant nations, but of course it's called a "charity" to fool the **kuffar**, so the practice won't stop.

Zandaqa: Heresy. Apostasy. See: **Ridda, Murtad**.

ZFA: Zakat Foundation of America. Purports to help the poor in the world, but it does not; it supports **jihad**. One of the founders: **Yusuf al-Qaradawi**, first among pro-Sharia Egyptian Muslims.

Zinaa: Adultery. Fornication.

Zindiq [pro: *zendeek*]: Atheist.

Zuhr [pro: *thohor*], also Dhuhr: Noon prayers.

RESOURCES/BIBLIOGRAPHY

Ali, Ahmed (translator). *Al-Qur'an*. Princeton: The Princeton University Press, 2001.

Awdi, Nicholas, and K. Smith. *Arabic Practical Dictionary*, 13th printing. New York: Hippocrene Books, 2010.

Emerick, Yahiya. *What Islam Is All About*. Lebanon: Noorart, Inc., USA, 1997; reprint, 2007.

Gaffney, Frank & contributing authors. *Sharia the Threat to America, the Report of Team B-II*. Washington DC: The Center for Security Policy, 2010.

Glassé, Cyril. *The Concise Encyclopedia of Islam*. San Francisco: Harper Collins San Francisco, 1991.

Hughes, Thomas Patrick. *A Dictionary of Islam*. London: W.H. Allen & Co., 1885. Reprinted 1996, Laurier Books, Ottawa, CN.

Keller, Nu Mim Ha (translator). Ahmad ibn Naqib al-Misri, author; died, 1368. *Reliance of the Traveller*. Maryland: Amanda Publications, 2008.

Malik, S.K., Brigadier. *The Quranic Concept of War*. New Delhi: Adam Publishers & Distributors, 2008.

McCarthy, Andrew C. The Grand Jihad. Encounter Books, New York, 2010

Rashid, Ahmed. *Taliban*. New Haven, Indiana: Yale University Press, 2000.

Siddiqui, Shamim. *Methodology of Dawah Elallah in American Perspective*. Maryland: International Graphics, 1989.

Solomon, S., & E. Al Maqdisi. *Modern Day Trojan Horse*. Charlottesville, VA: ANMPress, 2009.

Solomon, S., & E. Al Maqdisi. *The Mosque Exposed*. Charlottesville, VA: ANMPress, 2006.

Spencer, Robert. *The Complete Infidel's Guide to the Koran*. Washington, D.C.: Regnery Publishing, 2009.

Stakelbeck, Erick. *The Brotherhood*. Washington, DC: Regnery Publishing, Inc., 2013.

Warner, Bill. *Sharia Law for the Non-Muslim*. TN: CSPI, Inc, 2010.

Winn, Craig. *Prophet of Doom*. Canada: The Winn Company, LLC, 2004.

Primarily Islamic Sources used:

http://en.wikipedia.org/wiki/Glossary_of_Islam

http://corpus.quran.com/wordbyword.jsp?chapter=2&verse=190

http://www.scribd.com/doc/40004499/English-Arabic-Words-Meaning

http://www.islamicport.com/islamic_terms/d.html

http://www.islamcan.com/dictionary/index.shtml

http://www.dar-us-salam.com/**TheNobleQuran**/index.html

http://quod.lib.umich.edu/cgi/k/koran/koran-idx?type=DIV0&byte=282392

http://www.wikiislam.net/wiki/List_of_Abrogations_in_the_Qur'an

http://chronquran.blogspot.com/search?updated-max=2011-01-1T23:59:00-08:00&max-results=1

http://www.haqislam.org/the-fruit-of-belief-and-tawakal/

Most common blogs, websites, and webzines used:
American Thinker   (www.americanthinker.com)
Answering Islam   (www.answering-islam.org)
Answering Muslims   (www.answeringmuslims.com)
Atlas Shrugs   (www.atlasshrugs.com)
Bare Naked Islam   (www.barenakedislam.com)
Center for Security Policy   (www.centerforsecuritypolicy.org)
Citizen Warrior   (www.citizenwarrior.com)
(The) Clarion Project   (www.theclarionproject.org)
Creeping Sharia   (www.creepingsharia.com)
Daniel Pipes (www.danielpipes.org)

Discover the Networks   (www.discoverthenetworks.org)
FaithFreedom   (www.faithfreedom.org)
Family Security Matters   (www.familysecuritymatters.com)
Frontpage Mag   (www.frontpagemag.com)
Gatestone Institute   (www.gatestoneinstitute.org)
Global Muslim Brotherhood Daily Watch (www.globalmbwatch.org)
(The) Hudson Institute (www.hudson.org)
Investigative Project on Terrorism   (www.investigativeproject.org/)
JihadWatch   (www.jihadwatch.org)
Middle East Forum (MEF)   (www.meforum.org)
Middle East Media Research Institute   (www.memri.org)
MoneyJihad   (http://moneyjihad.wordpress.com/)
Political Islam   (www.politicalislam.com)
Public Policy Alliance (www.publicpolicyalliance.org)
Radical Islam (www.radicalislam.com)
Religion of Peace   (www.thereligionofpeace.com)
Sharia Finance Watch   (www.shariahfinancewatch.org/blog/)
SultanKnish (http://sultanknish.blogspot.com/)
Understanding the Threat (www.understandingthethreat.com)
World Threats (www.worldthreats.com)

Public Information: There is no doubt I have not listed all the websites and web pages and blogs I used in my search; I interpreted the information as I needed to and as I understood it. As is clear in the text, I also often gave direct credit within a definition or explanation, or a link to an article.

CPSIA information can be obtained at www.ICGtesting.com
Printed in the USA
LVOW04s0728260814

400626LV00001B/2/P